HEGEL AND THE LOGICAL STRUCTURE OF LOVE

TRANSMISSION

Transmission denotes the
transfer of information,
objects or forces from one
place to another, from
one person to another.
Transmission implies
urgency, even emergency:
a line humming, an alarm
sounding, a messenger
bearing news. Through
Transmission interven-
tions are supported, and
opinions overturned.
Transmission republishes
classic works in philoso-
phy, as it publishes works
that re-examine classical
philosophical thought.
Transmission is the name
for what takes place.

HEGEL AND THE LOGICAL STRUCTURE OF LOVE
AN ESSAY ON SEXUALITIES, FAMILY AND THE LAW

Toula Nicolacopoulos
George Vassilacopoulos

re.press Melbourne 2010

re.press

PO Box 40, Prahran, 3181, Melbourne, Australia
http://www.re-press.org

© T. Nicolacopoulos & G. Vassilacopoulos 2010 (new edition)

First published by Ashgate Publishing Limited in 1999

The moral rights of the authors have been asserted

British Library Cataloguing-in-Publication Data
A catalogue record for this book is available from the British Library

Library of Congress Cataloguing-in-Publication Data
A catalogue record for this book is available from the Library of Congress

National Library of Australia Cataloguing-in-Publication Data

Author:	Nicolacopoulos, Toula.
Title:	Hegel and the logical structure of love : an essay on sexualities, family and the law / Toula Nicolacopoulos and George Vassilacopoulos.
Edition:	New ed.
ISBN:	9780980668384 (pbk.)
ISBN:	9780980668391 (ebook)
Series:	Transmission.
Subjects:	Hegel, Georg Wilhelm Friedrich, 1770-1831--Contributions in philosophy of family.
	Hegel, Georg Wilhelm Friedrich, 1770-1831--Criticism and interpretation.
	Families--Philosophy.
	Sexual ethics.
Other Authors:	Vassilacopoulos, George.
Dewey:	190

Designed and Typeset by A&R

This book is produced sustainably using plantation timber, and printed in the destination market reducing wastage and excess transport.

CONTENTS

Acknowledgments *vii*

1. Introduction 1

PART I

2. The essential nature and current condition of modernity 9

3. The modern turn to speculative philosophy 27

PART II

4. The development of the notion in Hegel's *Logic* 57

5. The judgement, the syllogism and objectivity in Hegel's *Logic* 69

6. The categories of logic and real philosophy 87

PART III

7. The categorical syllogism and the concepts of family, love and intersubjective identity 125

8. The family and personality: marriage and intersubjective identities 141

9. The family and personality: family capital, children and the family's dissolution 163

10. Sexism, heteronormativity and plural sexualities 177

11. The family and the law 197

Bibliography *213*

For Flora and Lucas

ACKNOWLEDGMENTS

This book was previously published by Ashgate Publishing Limited (ISBN 978-1-85972-657-0).

1. INTRODUCTION

Our aim in this book is to develop an Hegelian account of familial love. To this end we have three main objectives in mind. The first is to show that such a normative account offers a principled way of satisfactorily resolving current controversies concerning the sphere of intimate life. The second is to argue that this kind of resolution of questions of philosophical ethics depends upon a systemic reading of Hegel's thought. Our third objective is to lend support to the view that Hegel's philosophical system continues to be relevant to our times.

In his 'Preface' to the *Philosophy of Right* (1981, p. 1) Hegel invites his readers to judge his ethical and political philosophy by reference to 'the logical spirit' that grounds it. We believe that we have yet to see the results of strict compliance with this demand. What does compliance require? To be sure, in Hegel's view a proper assessment of the subject matter of his ethical and political philosophy presupposes acquaintance with his philosophical method, namely 'speculative knowing' as elaborated in his *Science of Logic*. However, Hegel also insisted that the practice of 'philosophical science', whether this involves the elaboration of its subject matter or the assessment of this elaboration, should take it that 'content is essentially bound up with form'. It is this understanding of the nature of the interrelation of the form of philosophical thought with its content that sets Hegel's speculative philosophy apart from other non-speculative approaches. These latter treat the form of thought as 'something external and indifferent to the subject matter' that it produces.

Indeed, in this respect Hegel's philosophy stands apart from the currently dominant approaches. By the late twentieth century philosophy has become anti-systemic, or 'post-metaphysical', to borrow a phrase from Jürgen Habermas (1992). According to Habermas (1992, p. 6), 'the specifically modern element that seized all movements of [twentieth century] thought lies not so much in the method but in the themes of thinking'. In other words, post-Hegelian philosophy has become theme centred. It seems to us that it is precisely in relation to this fundamental difference that Hegel's contribution will ultimately be judged against later philosophical developments. Our own reading of Hegel tries to give effect to the view that his philosophical science is a matter of the elaboration and assessment of the content of philosophy in its own internally related form.

Furthermore, it follows from the kind of reading of Hegel that we favour that modern theme centred philosophy is unnecessarily restrictive. Precisely because modern theme centred thinking privileges the content of philosophy over the relationship of form and content, it tends to favour the proliferation of ideas.[1] We would suggest that this kind of proliferation becomes unproductive in the absence of some principled way(s) for determining the criteria of assessment of rival positions. In this case, philosophy ultimately amounts to what Hegel calls 'the bad infinite', that is, to the seemingly endless elaboration of position after position in which fundamental differences are reduced to the contents of the advocate's operative assumptions. We can best illustrate this point by reference to contemporary debates within feminist and sexualities discourses about the ideas of family, sexuality and the law.

Of course, feminism has a long history of denouncing the institution of the family for its reinforcement of patriarchal power relations. Even so, as Susan Moller Okin (1997) notes, for the most part feminist critics of the family have been ambivalent about the value of family structures. More often than not, they have targeted specific family practices and have argued for example, for the elimination of sexual inequalities or of the conditions that perpetuate the exploitation of women's reproductive and household labour or of psychological oppression and violence against women. But what of the ethical significance of the family? Moller Okin (1997, p. 17) suggests that since families are 'neither all bad nor all good' they should be reformed rather than discarded. In a similar vein, Michelle Moody-Adams (1997) argues that modern family life is indispensable for maintaining stability and well being in our lives. But there are equally forceful arguments for the view that the modern western idea of the family is inextricably tied to ever more

---

1. For a discussion of the nature and effects of theme centredness on current political philosophical discourse see Nicolacopoulos, 1997, pp. 82-85.

subtle ways of ensuring women's subordination (cf. Purdy, 1997, p. 70 and f. 5). To complicate matters further, since the 1980s feminist discussions of issues relating to the family have been sensitised to the effects of differences of race, ethnicity, class and sexuality. From this perspective well meaning feminists calling for the reform (rather than abandonment) of the modern ideal of the family, can be criticised for effectively defending arrangements that perpetuate sexist and colonising power relations (cf. Zack, 1997, p. 45; Bradford and Sartwell, 1997). The modern ideal of the nuclear family in which white co-resident heterosexuals raise their biological children does not only perpetuate sexism, it also perpetuates heteronormativity (cf. Bradford and Sartwell, 1997, p. 117). By 'heteronormativity' we mean reliance on heterosexuality as the norm in both senses of moral norm and normal.[2] Heteronormativity has the effect of rendering sexualities that do not conform to the dominant heterosexual paradigm as naturally or morally inferior or deviant thus establishing a value hierarchy. In an influential paper, Gayle Rubin (1993, p. 11) has argued that in western cultures 'virtually all erotic behaviour is considered bad unless a specific reason to exempt it has been established'. She cites marriage, love and long term relationship as amongst the acceptable excuses. Rubin (1993, p. 13) identifies hierarchies of sexual value operating in a variety of discourses. Such hierarchies rationalise the well being of 'the sexually privileged' who, amongst other things, are heterosexual, married, monogamous, procreative and non-commercial in their relationships. In defining 'good, normal, natural sex' the qualities attributed to the dominant heterosexual class function as the measure of acceptability. To the extent that sexual practices approximate those belonging to the heterosexual paradigm their status as 'bad' is able to be contested. So, for example, whilst homosexuality has been subordinated to heterosexuality, long term lesbian and gay male couples' relationships occupy 'an area of contest' in 'a struggle over where to draw the line' between good and bad sex (Rubin, 1993, pp. 14-15).

Once acknowledged, the pervasive effects of heteronormativity seem to call into question the universal applicability of categories such as family, marriage and love, even after attempts to elim-

---

2. Heteronormative thought and practice insist on the strict correlation of male and female bodies, desires and gender roles. On this see Butler, 1990, pp. 20-21. See also Warner, 1993, pp. xxi-xxv. On lesbianism specifically see Ginzberg, 1992, pp. 74-75; Calhoun, 1994, pp. 563-568.

inate from them their sexism.[3] Consequently, issues like the legal recognition of same-sex relationships are complicated by the question of whether support for such recognition inevitably reinforces heteronormativity (cf. Robson, 1992b). The elimination of heterosexist bias in the law may not straightforwardly be a matter of the decriminalisation of homosexuality and of the removal of discriminatory barriers to the rights and benefits accorded (married) heterosexuals. For this might be to grant homosexuality legal status only in so far as it can be represented as approximating heterosexuality closely enough, thereby leaving in place the institutionalisation of sexual hierarchy.[4] On the other hand, good reasons can be given for denouncing the law's failure fully to recognise same sex relationships.[5]

In our view, such important ethical issues cannot be satisfactorily discussed and resolved in the currently dominant theme centred approach to philosophy. More often than not opponents are at cross purposes precisely because each takes for granted background assumptions that would be highly contestable were they to be considered from the point of view of the other. Yet, we currently lack any principled way(s) of addressing philosophical questions at this fundamental level.

We believe that Hegel's system can provide an appropriate conceptual framework within which to reflect upon and resolve basic questions pertaining to the logical structure of the key ethical concepts that define the sphere of intimate life. Indeed, an Hegelian account can not only be instructive as regards normative questions, but it can also allow for the diversity and open endedness of human experiences where appropriate.[6] Of course, Hegel's own claims about the family have been presented as a classic illustration of the intellectual endorsement of the sexism and heteronormativity pervading western cultures. When we refer to an Hegelian account we mean to invoke an understanding of the relationship between the form of philosophical thought that we take his system to be relating to the relevant philosophical content. We

---

3. Compare Moller Okin, 1989.

4. Cf. Polikoff, 1993. See also Sinfield (1994). He argues in favour of directing gay and lesbian energies to 'subcultural consolidation' in the light of welfare capitalism's limited ability to accord gays and lesbians equal legal status with heterosexuals.

5. Cf. Calhoun, 1997. Compare liberal defences of the legal recognition of same sex relationships by Kaplan, 1991, and Sunstein, 1994.

6. In this respect, our argument can be read as an indirect defence of Hegel against the charge that his system denies difference and contingency.

will be arguing that, contrary to initial appearances, the categorical form of the syllogism as elaborated in the *Science of Logic*, provides the conceptual resources to reformulate a Hegelian account of familial love. Such an account will permit us to redeem some of the categories that have been culturally linked to sexism and heteronormativity. It is in this sense that we will be appealing to Hegel's system.

We will undertake our reworking of Hegel's idea of familial love and the related concepts of marriage, sexualities, property, parenting and the law in Part III of the book. In Parts I and II we will prepare the groundwork for the development of our argument. Part I explains our reasons for thinking that Hegel's speculative system continues to be relevant to our times. Part II supplies an overview of our understanding of the workings of the *Science of Logic* and of its relationship to the categories of real philosophy. Whilst the discussions of Parts I and II form a necessary part of our elaboration of what we consider to be a defensible Hegelian account of familial love, each part of the book has been written allowing for the possibility that the reader may wish to begin from Part III. As a whole, this book represents a first approximation of what we take to be the enormous potential of the Hegelian system to be productively (re) thought in accordance with the demands of our age.

PART I

2. THE ESSENTIAL NATURE AND CURRENT CONDITION OF MODERNITY

Contemporary discourse on modernity has not said enough about the nature and limits of modernity's own givenness. In this chapter we will begin our analysis of this important yet overlooked aspect of modernity by drawing upon and developing a claim that Jürgen Habermas has advanced. It is worth noting at the outset that our limited discussion of modernity is not meant to illustrate the creative activity of speculative thought. Our aim is merely to clarify a basis for the view that speculative philosophy has continuing relevance in our times. With this in mind we note that Habermas (1987, p. 7) credits Hegel with the realisation that

> [m]odernity can and will no longer borrow the criteria by which it takes its orientation from the models supplied by another epoch; it has to create its normativity out of itself. Modernity sees itself cast back upon itself without any possibility of escape.

Habermas takes this idea to be the axis around which the Hegelian problematic is developed. It certainly brings to mind the image of the circle that Hegel often uses to refer to the movement of speculative thought. Modernity begins with itself in order, through its own self-generated efforts, to return to itself as an integrated and reflexive whole. Modernity is an essentially self-determining whole in this sense of being thoroughly self-related.[1]

Even so, because the modern period is marked by the differentiation of society into distinct political, economic and domestic spheres in the process of its self-determination, it gives rise to the

---

1. Given the limited purpose of our discussion of modernity, we leave to one side issues stemming from alternative readings of society, such as that offered by Castoriadis (1997). The comparative strength of our understanding of modernity is properly the subject matter of a comprehensive defence of our position which we will not attempt here.

question of the degree to, and grounds upon, which its differentiated spheres are to be (conceived as) integrated.[2] Furthermore,
with modernisation, the task of understanding the normative basis of society's integration increasingly becomes identified as taking place against the background of the disenchantment of the
modern world. It, therefore, becomes a task for the modern individual subject conceived as the legitimate source of the identification of meaning and value; modern individuals have to invest
a certain form of social organisation with value through autonomous critical reflection and action upon their social world.[3] Even
so, they can encounter their social totality as 'an open-ended unity
in the process of making itself' (Castoriadis, 1987, p. 89).

In this process of modernity's self-determination no aspect of
its being can be treated as a fixed and pregiven reference point.
What is, therefore, necessary is some awareness of tendencies
towards the naturalisation of aspects of its being. Agnes Heller
(1990, p. 145) aptly describes modernity's denaturalising process
as the deconstruction of 'the natural artifice'. Instituted society is
a man made construct that, nevertheless, appears to exist by the
arrangement of nature and this appearance needs to be progressively challenged and unsettled.

However, Heller (1990, p. 155) also implies that modernity's
denaturalising process has its limits whereas we take the view that
if modernity is to 'create its normativity out of itself' modern individuals, whether human beings or institutions, must develop and
embody the reflective awareness of what we might call an absolutely denaturalising process. This is because modernity gives rise

---

2. Cf. Kean, 1988. For a recent discussion of the emergence of modern civil society (the economic and domestic spheres) see Taylor, 1997, pp. 66-77.

3. Cf. Poole, 1991. Notice that even the contemporary debate between realists
and non-realists about the source of moral value is made possible by the predic-
ament of modern individual subjectivity. Such a debate takes place against the
background assumption that the questions posed by participants in the debate
are rationally resolvable without having to appeal to authoritative sources beyond
human reason. No matter where you locate the source of value, whether in the
subject (individual person or community) or the object (the independent world),
the problem and the act of locating it belong to those of us who are prepared to
rely only on our rational capacities and to be moved by their products. Because of
this modern context, it would not be helpful for someone participating in the contemporary realism versus non-realism debate to appeal, for example, to God's will
to settle the matter either way. See also Walzer (1987, pp. 1-32) on three paths in
moral philosophical inquiry: discovery, invention and interpretation. Differences
aside, modern versions of these three paths equally presuppose the individual's
critical reflective agency.

to its own givens. The claim, for example, that all human beings are, by nature, free and equal is a modern idea as far as its content is concerned yet its advocates must take its truth to be given in much the same way that the substance of non-modern ideas are taken by their advocates to supply a fixed and ultimate truth. What is called for, then, is a denaturalising process that is absolute in the sense that it affects both the content and the form of ideas. This is a necessary part of modernity's self-determination, not only because it distances modernity from appeals to 'models supplied by another epoch', but also because it can readily dismiss the givens that have occasion to arise within the modern world itself.

Despite its endorsement of the importance of resisting reliance on givens we want to suggest that Habermas' understanding of modernity's denaturalising drive is not as radical as it initially sounds. We shall argue that the basic task of modernity, as far as overcoming reliance on givens is concerned, is not merely to reject the content or substance of particular givens that derive from earlier social paradigms. It is rather to overcome givenness or the very idea of the given. Indeed, if the task of modernity were simply to overcome the particular givens to which it is externally related, rather than to overcome its very own givenness, it would be locked into a purely negative mode of rejection thereby undermining its essentially self-determining power or, to use Habermas language, its ability to create its own integrating norms.

In order to make out this claim, in the present chapter we will begin our discussion by explaining the difference between a mere reliance on particular givens and the condition of givenness. To this end we will draw a broad contrast between the function and presuppositions of particular givens in non-modern and modern conceptual frameworks and social paradigms. By linking the idea of givenness to the modern concept of particularity we will explain why givenness is an idea whose universal character cannot be reduced to that which is identified with any particular given, whether 'supplied by another epoch' or not. We will end this chapter by explaining how our analysis of givenness, in terms of the universality of particularity, reveals the distinctive shape of modern social interaction at its most abstract level.

MODERN AND NON-MODERN PARTICULAR GIVENS
Particular givens and universal modes of being
Particular givens can be found in both modern and non-modern ways of being. For example, in modernity particular ways of life

whose contents and ideals differ from one another can coexist and flourish in their own ways without too much questioning of their ultimate worth. Their being in the world can be grounded in the taken for granted presupposition that they are indeed worthwhile. Similarly, non-modern particular religious world views can exist alongside one another, though the content of their ideas differs dramatically. Each world view can even claim the status of being the ultimate, universal truth of worldly existence.

However, as we will explain below, modern and non-modern conceptual frameworks make sense of these givens in radically different ways and this has important implications for the modes of being available to moderns and non-moderns respectively. In the present context, the 'mode of being' of something refers to the universal form that it takes, as distinct from the particular content which gives it its concrete existence.

The mode of being of something always combines with the content of its being in order actually to exist in the world. Yet, in supplying the form of a concrete existent a mode of being also reveals the essential nature of a being in the sense of that which makes it the kind of being that it is. This essential nature can, in turn, be expressed in its fully realised terms or merely in the terms of its developmental process since it is always to be found somewhere in the process towards its realisation.[4] The mode of being of something may, therefore, accord with its essential nature to a greater or lesser degree.

Non-modern particulars

With the above clarificatory points in mind, and having drawn attention to the distinction between particular givens in modern and non-modern conceptual frameworks, we can now move on to consider the ways in which particular givens appear in a non-modern framework.

Non-modern reflection typically focuses on the subject matter that is being reflected upon, such as the nature of the divine, whilst taking for granted its methods and processes of inquiry. In doing so, it treats the unity of its subject matter and cognitive structures as a given.[5] Within this conceptual framework a particular given

---

4. The concept of the essential nature of something presents well documented conceptual problems when it is mistakenly taken to be a static concept that represents fixed and rigid substances. Cf. Grosz, 1992, pp. 332-344; Phelan, 1989; Moller Okin, 1994, pp. 5-24.

5. Hegel refers to this kind of reflection as 'the old metaphysic'. For an

is recognised having regard to the specific content of the entity in question. Consider, for example, an entity about which one advances a substantive proposition that is derived from a taken for granted world view. Significantly, no distinction is made between the content and the mode of being of the particular. There is, instead, a conflation of the questions of (a) what the particular is and (b) how it is.

This lack of differentiation between the content of a being and its form presupposes their undifferentiated unity. From the perspective of this kind of unity a certain kind of task is rendered invisible. This is the task of achieving the unity of the universal mode of being of something with its particular substantial content following a recognition of their difference. Indeed, because it lacks the moment of differentiation such an undifferentiated unity also functions as a universal given. Thus, for the non-modern what is universal is, implicitly or explicitly, understood in terms of what is particular and, conversely, what is particular is taken to be a given universal substance.

This resulting conflation of the universal and the particular has certain implications for the ways in which non-modern particulars can be related to each other. Note, firstly, that non-modern particular givens exist in a world of particular entities that, in one way of another, is ordered in accordance with their ungrounded claims to be universal. Secondly, two ways of consistently relating to such a world seem to be open to non-moderns whose conceptual framework is limited in the way we have been describing. One of these is to remain in absolute ignorance of the fact that the world is differentiated by particular world views. This possibility is illustrated by cases of the historical development of self-sufficient communities in complete isolation.

Another non-modern way of relating to the world is to impose the particular content of one's own world view upon the rest of the world in an effort to advance a universal cause through the elimination of particular differences that must inevitably be presumed to be based on falsehood or some kind of evil. Perhaps, the most vivid historical expression of this second possibility is the emergence of empires. In this second case, we readily encounter what Heller calls 'absolute absolutism'.

Absolutists claim that only the particular kind of truth they acknowledge is true, only the kind of action they recommend

extensive discussion of Hegel's understanding of its character and limits see Vassilacopoulos, 1994, pp. 23-31.

is proper, virtuous or right, while all alternative views and practices are either untrue or wrong. ... 'Absolute absolutism' makes the same statements as absolutism, yet it denies (to repeat: *not merely philosophically but also socially*) the right of others (other absolutists and relativists alike) to make a similar claim for the truth and rightness of their own theory or practice (Heller, 1990, p. 156).

Heller describes this familiar attitude in the context of making a point that is unrelated to our present discussion but she fails, nevertheless, to draw attention to the ultimate conceptual presupposition of absolute absolutism, namely the fact that it conflates its 'particular kind of truth' (the content of the convictions espoused) with that of the universal (the form in which this content is given). To this extent her discussion implicitly raises but does not address this important issue.

Differences aside, the above mentioned possible responses to the non-modern formulation of the particular given show that non-modern particulars are not, after all, in touch with their precise mode of being. Their mode of being, we want to suggest, is their implicit particularity. As a result of the undifferentiated unity of a particular being's mode of being and the content of its existence, the particular given is conflated with the universal so as to render invisible precisely that which makes it a particular, namely its particularity. If we are right about this, then a distinguishing characteristic of the non-modern conceptual framework is its lack of an effective concept of particularity. We will go on next to explore the meaning and significance of this concept in and for the modern conceptual framework.

Modern particularity

Modern reflection is marked by an inward turn that draws attention to the subject of reflection and to his or her methods and processes of reflection, that is, to the form of the subject's thought as distinct from its substantial content (cf. Taylor, 1987; 1992). Within this conceptual framework, the modern particular relates to itself as a particular individual in the sense of being a reflective agent that does not take for granted either the unity of his or her cognitive structures with the subject matter of reflection or the universality of the content of his or her concrete existence. So, for example, the representation by one world view of the nature of the relationship between human beings and divine existence translates into something that can become the spiritual conviction of a particular individual qua particular. Modern liberal language registers this kind of understanding of the particular when it refers to individuals and their religious views as private or non-public (cf. Rawls, 1993) and thereby disconnects them from the non-modern presupposition that they are (one with) the universal.

By relating to itself as a particular the modern individual gives expression to its mode of being as that of particularity. Precisely because it relates to itself as a particular the modern individual is in a position immanently to abstract from the specific content of its concrete existence and, so, to recognise itself in the terms of its purely abstract being. By engaging in such a process of abstraction the modern particular makes explicit the independence of its abstract or formal mode of being from the specific content of its concrete existence. At the same time, what is immanent to the individual qua particular is its non-identity with the universal. Its abstract mode of being must, therefore, be in the dimension of particularity understood as that which makes the particular individual a particular. Particularity is, therefore, not to be confused with whatever concrete particulars might be said to have in common. Nor is it the product of a process of abstraction in relation to which, having been undertaken from some external reflective standpoint, the particular individual might remain ontologically indifferent.

We have suggested so far that, on the one hand, the modern individual is negatively defined as not being identified with the universal as such and, on the other, it is distinct from that which gives the specific particular its specificity. Particularity is the mode of being of every modern particular individual irrespective of the content of its concrete existence. Particularity is, therefore, universal in the sense that it explicitly supplies the mode of being of every modern particular. Furthermore, unlike the non-modern particular, the modern particular incorporates an indispensable moment of differentiation between its universal mode of being (form) and its particular substance (content).

It follows from the above that a significant difference between the non-modern and the modern particular is that the latter's own ability to differentiate itself gives rise to the idea of particularity and, with this, comes the explicit differentiation of the formal universal and the substantive particular. This modern differentiation between form and content would not be possible in the absence of the modern individual's power to abstract from its concrete content. Nor would it be possible, consequently, to free up the formal universal from the non-modern condition of being conflated with the substantive particular.

At the same time, this difference in the way in which the modern particular relates to itself has some further implications for the modern conceptualisation of the relationship between the universal and the particular. On the negative side, we have already seen that the formal universal is freed up from the non-modern condition of being conflated with the substantive particular. On the positive side, however, new kinds of task emerge for the modern individual as a result of its having secured the universal's independence from the particular. On the one hand, qua particular it faces the challenge of supplying its universal, yet wholly abstract, mode of being with concrete content. In doing so the modern individual addresses the question of the substantive meaning of particularity. On the other hand, qua formal universal the modern individual faces the problem of how to restrict the modern particular's universalising tendencies. The independence of the universal from the particular invests an institutionalised formal universal with the power to demonstrate the nullity of the concrete particular if and when the latter (mis)represents itself as the substantive universal.

Next we want to argue that the incorporation into modern individuality of this kind of differentiation between form and content permits modern particulars to relate to each other through awareness of their particularity. Consider, firstly, the role that particularity plays in the relationships between modern particulars. By relating to its own particularity (in so far as it does not conflate its particular being with that of the universal) the modern particular relates to other particulars as one particular amongst others, that is, as a given particular amongst a plurality of given particulars. Instead of being absolutely ignorant of the differences between particulars, this way of relating renders the being of one particular given as a mark of the boundary and limit of the being of the other givens. So, the recognition of particularity marks a shift from attention to what something is as a specific entity, like the non-modern isolated community or the empire, to how one particular is located in a network of particulars.

Indeed, we want to suggest that the modern recognition of particularity inevitably focuses attention on a network of symmetrically related particulars. The modern social arrangement is one in which all relationships are potentially, if not actually, understood in non-hierarchical terms. As Heller (1990, p. 148) points out, the mark of such an arrangement of, 'symmetric reciprocity', as she calls it, is that even though it 'does not exclude a hierarchy result-ing ... men and women are not thrown into it by birth'. To see that this, in principle, non-hierarchical way of relating is open to the modern particular individual in virtue of the recognition of partic-ularity consider the way in which the competing claims of modern particulars are typically formulated and negotiated. When modern individuals claim a right against others, for example, to be treated as an equal or not to be dominated, on the face of it they invoke the universalist language of formal rights: 'everyone should be treated as an equal' and 'everyone's freedom should be respected'. What grounds the claim of one particular not to be subordinated to an-other or the view that one particular should not be attributed pri-ority at the expense of others? To be sure formal rights claims, such as the ones we have just mentioned, are typically defined in terms of the properties that particulars are said to have in com-mon. Significantly, however, rights are also viewed as properties that belong to a certain kind of subject, namely one for whom par-ticularity (that in virtue of which one is a particular) is the mode of being that he or she recognises in everyone. 'Everyone', under-stood as every particular in the relevant class, is always implicated in the advocacy of a formal right. Were it not for the fact that par-ticularity is the recognised mode of being of modern particulars it would not be possible to understand conflict between particulars in terms of competing formal rights claims.

Indeed, because particularity provides the mode of being of each modern particular, within modern social paradigms every particular must conform to this mode of being even if this means, as in the case of religious world views, reformulating and restrict-ing one's claims to universality. This kind of awareness of partic-ularity renders the modern particular in touch with its mode of being so that the way in which it relates to its content is inevitably shaped by the explicit differentiation between what it is (content) and particularity as its mode of being (form).

THE UNIVERSAL GIVENNESS OF MODERN PARTICULARITY

So far, we have been arguing that the abstract idea of particular-ity is at the heart of the modern differentiation between form and content and that these concepts are, in turn, to be understood re-spectively as the mode of being of something and the substance of its concrete existence. As the universal mode of being of mod-ern individuals, particularity provides a way of relating modern individuals qua particular givens in the sense of different substantive particular beings. At the same time, we have also suggested that the modern association of particularity with the universal that has acquired its independence from the being of the particular (hereafter 'the differentiated universal') also renders the universal formal.

Now we want to point out that this kind of differentiation between the formal universal and the substantive particular translates into a dichotomous division as distinct from a mere differentiation. Firstly, because, as we indicated above, the substantive particular is defined only in its negative relationship to the universal, the two are oppositionally defined. Secondly, given that the formal being of the differentiated universal is not dependent on any substantive particular, unlike the particular, the formal universal is self-determining. For both the above reasons the formal universal takes a privileged position relative to the substantive particular.

We want to suggest, finally, that from the vantage point of its privileged position the formal universal plays the role of a givenness that mediates the relationships between different particular givens. We have already suggested that the formal universal mediates the relationships between different particular givens. This activity reveals its givenness, as distinct from its being a particular given, in the sense that it plays an unavoidable organising role for particular givens. The formal universal in the dimension of particularity functions as the very framework within which the relationships between particular givens are inescapably formulated. Modern particular givens are located within the givenness of their particularity which is, in turn, identified with the givenness of the formal universal for the reasons suggested above. In this way each particular given is not merely limited by its particular content, as is suggested by Habermas' implicit reference to the givens of nonmodern social paradigms. The modern particular given is also importantly limited by the givenness of the formal universal to which it is subordinated. To illustrate these claims we will go on to consider the way in which the givenness of the formal universal is socially embodied by formally free personality.

Modernity as the realm of givenness

So far we suggested, firstly, that the universal mode of being of distinctively modern individuals is given by their particularity which gives rise to the idea of the formal universal and, secondly, that modern particularity is a universal givenness in the sense that it supplies the organising framework within which modern individuals inescapably interact as particular givens. In this section we want to develop this discussion by demonstrating how the universal givenness of modern particularity reveals the shape of modern social interaction at its most basic level. Once we have arrived at an understanding of this claim we will also be in a position to see that Habermas' interpretation of modernity needs to be radicalised as a result of having failed to appreciate this key feature.

Our claim that the universal givenness of modern particularity reveals the shape of modern social interaction at its most basic level presupposes that all modern individual units of agency, whether distinct centres of consciousness, such as human beings, or social collectives and institutions, relate to themselves as particular givens. Yet, our earlier analysis also recognises that whereas modern individuals can differentiate between their particular substance and that which is universal, due to the emergence of formal universality they are also in a position reflectively to identify with formal universality. So, it is worth noting at the outset that even those units of agency that reflectively identify with formal universality embody some kind of awareness of themselves as particulars. Take as an example the legal system of a political state. On one level, relative to its subjects it represents itself as a universal authority. Yet, on another level, within the world order relative to the legal systems of other political states it takes itself to be one particular given amongst others. So, on some level of their existence all modern individuals relate to themselves as particulars. Our claim is that, by doing so, they all affirm the universal givenness of modern particularity.

This said, we will focus our attempt to lend support to our account of modernity's current condition on a demonstration of the way in which the universal givenness of modern particularity is embodied in what we consider to be a paradigm case. This is the case of formally free personality. As we will try to show below, the modern idea of socially interacting formally free persons incorporates all the features characterising the relationship between distinctively modern individuals' universal mode of being (form) and their concrete existence (content) which we have presented above.

The first thing to note about persons as conceived in modernity is that their identities incorporate the differentiation of the universal from the particular. On the one hand, personality permits a basic appreciation of the universal in the universal's own terms because, as Hegel (1981, §35R) puts it, it

> begins not with the subject's mere general consciousness of himself as an ego concretely determined in some way or other, but rather with his consciousness of himself as a completely abstract ego in which every concrete restriction and value is negated and without validity.

A person's ability to abstract from and negate every aspect of his or her concrete existence permits the emergence of the subject's formal or 'abstract universality, the self-conscious but otherwise contentless and simple relation of itself to itself' (Hegel, 1981, §35). In other words, we can focus exclusively on our sense of self as distinct from any of the particular properties with which we might otherwise identify. This ability to abstract from all the content of our concrete existence effectively frees up the universal aspect of the subject's mode of being in the sense that its mode of being need no longer be conflated with any substantive particular (as is typical of the non-modern relationship of the universal and the particular). From the perspective of an achieved differentiation of the idea of formal universality from that of the substantive particular every concrete restriction and value lacks validity because no substantive particular can legitimately presuppose its universality as it must do in order that it be valid.

Furthermore, the ability to negate every aspect of the content of our concrete existence also gives rise to the universal's essentially self-determining power. In so far as a person's formal self-relation remains wholly unmediated it is absolutely self-determining. Nevertheless, such absolutely free personality is only an inward mode of being given that it is grounded in the simple relation of a self to itself. For this reason, as formally free persons we face the task of having to move ourselves beyond our merely subjective freedom. We need our absolute but inward freedom to become our objective condition as well given that it is our universal mode of being.

As the first and most basic step in this direction, persons must freely will their own specific content. Of course, one of the important features of life in the modern age is that persons can insist on making their own choices about values and aspects of life that are important to them. These are the things that define and give substantive meaning to our identities as concrete existents in the world. So, when we make such choices we reflectively relate ourselves to some substantive particular(s).

However, it is not enough for persons to see something in their external world as valuable in order that they make it their own. The process of making objective or externalising our self-determining power, initially at least, calls for a certain kind of understanding of our external world. We have to be able to think of it in terms that would permit us to act upon it, to transform it appropriately, in order that we might make a place in it for ourselves as self-determining beings. We need, in other words, to externalise our mode of being as formally free persons by identifying with particular properties.

From this reflective standpoint, the world appears as a set of substantive particulars with the potential to embody the mode of being of free personality. At the same time, the very nature of free personality implies that our relationship to any particular property with which we identify cannot be viewed as permanent. Because free personality is a universal mode of being it cannot be confined to any substantive particular. So it is that we not only identify with, but also can withdraw from any particular property that belongs to the external world.

What kinds of relationship do we affirm in making these conceptual moves? To begin with, by relating to particular property items in the way just described a person's activity in the world manifests the non-identity of particular property items with the formal universality of personality. Substantive particulars remain particulars irrespective of their relationship to the formal universal. Their mode of being is, therefore, particularity.

At the same time, the person's formal self-relation is, nevertheless, externally mediated by some particular property. So, in relating to particular properties we also affirm the non-identity of the formal universality of personality and our own substantive particular being. In other words, we, ourselves, exist in the world of particularity as substantive particulars and every particular that makes up the specific identity of the particular person falls outside the scope of the formal universality of personality.

Furthermore, persons relate to each other through their particularity. Consider as an example relationships that are supposed to be symmetrical and are themselves mediated by substantive particulars. Modern relationships based on the exchange of property items are a case in point. In exchange relations our motivation for acting may well be to fulfill our respective needs and desires. Significantly, however, this type of interaction presupposes that we relate to each other as given particulars amongst a plurality of such particulars. That is, what each one of us is as a particular person is treated as being independent of the other's substantive being. Because every substantive particular making up the specific identity of each particular person falls outside the scope of the formal universality of personality, persons' substantive understandings of themselves are given independently of their interactions with one another. The content of their respective specific identities neither informs nor is informed by that of others. In this sense each person's particular identity appears as given relative to the exchange relationship. The other person's particular identity acts only as the boundary of, or limit on, one's substantive being and as such it commands respect due to the supposed symmetry of the exchange relationship.

It follows from the above that exchange relations presuppose a certain kind of mutual recognition. In this case we recognise each other, not for the specifics of what we are as particular substantive persons, but for the very fact that we are particular beings. In other words, we affirm our mutual particularity, that which makes us particulars and not any substantive universal.

Exchange relations thus illustrate the way in which the modern world affirms the universal givenness of particularity as the effective mode of being of persons who, nevertheless, take their mode of being to be their freedom. By interacting through their particularity, they manifest the formal universality of their personality and this, in turn, is to affirm the mere formality of their free personality.

In so far as modernity links the universality of free personality to the universal givenness of particularity, in the way just outlined, modern persons' essentially self-determining power turns out to be limited and, therefore, ineffective. Because it remains merely formal it cannot be integrated with persons' particular substantive being which, in turn, remains unfree, or externally determined, to this extent.

This dual condition of formally free yet substantively determined personality is itself socially instituted in a number of different ways within the modern differentiated social spheres that we mentioned at the outset. We have already seen how modern individuals interact as particular givens. This is the case within the sphere of civil life that is governed by market relations that are, in turn, subject to the necessary interconnectedness of substantive particulars. Within the modern legal sphere the differentiation between the formal universality of free persons and the substantive particularity of determined beings translates into an explicitly dichotomous division. On the one hand, individuals are

attributed the status of legal persons and so are formally recognised as self-determining. On the other, they are treated as legal
subjects. That is, in being subject to the external authority of the
law they are determined as substantive particulars whose substance must remain within the limits set by the givenness of particularity. Although we cannot argue the point here, we believe
that a more extensive discussion of modernity's failure to integrate
the formal universal with the substantive particular would show
that this failure is socially instituted, not merely within the differentiated social spheres, but also in the very way that these spheres
of activity relate to each other. Indeed, it could be argued that an
appreciation of the source of modernity's failure to supply the necessary integrating norms is at the heart of any adequate solution
to the much criticised modern dichotomisation of the public and
private social spheres.

As the above brief remarks suggest, there are a number of
ways in which we could develop and lend further support to our
argument. Nevertheless, we hope to have said enough to convey
our reasons for thinking, firstly, that particularity is modernity's
universal givenness in the sense that it defines the reality which
makes possible and affirms the formal universality of its freedom
as the mode of being of persons and modern existents more generally. Secondly, because the modern differentiation between the
formal universal and the substantive particular translates into a
dichotomous division that privileges the former, the formal universal plays the role of a givenness that mediates the relationships
between particular givens and supplies the limits within which
they can function. We will refer to this view of modernity as 'modernity's current condition'.

Habermas revisited

If the analysis of this chapter is correct then Habermas' understanding of modernity proves to be inadequate. Recall that on
his interpretation modernity cannot borrow its norms from non-
modern models because its inescapable self-referentiality obliges
it, so to speak, to create its norms out of itself. We have argued,
however, that we can make sense of modernity's denaturalising
drive in terms of a process that negates particular givens against
the presupposed background of its and their own givenness. On
this analysis of its current condition, contrary to Habermas' assertion modernity may well dispense with pre-modern givens without at the same time resolving the problem of creating its own

integrating norms. Since the possibility of negating particular givens arises out of the achieved differentiation of the formal universal that remains dichotomously related to substantive particulars, this possibility does not, after all, depend on any reintegrating norms. Indeed, the current condition of modernity would suggest that precisely because it relies on the very idea of givenness modernity, not only does not, but cannot immanently create its integrating norms. Its position might better be described as one of striving to avoid disintegration (cf. Luhmann, 1981).

So, where does this leave Habermas' claim that modernity must immanently create its own integrating norms and what should we make of the view that modernity's self-referentiality is inescapable? To be sure, if modernity is an essentially self-determining whole, then this is a demand which it must ultimately be in a position to meet. As we indicated at the outset, we accept that the essence of modernity is to be self-determining. Yet, our discussion suggests that we should not take it for granted that the emergence of this idea either suffices to generate, or is evidence for the existence of, the material conditions in which it is realisable. Furthermore, if we accept the conclusion that in its current condition modernity cannot supply its integrating norms, then we need to determine what it is about modernity's current condition that must change. What would it mean for modernity to overcome its givenness as a precondition for the creation of its own integrating norms and the realisation of its self-determination? We will turn to this issue in the next chapter.

3. THE MODERN TURN TO SPECULATIVE PHILOSOPHY

In the previous chapter we suggested that we can take modernity to be an essentially self-determining whole without also accepting that its self-determining power can be fully realised in modernity's current condition. Suppose that in order to be genuinely self-determining modernity must achieve, rather than take as given, its inescapable self-referentiality and that this requires it to undergo an appropriate kind of development. Obviously, such a process of development would, in turn, need to involve modernity's positive power of determination, as distinct from its mere power to differentiate itself from non-modern epochs. Now, if modernity's inescapable self-referentiality is to become the achieved result of its own immanent determining activity, then the process towards this end must include the moment of its as yet unrealised self-referentiality. This moment, we believe, is given by the current condition of modernity that we discussed in the previous chapter.

In this chapter we want to elaborate this position by advancing the claim that the givenness of the formal universality of modern particularity constitutes the very process through which the idea of modernity's self-determination can come to be known as modernity's as yet unrealised principle. We would like to develop this claim by arguing, firstly, that the modern endorsement of formal universality (with the ideal of freedom) amounts to a denial of modernity's self-determination (hereafter 'modernity's self-denial'); and, secondly, that unsuccessful efforts to overcome modernity's self-denial give rise to the need for speculative thought. If the analysis that follows is sound, then we will be in a position to explain the continued relevance of speculative philosophy and, relatedly, of Hegel's philosophical system in our times.

MODERNITY'S SELF-DENIAL

In the previous chapter we linked the emergence of the givenness of the formal universality of freedom to the modern concept of particularity. Particularity, we argued is the universal mode of being of modern existents, including formally free persons. Because particularity ultimately gives rise to the givenness of the formal universal, in the sense discussed in the previous chapter, the substantive particular being of modern existents is limited by this givenness. As we saw, one of the implications of this dichotomous conceptual framework is that the particular being of modern existents is negatively defined as not being the universal. Now we want to argue that this conceptual framework also permits the emergence of a quite different understanding of the relationship between the particular and the universal and thus of relating substantive particulars.

The differentiated unity of universal and particular

The understanding we have in mind here is that of a differentiated unity between the universal and the particular as conceived from the reflective standpoint of modern existents' particular identities (hereafter 'a differentiated unity'). Within the framework of modernity's dichotomous division between the universal and the particular, modern existents are in a position simultaneously to recognise the differentiation between universal and particular and to deny the necessity of their dichotomous division. They are in a position to do so for two reasons. Firstly, as our earlier analysis suggests, the dichotomous division of the universal and the particular only appears to be necessary in the light of the givenness of formal universality. Accordingly, to the extent that modern existents are differentiated from, because subordinate to, this givenness, they need not identify with the reflective standpoint of formal universality. Secondly, from the reflective standpoint that is identified with formal universality any interpretation of the relationship between the universal and the particular, including their differentiated unity, is open to modern existents as long as this interpretation does not challenge particularity as the mode of being of the particular.

The modern concept of substantive universality What precisely does a differentiated unity amount to? Like the dichotomously related universal and particular, in a differentiated unity differentiation is no less a characteristic of the universal's self-determination. However, unlike the dichotomously differentiated universal which remains formal, here, the universal becomes an internally related substantive unity. This is because in the process of embodying the universal as its mode of being the particular explicitly relates its substance to the universal as the substance of the universal. In other words, this way of relating the particular (content) to the universal (form) affirms their essential interconnectedness. In this sense the universal incorporates the particular without subordinating it.

What we have here is a redefinition of the unity of the universal and the particular that we introduced in our discussion of non-modern particulars in the previous chapter. Unlike the non-modern undifferentiated unity, this modern redefinition incorporates the moment of differentiation into its idea of unity. In doing so, a differentiated unity enables particulars to relate to each other through their substantive universality without ignoring or denying the particularity of their being. For this reason the concept of individuality that emerges in this understanding of a differentiated unity is neither atomic nor static. As in the dichotomous relationship, particular individuals recognise the boundaries between particulars as an essential moment of what makes each particular a particular. However, rather than viewing them as a limit or restriction on their identity, they take the boundaries between particulars to be part of that which they must reflectively incorporate into their own identity. It is in such a process of becoming that particulars unite with each other through the universal actively making the latter their mode of being. The universal is thus substantively, and not merely formally, self-determining.

Modernity's self-denial The substantive universality of a differentiated unity emerges as more comprehensive than, and, therefore, as the truth of, formal universality. This is because the former incorporates the formality of the latter (the differentiated universal) and also includes a further dimension. It supplies a unity of form with its content. A differentiated unity is, therefore, the sort of relationship between particular and universal that is required for modernity's self-determined generation of integrating norms. Nevertheless, since in its current condition modernity insists on the recognition of universality in terms of its formality, modernity effectively denies the truth of universality. This, in turn, amounts to the denial of its own self-determination.

Furthermore, nothing in the givenness of formal universality that characterises modernity's current condition permits it to recognise this denial as a denial of its principle of self-determination. It is in this sense that modernity's denial is a self-denial.[1]

In its self-denial modernity can do no more than represent itself as merely restricting, rather than precluding, the social realisation of a differentiated unity. Yet to modern existents for whom the realisation of a differentiated unity is necessary for the realisation of their own self-determination, modernity creates a gap between substantive universality as their ideal mode of being and particularity as their real mode of being.

The modern ideal of freedom in solidarity and modernity's self-denial
In this section we want to lend support to the claims, firstly, that the concept of the differentiated unity which we have sketched above does indeed belong to modernity and, secondly, that its emergence in modernity marks modernity's self-denial in a distinctive way. To see that relations grounded in the idea of a differentiated unity emerge within the social conditions of modernity we will argue, firstly, that the concept of substantive universality that characterises a differentiated unity is embodied in the modern social ideal of freedom in solidarity. We will then go on to explain the sense in which failed efforts to realise this ideal affirm modernity's self-denial.

Freedom in solidarity and communal being Broadly speaking, freedom in solidarity presupposes a certain understanding of communal subjectivity. This latter can be understood in the light of either of two fundamental modes of human existence, those of having and being, in the sense in which Erich Fromm (1984) explicates their difference.[2]

---

1. Cf. Castoriadis, 1997, pp. 372-373. In the context of proposing a very different analysis of society's self-determination, he concludes his account of the imaginary institution of society by noting that contemporary society is, not only alienating to humans, but is characterised by 'self-alienation' given that it is not in a position to know itself for the autonomous, self-instituting social organisation that it is.

2. Fromm's work suffices to draw attention to a broad contrast between the two fundamental modes of human existence that structure modern conceptions of communal subjectivity and are presupposed by modern conceptions of freedom. It is worth noting, however, that understood in dialectical terms, the conceptual source of the distinction between being and having is Hegel's idea of mutual recognition as elaborated both in his 'early' and in his 'late' phases. Cf. Hegel, 1979 and 1977. See also Honneth, 1992. This idea has, of course, been reworked by influential thinkers from Marx to Habermas, including anarchist thinkers, like Bakunin. These latter authors can be understood as attempting to radicalise the concept of mutual recognition in anti essentialist ways that

Fromm (1984, p. 33) explains that the having and being modes of existence are,

> two different kinds of orientation towards self and the world, ... two different kinds of character structure, the respective predominance of which determines the totality of a person's thinking, feeling and acting .

The having mode of existence The more familiar in western culture, the having mode, is closely linked to notions of possessing and owning and is therefore associated with property, control and the need for power which this brings with it.[3] To be in this case is to have. The having mode coincides with an atomistic social ontology, that is, a division of the world into concrete individual substances identifiable independently of their (causal) relations. Thus 'I am a member of a community' means I, who am identifiable independently of my particular situation in the world, have certain ties or associations with a group identifiable in a similar way. The ways in which I can be (ideally) related to my community are constrained by this mode of existence. Subject relates characteristically to object in terms of the notions of possession (of properties) and the other associated terms that link the subject externally to the object.[4] When our mode of ex-

---

avoid the reintroduction of dichotomies in our ethical stance. Cf. Marx, 1978; Habermas, 1973; Kyrkilis, 1991. For the purposes of our present discussion of the notion of communal being we need not be concerned with specific disagreements and differences in approaches concerning the details of the notion of mutual recognition.

3. Wolff-Dieter Narr (1985, p. 36) attributes a similar understanding of modern social existence to the effects of 'the performances necessary for [industrial-capitalist] production' when he claims that they 'create a society of roles where the individual is important only as a bearer of attributes—with reference to this or that attribute but not to what these attributes constitute: the person.'

4. In an atomistic conception of the social order individuals' 'interactions with others consist in mechanistic collision and displacement, in competition for space' (Mathews, 1991, p. 40). Based on Newtonian science and being a theoretical elaboration of substance pluralism, this metaphysic takes isolated individuals to interact causally yet their relationships are logically contingent and external to the identity of each. (Cf. Mathews, 1991; Gare, 1995.) Social atomism is also related to the much discussed notion of 'abstract individualism'. According to Lukes (1973, p. 73), abstract individualism takes a number of forms. In one of these it posits the idea of a 'pre-social individual' in the sense that 'the relevant features [properties] of individuals ... are assumed as given, independently of a social context'. (Cf. Grimshaw, 1986, pp. 162-186.) In our view commitment to an atomistic social ontology is best understood as limiting all relationships to the various forms of relatedness that are available to what Hegel (1981, §234) calls 'external

istence is an orientation of having, our identity is structured in accordance with the immediate self-relation at the heart of the idea of formally free personality that we discussed in the previous chapter.

The being mode of existence In contrast to the above, the being mode of existence has as its fundamental characteristic, the productive use of human powers. To be sure, the characteristics of the modern ideal of personal autonomy, freedom from internal and external constraints and critical reason, are preconditions of the being mode.[5] Even so, what is crucial for it is that one be involved in non-alienated, productive activity, as distinct from 'mere busyness', in which one experiences oneself as an acting subject in the very process of being active (Fromm, 1984, pp. 94-95). This experience cannot be fully captured in description. Rather it is communicated only by sharing in it.[6] The practice of sharing and the willingness to make sacrifices for others are characteristic of this orientation. One who experiences herself in this way does not place affective importance on drawing clear boundaries between self and others and between 'the things' that might belong to each, since it is not a condition of the enjoyment of something that one 'have it' as in

---

existents', that is, to the modern world's externally related units of agency. There are three general forms of relatedness available to external existents: (1) the incidental relations of reciprocity that exist between mutually dependent needy persons where each is ultimately moved by the desire to satisfy his or her own needs (the paradigm embodiment of which is the means-ends rationality of market relations); (2) the formal relations of obligation that exist between an individual agent and any external object that the agent recognises as an authoritative body (the paradigm embodiment of which is moral responsiveness to recognised customary or natural law); and (3) the concrete relations existing between needy individual agents, on the one hand, and public, official and cooperative services on the other, which combine to create the concrete social context in which subjectively or intersubjectively defined needs are actually met (the paradigm embodiment of which is state welfare services and self-governing, cooperative services). For a defence of this claim and a detailed analysis of the logical structure that these three forms of relatedness are given in Hegel's philosophy see Vassilacopoulos, 1994, pp. 188-230.

5. For an account of 'dynamic' personal autonomy which accords with a being mode of existence see Fox Keller, 1985. This account of personal autonomy gives expression to the dyadic structure of reflective subjectivity. See also Castoriadis, 1997, pp. 101-104 and 107-108.

6. As Laing (1985, p. 53) puts it, 'human beings relate to each other not simply externally, like two billiard balls, but by the worlds of experience that come into play when two people meet. Here we wish to emphasise the existence of non-reducible 'we experience' within such worlds. Cf. Singer, 1991.

the having mode. On the contrary, this is what makes the experience of shared enjoyment possible (Fromm, 1984, p. 116).[7]

It follows from the above that when our orientation to ourself and the world is that of being, our claim to be members of a community or more precisely our claim to be communal beings, is not primarily a claim about something of value that we have or even about an association between two (causally interacting) entities, ourself and the community. On the contrary, 'communal being' refers to a mode of being in which one's orientation to self and the world is constituted by non-alienated productive activity. Thus, the statement signifies my situation in the world in such a way as to emphasise a necessarily intersubjective experience, that is, an ontological state of affairs that extends beyond what in the having mode might be identified as the boundaries of my self.[8]

Furthermore, communal being need not be restricted to the social field of interpersonal practices and institutions, the paradigm instances of which might be friendship and other intimate relationships (cf. Held, 1993). The necessarily interconnected character of the experience of communal being may extend to one's world as a whole. This means, firstly, that communal being may coincide with a holistic world view in which human society is viewed as an integrated yet differentiated system.[9] Secondly, it means that in the political institution of society intersubjective relationships and the relationships of subjects to objects must be mediated by the value of solidarity.[10] So, irrespective of how else

7. Shared experience in the sense of participation with others is what Mae Brown (1985, p. 134) refers to when she explains that her commitment to feminism is not constituted by her having certain convictions: 'I am no longer tied to feminism by merely conviction or ideology. I am bound by a knot which I tied over time with other women'.

8. One might object that boundaries are crucial for the development and maintenance of ego identity. We do not want to dispute this. However, the point here is that when one's particular self is understood in terms of solidarity with other selves, then the boundaries between selves do not function as something to be protected but as what permits each self to move beyond them. We will return to this idea in Part III of the book when we focus attention on the intersubjective character of the loving self.

9. For recent attempts to develop holistic ontologies, understandings of scientific knowledge and dialectical logic see Gare, 1995; Mathews, 1991; Merchant, 1990; Skolimowski, 1992; E. E. Harris, 1987.

10. Cf. Dean, 1996; Oldfield, 1990, pp. 25-27 and Ch.7; Jordan, 1989, pp. 67-86. In our view two features of citizen solidarity are of special importance for communal being when compared to other values such as care and love. First, solidarity is subjectively mediated in the sense that individual subjects' reflectively endorse their relationships of solidarity. Second, solidarity is capable of being

one defines the specifics of the structure of the political life of a community, communal being necessarily includes a political dimension. This dimension is captured by the ideal of freedom in solidarity.

Freedom in solidarity and the concept of substantive universality Freedom in solidarity is grounded in the dyadic structure of subjectivity. This makes it necessarily intersubjective in the following sense. The reasoning processes ideally involved in the definition, and not just in the realisation, of political values are necessarily (potentially, if not actually) intersubjective in a way that gives expression to relationships of mutual responsiveness, responsibility and accountability.

What we have in the case just described is a mature expression of that which Hegel (1985, §436) calls 'the affirmative awareness of self in another self'. In Part III of the book we will develop and illustrate these claims about the structure of subjectivity and explain their Hegelian connections. For now, the general point to note is that the communal subject embodies a universal self-relation. However, unlike the merely formal universality of the subject who in the having mode of existence can only be immediately self-related and, hence, externally related, this universal self-relation incorporates the particular self. In the being mode one's particular self relates to its universality as that through which one is united with another particular as a particular. One's particular substance is, therefore, recognised as the universal substance through which particulars unite with each other. In this way communal subjectivity embodies the substantive universality characterising the differentiated unity of universal and particular.

The struggle to realise the ideal of freedom in solidarity

From the above outline we can see how the ideal of freedom in solidarity presupposes a distinctively modern concept of substantive universality which is at the heart of a differentiated unity. In doing so it also gives rise to an alternative conception of the mode of being of modern existents. From the reflective standpoint of individuals who, implicitly or explicitly, appeal to substantive universality as their mode of being (hereafter 'visionary moderns') formal universality represents an incomplete understanding of modern

---

institutionally mediated, for example, through the mechanisms of government. This said, we leave open the question of whether or not the nation-state is an appropriate model of political community.

self-determination. Consequently, as far as visionary moderns are concerned, there is no reason why they should restrict the determination of their particular being to its negative definition, as is the expectation in modernity's current condition. They see the realisation of their self-determining nature as unavoidably tied to the realisation of ideals, like freedom in solidarity, that embody substantive universality. Starting with the French Revolution, the last two hundred years have witnessed repeated struggles to realise some vision of freedom in solidarity in (an implicit) defiance of the givenness of formal universality (hereafter 'visionary struggles'). Such visionary struggles represent attempts to lead us, in one way or another, in the direction of a radically transformed social order in which our social existence and our mode of being might accord with each other and with our self-determining essence. Visionary moderns can be viewed as the bearers of an as yet unrealised mode of being that actively must be brought into being, as it were. In this way they embody modernity's future orientedness.[11]

Yet in modernity's current condition (within the realm of particularity that is governed by formal universality) only a limited space can be made available to those who would espouse ideals embodying substantive universality. Indeed, the availability of this space is made conditional upon their remaining within the limits set by the recognition of the formal universality of particularity. This means that the acceptable pursuit of the ideal of freedom in solidarity must be restricted to the internal operations of small scale associations that do not thereby oppose the mode of organisation that defines modern society's public domain (cf. Rawls, 1993). Accordingly, what we have is an antithesis between the conditional space that is created for ideals embodying substantive universality and what we might call the unconditional aspirations of the bearers of such ideals.

Three readings of visionary struggles How might we interpret the objective significance of the agonistic co-presence of formal and substantive universality described above? One might interpret the antithesis as confirmation of Habermas' thesis that modernity cannot escape the task of setting and realising its own integrat-

---

11. For an exposition of visionary moderns' attitude and motivations see Castoriadis (1997, pp. 91-93). This outline captures the subjective experience of visionary moderns irrespective of whether or not they share Castoriadis' philosophical presuppositions (1997, pp. 74-75) or his precise conception of 'the revolutionary project' as praxis in his sense of this term (1997, pp. 77-78).

ing norms. Despite the many unsuccessful attempts to realise this task, it continues to be critically reformulated against the background conviction that its proper formulation and ultimate realisation will prove the indispensability of the view of modernity as essentially self-determining.

This interpretation attributes the unsuccessful struggles of visionary moderns to a necessarily practical process that must be guided by the conditions of modernity. For example, Castoriadis (1997, p. 77; pp. 95-101) maintains that, although a genuinely revolutionary politics has not existed until now radical social transformation is rooted in 'the crisis of established society' as lived by the masses.

> The crisis is due to the fact that it [established society] is at one and the same time a protest ... Labour conflict, the destructuring of the personality, the collapse of standards and values are not and cannot be lived by people as mere facts or as external calamities, they also give rise to responses and to intentions and the latter, while they complete the shaping of the crisis as a genuine crisis, go also beyond the crisis itself (Castoriadis, 1997, p. 99).

The view just sketched represents one of three possible interpretations of modernity's current inability to generate its own integrating norms. A second interpretation might insist that all visionary struggles must fail precisely because the task is utopian in the sense of being unrealistic. Underlying this position is the view that the dichotomous differentiation of the universal and the particular is axiomatic for the human condition and that modernity's current condition cannot therefore be transcended. Some go so far as to insist that the liberal social order that modernity has already instituted represents, not only the most advanced to date, but the final social paradigm (cf. Fukuyama, 1992; Ryan, 1997, p. 308).

From this perspective radical attempts to reshape the modern world amount to regressions to non-modern ideals that fail to give due weight to modern individuality. The second interpretation would have it that the apparent failure of the western political and intellectual tradition to elaborate and institute a modern non-liberal conception of freedom leaves us with only one rational choice. We should insist on refining modern liberal individualist social practices and institutions.

A third interpretation shares with the first the view that the substantive universality underlying the ideal of freedom in solidarity defines the essential nature of modernity. Yet it also shares with the second the view that visionary moderns' failure to realise this ideal is unavoidable. However, it does not share with the first interpretation the conviction that a visionary struggle might succeed some time in the future if it can (a) identify and harness appropriately the powers of genuine agents of radical social transformation and (b) grasp the proper connections between such agents, their transformative powers and the current conditions of modernity. Nor does it share with the second interpretation the conviction that the current conditions of modernity represent the final social paradigm. On this third interpretation, even though agent-centred visionary struggles cannot hope to succeed, this does not tell against the utopian project of modernity understood as the transition to a social paradigm in which, having overcome its givenness, modernity generates and realises its own integrating norms (hereafter 'the project of modernity').

The third interpretation of the failure of visionary struggles supplies an understanding of the objective significance of this failure in terms of its (implicit) affirmation of modernity's self-denial and the consequent emergence of speculative awareness. In order to spell out this understanding we need to explain, firstly, what it is about visionary struggles that leads them to fail unavoidably, if this is not due to the fact that they mistakenly oppose the final social paradigm; and, secondly, the sense in which, far from being misconceived, the project of modernity can, nevertheless, be understood as still in the process of being realised.

Why visionary struggles fail unavoidably In our view to appreciate the genuine limits of visionary struggles we must have regard to the way in which the identity of visionary moderns relies upon the concept of substantive universality that characterises a modern differentiated unity. If our analysis above is correct, when, whether individually or collectively, visionary moderns demand a new social reality they implicitly or explicitly represent themselves and each other as becoming united through their substantive universality. In thus effectively willing their substantive universality they set their ideal mode of being as an aim to be realised. For example, the visionary modern might say, along with Castoriadis (1997, p. 100),

> [i]f we assert the tendency of contemporary society towards autonomy, if we want to work for its realisation, this is because we are asserting autonomy as a mode of being of humans, that we are ascribing value to it, that we are recognising it as our

essential aspiration and as an aspiration that surpasses the pe-
culiarities of our personal constitution.[12]

To work for the realisation of contemporary society's autonomy is
to aspire to bring about radical social transformation 'by means of
the autonomous action of individuals' (Castoriadis, 1997, p. 77).
The aspiration to work in this way at once invokes the universal aspect of our being and the non-formality of this universality given
the presupposition of the need for radical change from the current
condition of modernity which, after all, recognises universality in
terms of the formality of freedom.

One might, of course, insist, as Castoriadis (1997, p. 78) implies, that the universality in question is not substantive in the
sense of being capable of being 'fixed in "clear and distinct" ideas'
that stand over against reality as if ready to impose themselves
upon it. Being a project and an aim to be realised, the content of
the mode of being of visionary moderns is concretely given in an
ensemble of phenomena, such as tendencies in people's work towards cooperation and collective self-management. Despite lend-
ing themselves to ambiguity, such tendencies signal 'the possibility and the demand for autonomy' (Castoriadis, 1997, p. 99).

Let us grant that we should not conflate (a) visionary moderns'
self-determined willing of substantive universality in the sense of
a mode of being that is not reducible to an empty form with (b)
appeals to rigid predetermined categories of substance. What we
want to argue is that this first sense of individual willing nonetheless fails to appreciate the preconditions of a successful exercise of
particular wills' self-determining powers. More specifically, substantive universality must pre-exist acts of particular willing in
a way that permits it to function as the framework within which
to undertake the individual and collective will formation in question. This means that in order to function as the mode of being of
particular individuals, substantive universality must not only be
socially instituted but it must be appropriately socially instituted.

To be sure, visionary moderns can readily point to a number
of social phenomena that signify a substantively universal mode of

12. An advocate of Castoriadis' position would likely object to our association
of this demand with an appeal to a mode of being that we regard as ideal given
his unwillingness to recognise the existence of a gap between 'idea' and 'reality'
in the explication of the nature of the revolutionary project (Castoriadis, 1997, p.
78). Nevertheless, for reasons that we cannot go into here we think that we can
usefully and consistently rely on the distinction we drew above between an ideal
and a real mode of being to signify the sort of gap between 'representation' and
'realisation' that Castoriadis (1997, p. 78) acknowledges.

being in modernity's current institutional arrangements. We have already mentioned tendencies toward cooperation and self-management in the sphere of production. Drawing on the sphere of intimate life, we could invoke as further examples the social practices that give concrete shape to feelings of love and care for others. In each of these cases visionary moderns can readily set their ideal mode of being as an aim that they can realise as particular self-determining individuals in the current condition of modernity. The substantive universal can thus become the actuality within which visionary moderns' acts of common willing exhibit the creative force which Castoriadis and others envisage.

Still, despite the fact that such social phenomena give a determinate shape to visionary moderns' ideal mode of being within the modern world in its current condition, the substantive universality that they embody is limited in one crucial respect. Its actuality rests on the presupposed givenness of modern particularity. This would explain why, as the above examples suggest, in modernity's current condition the concrete expression of visionary moderns' substantive universality appears in institutions and social practices whose particularity is not thereby challenged. We readily recognise it within small scale associations, such as the family, the local cooperative or the trade union. What we do not seem to be able to show, however, is how visionary moderns might successfully set their substantive universality as an aim to be realised in and for the political institution of their society as a whole, as distinct from the political institution of this or that particular modern existent (such as the market or the legal system).

Irrespective of their aspirations, the actualisation of visionary moderns' ideal mode of being remains objectively limited to the presupposed givenness of the particularity of modern existents. This is because the mode of being of the world as a whole is not something that can be created out of acts of particular willing alone, even if this particular willing is conducted in common. Even though the particularity of individual willing must be involved in the creative realisation of the mode of being of the world as a whole, this mode of being is not properly reducible to that of particular existents within the world. When visionary moderns set their ideal mode of being as their aim to be realised in the name of modernity's self-determination they would appear to be conflating the realisation of (a) the substantive universal as the mode of being of particular existents with (b) the substantive universal as what we might call an all-informing mode of being. Whereas the first may well be within the range of our effective powers of self-determination under the current condition of modernity that is, after all, defined by the givenness of particularity, the second need not. Since visionary moderns equally presuppose the givenness of particularity, when they invoke the substantive universality that characterises their ideal mode of being in order to oppose the formality of modern universality, they do not thereby pose any threat to particularity as the real mode of being of modernity.

If the above analysis is correct, then visionary moderns cannot fully realise their aim within modernity's current condition. Perhaps they must wait for modern instituted society to reach a new level of maturity as a result of which it might supply the conditions in which, instead of merely opposing the formality of modern universality, visionary moderns might contribute to the overcoming of particularity as modernity's real mode of existence.

This said, we can still think of modernity in its current condition as having reached an important level of maturity with the emergence of the moment of its self-denial. This is because the subjective affirmation of its denial plays a critical role in rendering explicit that its self-determining essence is, after all, a project in need of realisation. The failure to realise the modern ideal of freedom in solidarity affirms modernity's self-denial in the sense that unsuccessful attempts at radical social transformation render the objectivity of modernity's self-denial visible to subjective awareness. What is otherwise already a matter of denied self-determination becomes capable of being known as such to modern subjects. By making explicit that which it denies, modernity gives rise to the possibility of being known as that which is in the process of becoming an essentially self-determining whole. In the next section we will try to spell out the reflective process that this knowledge can trigger and from which, we will suggest, visionary subjects might reasonably turn to the practice of speculative philosophy in the current condition of modernity.

THE TURN TO SPECULATIVE PHILOSOPHY

Our aim in this section is to explain how a certain way of understanding the emergence of speculative awareness in the current condition of modernity allows us to see, in very broad terms, how speculative awareness is appropriately placed to supply us with genuine knowledge of the world assuming from the outset that the world is an essentially self-determining whole. We believe that such knowledge develops out of a reflective standpoint that has good reason, not only to see modernity as currently being in self-denial, but also to situate modernity's self-denial in a developmental process that treats this denial as the necessary moment of its as yet unrealised self-determining power. Both these claims are of course controversial and we do not mean to imply that they are in any way (capable of being) settled prior to, and independently of, the full elaboration of a speculative philosophical system that has adequately formulated and justified its understanding of modernity's essential nature. What we hope that our discussion will show is that, despite the currently dominant belief to the contrary, we should not abandon the speculative approach to the development of philosophical knowledge on the ground that its methods and criteria of adequacy are irrelevant to the problems of our world.

The experience of worldly alienation

The failure of visionary subjects to realise their ideal mode of being renders visible the resilience of modernity's current condition against such struggles. Nevertheless, we want to suggest that this failure does have the power to transform the relationship of visionary subjects to modernity. The former might no longer see themselves as the bearers of transformative powers adequate to the task of realising their ideal mode of being in modernity. For this reason such visionary subjects can become alienated from our current reality as a whole. As a result of its repeated lack of responsiveness to the demands of visionary moderns the current condition of modernity may appear before them as what we might call the world of denial. That is, what was previously understood as a totally interconnected field of potential doing (cf. Castoriadis, 1997, pp. 71-75; pp. 86-90) comes to be experienced as the very negation of such doing.

This world of denial is not restricted to that which is external to the particular being of visionary subjects. Instead, it not only includes all the particular properties making up their concrete identities and from which they are in a position to abstract, but it extends to the formal self-relation with which they otherwise identify consistently with modernity's recognition of their formal freedom. Their identity as particulars and as individuals is implicated in the experience of worldly alienation because, as we argued above, this identity gives expression to their real mode of being whereas this mode of being, the formal universality of particularity, is itself the source of modernity's self-denial. Because the world of denial extends to visionary subjects' very own existence within it, they can become alienated from their own existence, including their formal self-relation, as much as from the rest of the world. When such a process of negation takes hold visionary subjects become what we can call 'totally alienated subjects'.[13]

The transition to speculative awareness

How does one move from the reflective standpoint of the totally alienated subject to the reflective standpoint of speculative awareness? As a result of the discord between the concept that we take to be our ideal mode of being (the substantive universality of differentiated unity) and the real mode of being that our current reality recognises in us (the formal universality of particularity), the object of our reflection shifts from the mode of being we have sought to realise as the true mode of being of our world to the very meaning or notion of our own and the world's mode of being. This is a strictly conceptual refocussing of our attention on this meaning as a potentiality in the sense of that which, being in the process of being realised, is not yet.

Furthermore, because the world of denial includes our own existence within it, in the sense discussed above, in this conceptual refocussing we are left with the notion of that with which we continue to identify, namely the reflective self-relation that we earlier examined in connection with the ideal of freedom in solidarity. However, as a result of the experience of total alienation this notion can be nothing more than the pure awareness of reflective self-relatedness; the meaning of our reflective self-relation can include no empirical determination whatsoever. Pure awareness in this speculative sense is the kind of awareness in which to address the meaning of the world's potential mode of being as such.

The possibility of speculative knowledge Speculative awareness can become the cognitive perspective from which to know the world because it is meaning or conceptuality as derived from our totally

---

13. This idea of total alienation contrasts with that which views the members of a certain interest group as being socially marginalised or excluded from the general class of recipients of social benefits of some kind. Cf. Jordan, 1989, pp. 90-107. As a late twentieth century phenomenon the experience of total alienation grows out of the realisation that neither the traditionally Marxist, nor the New Left social movements' efforts to create stable revolutionary identities have succeeded. Cf. Laclau, 1994, pp. 1-10; Seidman, 1993, pp. 103-142. Dunn (1993, p. 122) echoes this sentiment when he suggests that in the late twentieth century, 'what has been deleted from the human future ... is any form of reasonable and relatively concrete social and political hope'.

alienated relationship to the world, in the sense explained above. (It is not to be confused with concepts that might be used to represent this relationship.) If speculative awareness can provide the meaning of the world's potential mode of being, the world cannot but reveal itself when reflected upon from the cognitive perspective that is supplied by its own mode of being. Such conditions of knowing reveal the world's essential knowability.

Speculative awareness in its absolute negativity It follows from the above brief remarks that when our awareness becomes speculative it is an absolute negativity in the sense that its being is wholly indeterminate. However, it is also not unmediated given the process of its emergence that we have sketched. Furthermore, if speculative awareness is, after all, the kind of awareness from which to resolve the problem of the meaning of the world's (potential) mode of being, it must construct this meaning immanently. This means that speculative awareness begins with awareness of its lack of determinate being and of its need to determine itself as, or to become, the notion of the world's mode of being. This is the sense in which speculative awareness becomes speculative.

The cognitive structure of speculative awareness

Because speculative awareness must construct the meaning of the world's mode of being immanently, this meaning must be drawn out of its pure self-relation. To do this speculative awareness must treat itself as absolutely self-determining. What is the structure of its self-determining cognition? Hegel (1975, §160A) notes that speculative awareness

> must be considered as a form, but it is a form that is infinite and creative, one that both encloses the plenitude of all content within itself, and at the same time releases it from itself.

We want to suggest that the interplay between the concepts of the universal, the particular, and the individual supplies the structure of speculative awareness' self-determination. Indeed, we think that it is for this reason that Hypolite (1989, pp. 80-81) is correct in maintaining that this interplay is 'the basis of Hegel's entire philosophical system'. In its self-determination speculative awareness must think of itself as supplying its own mode of being (form) in that it must treat its thought as being created out of, and revealed to, itself. Such an all encompassing and immanent process of creation and revelation is available to that which is universal. Understood in this way, the universal is not only that which has abstracted from every concrete determination but it also potentially incorporates every possible determination. Speculative awareness is thus not just the universal mode of being. Because the concept of determinateness is indispensable to its universal self-relation it is also the concept of the particular. Awareness of the particular as having the universal as its own mode of being, in turn, renders speculative awareness an individual.

The most elementary formulation of the self-determining power of speculative awareness is given by these three concepts. Their interplay constitutes the meaning or notion of speculative awareness. For this reason, irrespective of the precise determination that speculative awareness gives to itself through the development of its concepts, its determination must always involve some interrelationship of the universal, the particular and the individual.[14]

HEGEL'S PHILOSOPHICAL SYSTEM

So far we have suggested that the aim of speculative philosophy is to become the notion of the world's mode of being. We tried to show, not only why this understanding of philosophy has continuing relevance for our times, but also that the need for it is derivable from a certain way of experiencing the current condition of modernity. We suggested that the experience of total alienation gives rise to speculative awareness that is aware from the outset of its notion and its purpose: (i) its notion is that of unconditional self-determination as given by the interplay between the concepts of the universal, the particular and the individual; and (ii) its purpose is fully to determine itself as the meaning of the world's mode of being in order to come to know the world as embodying this meaning. Our aim in this final section is to explain how these ideas are connected to our reading of Hegel's system.

14. The relationship between the universal, the particular, and the individual is elaborated in the second volume of the *Science of Logic* after the development of the categories of being and essence. From this one might conclude, mistakenly in our view, that we have misinterpreted Hegel's view of the cognitive structure that initially defines speculative awareness. Note, however, that according to Hegel, irrespective of our awareness 'we cannot begin with the truth, because truth, when it forms the beginning, rests on bald assurance, whereas the truth that is thought has to prove itself to be truth at the bar of thinking' (Hegel, 1975, §159A). So, there is a sense in which the concept that constitutes speculative awareness in its beginning must nonetheless come into being that is justifiably known because it is the result of its own self-determining thinking activity. This requirement explains how it is possible for philosophical science at once to begin as the unity of its three categories and to undertake the construction of these categories well into the categorial development that takes place in the *Science of Logic*.

First, we will explain why the realisation of the aim of speculative philosophy, as we have outlined it above, calls for a systemic approach like Hegel's and, then, we will offer an interpretation of the role and general significance of the main parts of Hegel's system. Though this is not the place to offer any detailed defence of our claims, especially concerning issues that are very controversial within Hegelian scholarship, we hope that our suggestions will suffice to indicate our general understanding of the wider framework within which the more detailed discussions of Parts II and III of the book take place.

The necessity of Hegel's system

On the first of these issues, we maintain that a systemic approach like Hegel's becomes necessary because it supplies the progressive self-determined construction of conceptual relationships in which being and the notion of the world's mode of being can come to accord with each other. This is implied in Hegel's remarks in his 'Preface' to the *Phenomenology of Spirit* (1977, §26) when he notes that 'the ground and soil' of philosophy is 'pure self-recognition in absolute otherness'. The state of 'pure self-recognition' characterises speculative awareness whose cognitive structure is the unity of the universal, the particular and the individual, when it first comes on the philosophical scene. Unlike the immediate awareness characteristic of the merely formally self-related being, speculative awareness does not just affirm its being. Rather, it recognises itself in its notion. At the same time, due to the purposive nature of speculative awareness that we mentioned above, this self-recognition must also be accompanied by an awareness of its being 'in absolute otherness', that is, as being the absolute indeterminacy of a being that is not yet. The tension between these two seemingly incompatible elements of pure self-recognition and absolute otherness permits speculative awareness to construct its being progressively in accordance with its notion and this is what renders speculative philosophy holistic and systemic.

Where does the system of speculative philosophy begin? From what we have said so far, one might think that the emergence of speculative awareness leads directly to the process of determining the notion of the world's mode of being. However, were speculative philosophy to proceed like this it would fail to take into account an important aspect of the emergence of speculative awareness. Due to the very immediacy of its emergence speculative awareness must first confront the givenness of the presupposition that it is indeed appropriately positioned to make a philosophical beginning. For this reason speculative philosophy faces a preliminary task of coming to know its cognitive perspective to be true to its purpose. In our view this is achieved by undertaking the reflective process in the *Phenomenology of Spirit*.[15]

Phenomenology of Spirit

The stated aim of the *Phenomenology of Spirit* is to introduce absolute knowledge to consciousness as the truth of consciousness. Absolute knowledge in the manner we understand it here is another way of referring to the cognitive perspective of speculative awareness. Absolute knowledge is knowledge that is given within an epistemic and ontological framework that recognises the essential unity of (knowing) subject and (known) object. In contrast, the phenomenological consciousness is dichotomously structured. In the latter the known object exists indifferently to the knowingness of the knowing subject whilst the knowing subject is aware of this indifference. In the subject-object dichotomy consciousness treats the object of its knowledge as being independent of the subject's knowing in this sense. Due to this presupposed independence of the object of knowledge from the fact of its being known by the subject, the knowledge that consciousness generates must appear to be relative to its object (hereafter 'relative knowledge'). Relative knowledge is the product of consciousness' necessarily formal awareness in the sense of an awareness that lacks essential content and thus derives its content externally. Despite this formality of the phenomenological consciousness and the related relativity of its knowledge, the completion of the phenomenological process that takes place in the *Phenomenology of Spirit* is supposed to demonstrate the unavoidable implicit reliance of consciousness on absolute knowledge. Absolute knowledge is ultimately presented as the justified perspective from which to come to know the world and this includes the world of relative knowledge that is generated by consciousness' formal awareness.

The phenomenological consciousness and speculative awareness How is the above mentioned aim of the *Phenomenology of Spirit* related to our claim in the previous section that Hegel's system presupposes the emergence of speculative awareness? We have suggested that the emergence of this kind of awareness stems from the fact

---

15. For an alternative systemic reading of the role and significance of Hegel's *Phenomenology of Spirit* see Harris, 1995.

that the would-be speculative philosopher's empirical self is taken
to be an integral part of the very world that denies the mode of being whose meaning speculative philosophy sets itself the task of
constructing. Precisely because this world is structured dichotomously the subject-object dichotomy is at home in it. So, it seems
that, as an empirical self that belongs to this world, the would-be
speculative philosopher is identified with the phenomenological
consciousness to this extent.

At the same time, there appears to be an important difference
between the two kinds of awareness as we have presented them
above. This difference lies in the fact that whereas the would-be
speculative philosopher's empirical self has embraced the cognitive perspective of speculative awareness, the phenomenological
consciousness only becomes self-consciously aware that its cognitive perspective is that of speculative awareness as a result of work-
ing through the phenomenological process. Let us consider this
apparent difference taking further note of Hegel's remarks in his
'Preface' to the *Phenomenology of Spirit:*

> pure self-recognition in absolute otherness, this Aether as
> such, is the ground and soil of Science or knowledge in gener-
> al. The beginning of philosophy presupposes or requires that
> consciousness should dwell in this element (1977, §26).

(In this context 'science' refers to speculative philosophy that is
genuinely self-determining.) We have already indicated what we
take Hegel to mean by the condition of 'pure self-recognition in absolute otherness' and why this condition should be understood as
a basic precondition for the emergence of speculative awareness'
cognitive perspective. Now we want to suggest that the 'dwelling'
of 'consciousness', that Hegel suggests is presupposed for a philosophical beginning, should be understood in terms of the would-
be philosopher's willingness to embrace the cognitive perspective
of speculative awareness. As we noted in the previous chapter,
speculative awareness arises out of the totally alienated subject's
relationship to the dichotomously structured world and out of the
would-be philosopher's willingness to go beyond his or her formal
awareness. That is, having emerged, the cognitive perspective of
speculative awareness promises the capacity to reveal the meaning of the mode of being of the philosopher's empirical self and of
his or her dichotomous world. Yet, as our analysis also suggests,
this promise can be made only when the empirical self that is con-
fronted by speculative awareness is itself implicated in it. The former must have the strength to allow the very thing that ensures

its existence in the world, namely its formal self-relation, to be absorbed into the abstract reflective process undertaken from the cognitive perspective of speculative awareness. Without the empirical self's unconditional opening to, or dwelling in, speculative awareness it would not be possible for speculative awareness to 'come on the scene'.

Still, even though it is necessary, the requirement that consciousness dwell in the element of speculative awareness does not suffice to ensure a genuinely philosophical beginning. Hegel (1977, §26) indicates as much when he says

> [s]cience on its part requires that self-consciousness should have raised itself into this Aether in order to be able to live— and (actually) to live—with Science and in Science. Conversely the individual has the right to demand that Science should at least provide him with the ladder to this standpoint, should show him this standpoint within himself.

The merely immediate emergence of speculative awareness cannot fully satisfy the presupposition that consciousness dwell in the element of speculative awareness precisely because it emerges merely immediately. Rather than proceeding directly with the elaboration of its notion, speculative philosophy must therefore turn backwards, so to speak, in order to reconstruct what it presupposes in a way that overcomes the original givenness of this presupposition.

The would-be philosopher's act of immediately embracing speculative awareness does not suffice to justify the claim that absolute knowledge is indeed the truth of relative knowledge given that this act of embracing has not itself been justified. After all, the self which identifies with this claim is only the would-be philosopher's particular empirical self. This self, as we explained in the previous section, is still implicated in the real mode of being (the formal universality of particularity) that is recognised in the current condition of modernity. In contrast, absolute knowledge claims to be the truth, not only of some particular self and its world, but also of the very idea of the self in its dichotomously structured world. The immanent development of the speculative philosophy thus presupposes that speculative awareness can properly be embraced by the philosopher's empirical self taken as a universal (hereafter 'the empirical self as such').

If this suggestion is correct, then, the particular empirical self's initial act of embracing speculative awareness has to be understood as something with which the empirical self as such needs ultimately to be identified. At the same time, a justification is required for the claim that absolute knowledge is the truth of the cognitive perspective of the empirical self as such. Without it speculative philosophy cannot be justifiably developed as the immanent truth of the empirical self and its world.

Precisely because absolute knowledge cannot ultimately ground the truth of its claim in the mere fact that the would-be philosopher has immediately, albeit immanently, embraced speculative awareness, through his or her particular empirical self, speculative awareness must itself be shown to be the truth of the empirical self as such. This is what Hegel has in mind when he says that 'self-consciousness should have raised itself into this Aether'. To meet this demand for justification the particular empirical self must, in turn, be reconceptualised. This reconceptualisation should be able to demonstrate the truth of speculative awareness' presupposition that the empirical self as such can properly be embraced.

The phenomenological consciousness is in a position to address this demand for justification because in the *Phenomenology of Spirit* it gives expression to the empirical self as such. The phenomenological consciousness enables us to reflect upon consciousness, understood as the empirical self as such in all the different configurations that it can possibly take. The aim is to determine whether it can sustain itself, in any of its configurations without having to rely on the absolute knowledge of speculative awareness. If consciousness, thus understood, cannot but rely on absolute knowledge as its truth, then absolute knowledge can proceed from its speculative perspective to determine itself as the truth of consciousness' relative knowledge and, hence, as the justified perspective of the empirical self and its world. In this way, the *Phenomenology of Spirit* provides the would-be philosopher with the 'ladder' with which to raise himself or herself (i) out of the limits that are otherwise imposed by his or her dichotomous thought and (ii) justifiably into the cognitive perspective of absolute knowledge.

Absolute knowledge through the idea's cycles of development

At the completion of the phenomenological process the notion is ready to develop its categories as absolute knowledge. According to Hegel, absolute knowledge is given by 'the Idea' (cf. Hegel, 1975, §14). The 'idea' refers to the kind of reflectively self-determining awareness that provides itself with its notion and its being. So, at any given moment in the philosophical system the idea is speculative awareness that has become the kind of reflective being that has resulted solely from the power of its self-determination.

The idea unfolds in three cycles of development that are carried out in the *Science of Logic*, *Philosophy of Nature* and *Philosophy of Mind*. These are respectively characterised as 'the science of the Idea in and for itself', 'the science of the Idea in its otherness' and 'the Idea that returns into itself out of its otherness' (Hegel, 1975, §18). What role do these developmental cycles play? Our earlier analysis suggests a general response. One of the tasks of speculative philosophy must be to determine itself as the meaning of the world's mode of being. Furthermore, once this task is completed the idea must come to know the world as embodying the meaning of the world's mode of being. These two tasks can be said to be undertaken, first, in the logical categorial progression of the *Science of Logic* and, then in the *Philosophy of Nature* and the *Philosophy of Mind* that respectively deal with the categories of nature and social life (hereafter 'real philosophy'). But why are the three developmental cycles necessary and how do they relate to each other? In our view the answers to these questions presuppose an appreciation of two complementary aspects of the categorial progression. These are what we might call the notion's anticipatory and retrospective dimensions.

We have already explained the sense in which speculative awareness has an overall purpose. The idea's absolute immanence permits it never to lose sight of this purpose. Since the idea is aware of its immanent purposiveness from the start of its development, it repeatedly finds itself anticipating its movement from one developmental stage to the next until the full realisation of its overall purpose. At the same time, the retrospective knowledge of its exact position at every point in its progression is equally necessary for the idea's overall development. To put the same point differently, the idea's completion of its task within any one developmental cycle without the memory, so to speak, of its overall purpose would render it blind to the overall significance of its achievements.

We want to suggest that the idea's anticipatory and retrospective dimensions tie together its three developmental cycles in a way that gives each cycle its necessary place in the system. We will briefly consider the three developmental cycles in order to illustrate the claims (1) that these two dimensions enable the idea to have regard to its overall purpose at appropriate points in the categorial progression; and (2) that the necessity for each of the three cycles can be explained by reference to the fact that the idea's overall purpose comes into play as a result of its retrospective and anticipatory dimensions.

Science of Logic   We have already suggested that the idea's overall purpose explains why the *Logic* must form the first of the idea's developmental cycles. Recall that the idea's overall purpose is fully to determine itself as the meaning of the world's mode of being in order to come to know the world as embodying this meaning. The logical categorial development makes explicit the meaning of the world's mode of being in the element of its pure self-recognition, that is, in pure thought and as pure thought. This is what Hegel means when he says that in the *Logic* the idea develops and completes itself 'in and for itself'. So, we can say that the *Logic* begins by anticipating the idea's first major task, namely the development of the notion of its self-determining power in the element of its pure self-recognition.

When the notion has fully determined itself in the element of pure thought it justifiably becomes the logical idea, that is, the idea that retrospectively knows itself to be complete in this respect. However, as a result of the logical idea's retrospection that brings the idea's overall purpose into view once more the logical idea also knows itself to be merely abstractly realised. This is because it is the meaning of the world's mode of being that is not yet actualised as knowledge of the world. The idea's retrospection renders visible the merely abstractly achieved unity of thought with its being. To summarise: on completion the logical idea is aware of two aspects: first, it has fully determined itself in the element of its pure self-recognition; and, second, it has only achieved this self-determination as an abstract principle that wholly lacks existential determinateness.

The transition to the Philosophy of Nature   The above mentioned dual aspect of the completed logical idea is crucial to an appreciation of the basis for the idea's movement to the next developmental cycle, that of reflection into nature. For, whereas the completion of the *Science of Logic* is necessary for the transition, the rationale underlying the latter cannot be understood simply by reference to the logical idea's completed self-determination. The fact that the completed logical idea is wholly abstract and lacks existential determinateness ultimately requires the idea to anticipate its development through the categories of nature. Why is this the case?

In recognising itself as a being that lacks existential determinateness, the idea immediately becomes the other of the logical idea or, as Hegel puts it, 'the idea in its otherness'. This is because its abstract being is that of a being that does not know itself to be the embodiment of the notion of the world's mode of being. Existence which is thus distanced from the meaning of its mode of being is external to itself; it lacks self-determination. So, the idea in its otherness becomes the idea of necessity or nature. The *Philosophy of Nature* is thus the full elaboration of the idea's self-externality.

Philosophy of Nature In the *Philosophy of Nature* the idea gives itself existential determinateness through the categories of nature. Here we want to suggest that because the idea must move through the realm of necessity immanently to it, this movement is not itself determined by the preceding logical categorial progression. Even though the reflection in the *Philosophy of Nature* is not devoid of logical categorial determination, the development of the categories of nature cannot progress in accordance with the movement defined by the logical progression. For, this would amount to reflection upon the world of necessity with the aid of the idea's self-determining categories. This, in turn, would defeat the purpose of the idea's development in its otherness. For, the idea must become that in which its self-determining power can be realised.

In the *Philosophy of Nature* the idea of nature is transformed from mere existence that is external to itself to the kind of being that is retrospectively in a position to know itself as being in accordance with its own notion. This is what Hegel means when he refers to 'mind' as the idea that has returned 'into itself out of its otherness'.

The Philosophy of Mind In Part II of the book we will set out what we consider to be the main aspects of the process through which the categories of mind are progressively developed into a system of social and ethical life. Here we note one final advantage of our reading of the way in which the overall purpose of Hegel's system ties together its various developmental cycles through the idea's retrospective and anticipatory dimensions. Because we can make sense of the necessity for the systemic transition from the *Logic* to the *Philosophy of Nature* in the way we just outlined, we are also in a position consistently to advance a certain view of the relationship between the *Logic* and the *Philosophy of Mind*. This is the view that the shape and direction of the categorial progression in the *Philosophy of Mind* is determined by the nature of the idea's progression through the *Logic*. To offer a partial defence of this reading, Part II of the book we will begin with an overview of the main aspects of the *Logic*.

PART II

4. THE DEVELOPMENT OF THE NOTION IN HEGEL'S *LOGIC*

This chapter will provide an overview of the notion's development in thought and as pure thought or, to use Hegel's (1975, §19) words, of thought 'in the sense of the self-developing totality of its laws and peculiar terms'. Let us begin by considering what Hegel (1989, p. 69) says about the nature of the notion's initiation into this developmental process.

> Now starting from this determination of pure knowledge, all that is needed to ensure that the beginning remains immanent in its scientific development is to consider, or rather, ridding oneself of all other reflections and opinions whatever, simply to take up, *what is there before us.*

According to this statement, if we focus our attention on 'what is there before us' we can ensure the immanent beginning of a scientific development of the notion's unfolding because we start from the 'determination of pure knowledge'. What precisely is this determination? Following from our discussion in Chapter 3 we can answer this question by turning to the cognitive structure of absolute knowledge. Recall that speculative awareness takes its notion to be the differentiated unity of the universal, the particular and the individual that is yet to be realised.

The question to be addressed now is what role does this categorial interplay play in the starting point of the notion's logical development. Is 'what is there before us' the notion, as Hegel refers to it? If it is, should we expect absolute knowledge to begin with its notion and to go on from there to consider the question of its realisation? What should we make of the fact that the *Science of Logic* consists of three 'parts' of which only the third and final part, 'The Doctrine of Notion and Idea', explicitly addresses this question of the notion's realisation? We want to suggest that from the outset absolute knowledge takes the differentiated unity of the universal, the particular and the individual to be its notion but in doing so it is, nevertheless, also aware that it has yet to think this unity in and as pure thought. From this perspective, the first two cycles of development in the *Logic* function as prerequisites for the notion's readiness to tackle the question of its realisation.[1]

BEING AND ESSENCE

These cycles are developed respectively in 'The Doctrine of Being' and 'The Doctrine of Essence' (Hegel, 1975, § 83). Here, the notion is referred to as 'implicit' and a 'show' respectively. More specifically, the 'Doctrine of Being' is 'thought ... in its immediacy' which corresponds to 'the Notion implicit and in germ', whereas in the 'Doctrine of Essence' we have 'thought ... in its reflecting and mediation' which corresponds to 'the being-for-self and show of the Notion' (Hegel, 1975, §83). The development of the notion through 'Being' and 'Essence' shows it justifiably to be their truth. Even so, Hegel (1975, §159A) notes,

> [w]hen ... the notion is called the truth of Being and Essence, we must expect to be asked why we do not begin with the notion? The answer is that, where knowledge by thought is our aim, we cannot begin with the truth, because the truth, when it forms the beginning, must rest on mere assertion. The truth when it is thought must as such verify itself to thought.

Although the notion is the truth of 'Being' and 'Essence', before beginning its explicit development it has to show itself to be this truth. We can see why this is necessary by briefly considering the categorial character of 'Being' and 'Essence'.

According to the *Encyclopaedia Logic* 'in Being everything is immediate, in Essence everything is relative' (1975, §111A). The categories that correspond to 'Being' are oblivious to any kind of relation and are absorbed in their own immediate, that is unreflective, self-unity. In 'Essence' each category retains its unity without however being exhausted in this unity in that its relation to an other category is acknowledged (1975, §111A). However, this acknowledgment has an external character. In 'Essence' the coexistence of unity and differentiation does not amount to the differentiated unity of the notion.

> The terms in *Essence* are always mere pairs of correlatives, and not yet absolutely reflected in themselves. ... hence in essence the actual unity of the notion is not realized, but only postulated by reflection (Hegel, 1975, §112).

1. See also Burbridge, 1995.

So, in 'Essence' we have the external relation of unity and differentiation whereas in 'Being' we have only a unity which is oblivious to differentiation. If this account is correct then 'Being' and 'Essence' would appear to be the moments of the notion, not in their unity but as abstracted from it. Recall that the main characteristic of the notion's cognitive structure is that it is a differentiated unity. It is the unity of the moments of unity and differentiation. In 'Being' and 'Essence' these two moments are formulated so as to exhibit the condition of their abstraction from their unity.

As moments of the notion, 'Being' and 'Essence' can also be described as the (knownness of the) object and the (knowingness of the) subject respectively. Their unity constitutes the notion's being as absolute knowledge. 'Being' is not the object of knowledge in abstraction from the knowing subject in the sense of an object existing independently of the subject. Nor does 'Essence' express the reflective activity of a subject apart from the object of cognition. Rather each expresses the unity of knowing and known (absolute knowledge) from a different angle. In 'Being' this unity is exhibited from the side of the known; the knownness of the object is immediate presence. In 'Essence' we see the unity from the side of its knowingness; this is relation. These two angles come together in the perspective of the unity that is exhibited in the 'Doctrine of the Notion and Idea'.

Justifying the notion in being and in essence

The above understanding of 'Being', 'Essence' and their relationship to the notion allows us to see why Hegel thinks it necessary for the notion to justify itself as their truth. Were the notion to begin its realisation as a differentiated unity it would have had to presuppose itself as the truth of its moments. That is, it would have to assume that it is the truth of both a unity which is without differentiation and a differentiation that is externally related to unity. In this way, thought would merely have assumed the truth of its notion rather than having derived it immanently, as is the mark of the development of scientific philosophy.

In order to engage in a justificatory process of the kind just referred to absolute knowledge must in some sense already possess that which is to be justified but it must also be immanently aware of the need of justification. In other words, the notion must be both a differentiated unity and one that incorporates the awareness of the need to justify itself as the truth of its moments. This is precisely the situation in which absolute knowledge finds itself.

It initially encounters itself as a categorially differentiated unity yet this awareness of itself also makes explicit the need to justify itself in pure thought. When it is sought to be met in and as pure thought this need for justification is not external because absolute knowledge simultaneously reveals its notion to itself and challenges the validity of what is expressed in this revelation thereby raising the question of its authentication. So, the requirement that the notion justify itself by emerging as the truth of its moments is an integral part of the development of the notion's determinate being as fully self-determining. The notion's awareness of itself as a differentiated unity of the indeterminate categories of the universal, the particular and the individual must, therefore, be unavoidably accompanied by awareness of the task of reflecting on the being of thought that is nonetheless unthought in the sense of a being that is non-self-determining.

THE DOCTRINE OF THE NOTION

We suggested so far that it is only at the completion of the developmental cycle making up the second part of the *Science of Logic* that the notion determines itself as that which seeks its realisation. For this reason it is only from this point on that it can justifiably treat itself as the starting point of the process that confronts the question of its realisation. The notion fully determines its otherwise indeterminate differentiated unity in the third cycle, developed in 'The Doctrine of Notion and Idea'. As the references to both notion and idea in the title of this third cycle suggest, at this point the notion undertakes a developmental process that eventually gives rise to the objectified notion that Hegel calls the 'idea'. In the third part of the *Logic* we have 'thought in its return into itself, and its developed abiding by itself' that corresponds to 'the Notion in and for itself' (Hegel, 1975 §83).

In an explanatory remark concerning the emergence of the notion in this sphere of its freedom Hegel notes the following.

> The Notion, when it has developed into a *concrete existence* that is itself free, is none other than the *I* or pure self-consciousness. True, I *have* notions, that is to say, determinate notions; but the *I* is the pure Notion itself which, as Notion, has come into *existence* (Hegel, 1989, p. 583).

Even though the notion has 'come into existence' as self-determining this existence is still incomplete to the extent that it is still a derivative or relative existence. In spite of having emerged as the absolute unity of unity (being) and difference (essence), it has only determined itself as their truth and has not yet determined itself as notion. As self-determining the notion 'must itself posit what it is'. In other words, the notion which is a positedness because it 'has come to be' through the development of its moments of unity and differentiation, must now develop itself as this differentiated unity:

> this reality [of the notion's positedness] does not yet possess the determination of being the Notion's *own, self-evolved* determination; it fell in the sphere of necessity; but the Notion's own determination can only be the result of its *free* determining, a determinate being in which the Notion is identical with itself, its moments also being Notions and *posited* by the Notion itself (Hegel, 1989, p. 596).

The self-determining notion must now construct its differentiated unity from the perspective of its truth. This means that it must engage in a process the result of which will be to arrive at the differentiated unity of the universal, the particular and the individual, this time as determined by the notion.

The notion of the notion as the unity of universal, particular and individual

For Hegel the requirement that the notion determine its differentiated unity amounts to the requirement that the 'Notion of the Notion' be developed (1989, p. 582). The 'notion's notion' refers to the principle of the notion understood as that which makes it the notion at its most abstract or universal level. Hegel refers to this as the 'universal Notion'.

> The universal Notion, which we have now to consider here, contains the three moments: *universality, particularity,* and *individuality*. The difference and the determinations which the Notion gives itself in its distinguishing, constitute the side which was previously called *positedness*. As this is identical in the Notion with being-in-and-for-self, each of these moments is no less the *whole* Notion than it is a *determinate* Notion and *a determination* of the Notion (Hegel, 1989, p. 600).

In this process of self-determination the notion is 'universal' because it presents itself as the truth of every step making up the process. The claim that 'each of these moments is no less the *whole* Notion' means that each moment must incorporate the others. According to Hegel (1975, §164)

> ... the universal is the self-identical, with the express qualification, that it simultaneously contains the particular and the individual. Again, the particular is the different or the specific

character, but with the qualification that it is in itself universal and is as an individual. Similarly the individual must be understood to be a subject or substratum, which involves the genus and species in itself and possesses a substantial existence.

The process in question takes the universal, the particular and the individual to be stages which are 'determinations' of the notion. At the same time each one of these categories is a form of the 'determinate' notion, that is, one form of the notion's differentiated unity. In other words, the justified notion is the differentiated unity that aims at determining itself as this unity.

The rationale underlying this development can be put as follows. Precisely because it is merely self-determining, as distinct from already self-determined, the notion both anticipates the realisation of its self-determination and is ready to realise what it anticipates. In its attempt to realise its self-determining power, the notion enters a developmental process the principle of which is the differentiated unity of the universal, the particular and the individual. (For ease of reference we can simply refer to the differentiated unity of these three categories as 'the categorial differentiated unity'.) The abstract unity of universality corresponds to the notion that, in anticipating its realisation, is not yet and, so, is as otherness expressed by the particular. In transcending its otherness the notion reflectively knows itself as self-determining and is thereby the individual. Given that the notion is the categorial differentiated unity that anticipates its determination, it begins with the moment of universality which becomes the abstract expression of the differentiated unity. In this way, the universal is 'the whole Notion' and at the same time, a moment of the notion's development. The same holds for the particular and the individual, the first of which expresses the differentiated unity in its determinate otherness whilst the second expresses the accomplished categorical differentiated unity.

So the notion must begin with the moment of universality in which it is abstractly self-related in a way that includes both determinateness (particularity) and awareness (individuality) since it is the truth that is at the same time unrealised. From universality the notion moves to particularity. According to Hegel (1989, p. 606), 'the particular is the universal itself but it is its difference or relation to an other, its *illusory reference outwards*'. It eventually realises 'the return into itself' (Hegel, 1989, p. 621) in the moment of individuality which is 'the notion reflecting itself out of the difference into absolute negativity' (Hegel, 1989, p. 601). The difference expressed by the fact that the notion is related to the particular as its other is transcended when the notion reflectively knows that the essence of the particular is to embody the universal. The reflective awareness expressed by individuality reveals that the notion is not simply immersed in its determinateness; it knows itself to be its own creation. The truth of the notion's embodiment (the truth of its particularity) is the fact that in it and through it the universal is united with itself as both the determinate universal and the universal that is responsible for its determination. This is why Hegel calls the individual the absolute determinateness. The absolute negativity initially expressed in universality is explicitly shown in individuality to be the factor that determines the differentiated unity of the notion. In the categorial differentiated unity formulated by the moment of individuality the notion returns to the absolute negativity of universality through particularity and it is in this regard retrospective. The notion is an individual that has accomplished its anticipated self-reflective determination.

The logical progression from the universal through the particular to the individual

The movement from the moment of universality that is itself a categorial differentiated unity (hereafter 'the U moment') through the unity of particularity (hereafter 'the P moment') to that of individuality (hereafter 'the I moment') exhibits the principle of the notion's process of becoming. This aspect of the logical structure can be said to guide the progression through 'The Doctrine of the Notion and Idea'.

If this interpretation is correct then the development in 'The Notion', the beginning of 'The Doctrine of the Notion and Idea', must be (at least part of) the U moment of the doctrine's cycle of development. The last section, 'The Idea' must be (at least part of) its I moment. Indeed in the scheme we want to propose the notion's I moment is fully constituted by this stage whereas the notion reaches this stage through the P moment which is developed as 'The Objective Notion' in the stage of 'Objectivity'. We can refer to the kind of movement just described, from the U moment through the P moment to the I moment, as a 'U, P, I progression'. (Cf. Gaskins, 1990, pp. 414-416).

We can make sense of the transition from one developmental stage to the next, whether between developmental cycles or within a cycle, having regard to whether, and in what combination, the notion is (a) anticipatory and, hence, abstract relative to its end; (b) in otherness, in so far as it has yet to determine its being; or (c) retrospectively aware of itself as whatever it has determined itself to be. Consider the movement within the U moment of the most comprehensive cycle of development within the *Logic*. The three stages that are involved here, 'The Notion', 'The Judgement' and 'The Syllogism', are equally stages of abstractness given their anticipatory role in the most comprehensive cycle of development within the *Logic*.[2] On the other hand, they are also related to each other as the three moments of a U, P, I progression. The U moment of abstractness, 'The Notion', expresses the notion's absolute indeterminacy. The P moment of abstractness, 'The Judgement', expresses the notion's complete loss in externality given the otherness of this moment in abstractness. That is, the notion immanently introduces itself into otherness by establishing its inner identity in otherness. However, in doing so, it posits the determinateness of its abstractness and thereby moves to the I moment of abstractness, which is its reflective moment.

The I moment of abstractness, 'The Syllogism', expresses the notion's opposition of its mediating unity to its externality due to its formality. The notion thereby exhibits its full determinateness as abstractness. Through this relation of opposition its inner abstract unity (the absolute indeterminacy of the accomplished notion's differentiated unity) is reflectively equated with externality (the being to which the syllogistic form is related as the mere form). As a result of this equation in 'The Syllogism' the notion is posited as the essence of its other and thereby moves to 'Objectivity', the P moment of the most comprehensive cycle of development within the *Logic*.

As the P moment of its developmental cycle, 'Objectivity' incorporates the determinateness of its U moment which is made explicit in the latter's reflective I moment, that of 'The Syllogism'. The determinateness of the notion as the essence of otherness is thus exhibited with the emergence of the objective notion. The task of 'Objectivity' is then to become the self-determining identity of externality. Since it is not yet this identity the movement to objectivity gives rise to a new developmental cycle with its own anticipatory and retrospective moments.

In this way the notion develops through its first reality, that of the development of the subjective notion to objectivity, and, then through its second reality, that of the development of the

2. We adopted this understanding after consideration of comments by G. Marcus on Vassilacopoulos, 1994.

objective notion's subjectivity. At the completion of the development through these two realities the notion becomes the self-determining identity of its externality from which externality it is thus distinguished. It thereby passes into 'The Idea', the I moment of the most comprehensive developmental cycle within the *Logic*.

This reading of the development of the notion's first and second realities implies three things about the nature of any particular point in the developmental process. Firstly, such a point constitutes one moment of a U, P, I progression. Secondly, it is also part of the U, P, or I moments of the cycles of development from 'The Notion' to 'The Syllogism' or from those within 'Objectivity'. Finally, the particular point of the developmental process is an aspect of either the U moment or the P moment constituting the most comprehensive logical cycle. For example, the 'Judgement of Existence' is to be understood as simultaneously bearing the features of (i) the U moment of the cycle of development that ends with the 'Judgement of Necessity' as this cycle's I moment; (ii) an aspect of the P moment of the cycle of development from 'The Notion' to 'The Syllogism' in so far as it is incorporated into the true form of the judgement; and (iii) an aspect of the U moment in the cycle of development from 'The Notion' to 'The Idea' to which 'The Judgement' as a whole belongs.

On this view any particular point in the system is not merely to be understood as manifesting features which belong to it in virtue of its position in the notion's developmental process. Such a position should not be taken as one point in one cycle of development but rather as a point in a number of cycles operating at different levels. These different levels need to be taken into account in order to understand the features manifested at any particular point in the system.

We can demonstrate the merits of our proposed reading of the logical structure by indicating how it serves to explain transition points in the *Logic*. Indeed in the absence of this kind of explanation these transitions either remain unaccounted for or are only explicable by reference to conditions external to the system. Some commentators on the *Logic* believe that this latter is the only kind of justification that is available to the Hegelian system. For example, Zimmerli (1989) advances such a position regarding the justification of Hegel's subjective logic. We believe, however, that we are left with Zimmerli's conclusion only if we fail fully to appreciate the implications of a reading that takes seriously the complex relationships between the various levels of U, P, I progressions within the logical system's cyclical development. The partial defence of our reading, in the next chapter, will begin with a presentation of the general character and stages of the developmental process that the subjective notion undergoes in order to restore itself in its other and thereby to posit itself as the objective notion.

5. THE JUDGEMENT, THE SYLLOGISM AND OBJECTIVITY IN HEGEL'S *LOGIC*

In the previous chapter we made the point that the notion, whose absolute identity has been formulated by the moment of individuality, enters the realm of otherness. This, we explained, constitutes the P moment of a U, P, I progression that unfolds within the overall U moment of 'The Doctrine of the Notion'. According to the *Science of Logic* (1989, p. 621), at this stage otherness expresses the notion's immediate loss of self:

> individuality is not only the return of the Notion into self, but immediately its loss. Through individuality, where the Notion is internal to itself, it becomes external to itself.

Hegel (1986, p. 99) also refers to this kind of externality as that which 'destroys' the notion.

THE JUDGEMENT

According to the *Science of Logic*, the notion's externality is initially exhibited in the form of the judgement. The transition to this form is presented as follows.

> Because it [the notion] is absolute negativity, it sunders itself and posits itself as the *negative* or as the *other* of itself; and further because as yet it is only the *immediate* Notion, this positing or differentiation is characterised by the fact that the moments become *indifferent to one another* and each becomes for itself; in this *partition*, its unity is still only an external *connexion*. As such *connexion* of its moments, which are posited as *self-subsistent* and *indifferent*, it is *judgement* (Hegel, 1989, p. 599).

It is worth noting here that commentaries on Hegel's analysis of the judgement offer very little by way of a discussion of the reasons for the transition from 'The Notion' to 'The judgement'.

Indeed, references to the notion's overall movement through the judgement's developmental process are largely descriptive rather than explanatory. For example, Taylor (1983, p. 306-308) suggests that for Hegel the transition to the judgement is necessitated by 'the requirements which are posed by the ontological Concept' but he does not say why these are supposed to be met by the form of the judgement in particular. Marcuse (1987), on the other hand, introduces his brief discussion of the judgement by suggesting that the transition to it should be understood in the light of the 'species process' undergone by the notion. In his interpretation Marcuse mentions the 'principle' or 'notion of the notion' but he does not explain its precise role in the transition to the form of the judgement.[1]

To appreciate the role of the judgement and the necessity of its emergence for the notion's development we must bear in mind the relevant condition of the subjective notion. The subjective notion is not only immanently negated but its negation is immediate and due to the notion's very formality. In the form of the judgement the notion is the other, immediate loss, of itself. As such it is immediately the differentiatedness of its moments. These moments, the categories of the universal, the particular and the individual, have not yet been concretely determined by the notion as internally related. Individuality is only individual, universality, only universal and so too with particularity. The notion's unity thus appears only as an 'external connection' of 'self-subsistent and mutually indifferent' categories. The absolute absence of internal categorial relation marks the 'loss' and 'destruction' of the notion given that the notion has formally determined its absolute identity as the categorical differentiated unity. Having become immediately 'external to itself' the notion's reflection upon its reality, the reality of its self-loss, must be exhibited as an external, as opposed to absolute, reflection. This is because that which is reflected upon is the lack of internal categorial relation. According to Hegel (1986, p. 99),

> [i]n the judgement 'otherness' comes into the Notion. Judgement is a subjective affair; Subject and Predicate appear as indifferent, apart, external and are first brought together by us externally.

---

1. Compare Burbridge, 1995, p. 124. This tendency in the secondary literature merely to describe the transition process rather than to offer an explanation for it is not limited to discussions of the judgement but extends to the discussion of transition points of the *Logic* generally. Cf. E.E. Harris, 1983, pp. 226-238; Johnson, 1988, pp. 169-179. In what follows we make an attempt to redress this problem by offering an explanation for the supposed necessity of the notion's transition to the form of the judgement.

> *We* have here a Subject and here a Predicate which *we* attribute
> to the Subject.... In judgement there is a separation of Subject
> and Predicate, of the matter in hand and reflection.

For the negated notion relatedness is present only as a connection
that we who reflect in the form of the judgement make externally
to the mutually indifferent categories.

According to Hegel (1975, §166),

> [i]n its abstract terms a judgement is expressible in the propo-
> sition: 'The individual is the universal.' These are the terms
> under which the subject and the predicate first confront each
> other, when the functions of the notion are taken in their im-
> mediate character or first abstraction.

The suitability of these terms of the judgement for exhibiting 'the
notion in its particularity' (1975, §166) can be appreciated if we
bear in mind the retrospective achievement of the notion that constitutes the I moment of 'The Notion'. Taken retrospectively the
notion's U, P, I progression within 'The Notion' has given the notion the status of a self-determined individual. Recall that the individual finds its universality in the determinateness of the particular. Now, in the realm of its self-loss this determinateness of the
particular must be absent. The absence in question is exhibited
by the absence of the particular as one of the terms of the judgement's propositional form. The individual thus appears to be connected to its essence, as exhibited by the universal in the position
of the predicate, simply through the abstractness of the copula.
The judgement's abstract form makes no reference to a third category. It, therefore, manifests the notion's first reality as the reality
of immediate loss or destruction by taking a form in which there
is absent the determinateness (particular) which brings together
the reflective notion (individual) and its essence (universal) in the
notion's retrospection.

The form of the judgement manifests the differentiated unity
of the notion only in so far as its terms exhibit differentiated categories that are related through the copula. Because the copula of
the judgement is indeterminate this unity is not yet the posited
'pregnant *unity* of subject and predicate ' (Hegel, 1989, p. 630).

> To restore this *identity* of the Notion [categorial differentiated
> unity], or rather to *posit* it, is the goal of the *movement* of the
> judgement ... since subject and predicate are *in and for them-
> selves* the totality of the Notion (Hegel, 1989, p. 630).

This 'goal' together with whatever is required for its realisation are
anticipated at the beginning of the movement in question in a way

that makes this movement possible and necessary. In order to restore its identity the notion must immanently transcend its self-
loss. This immanent transcendence requires that what is anticipated is, firstly, posited and, secondly, developed. In this way the
notion establishes its presence in order thereby to show the judgement's form to be its own reality. This task calls for the development of the judgement as 'truth' in the sense of a correspondence
of the notion to the reality of its object. The anticipation in question is that of the notion's truth understood as the 'doubling' of
'one and the same object', that is, as the unity of individual subject
with its universal essence (Hegel, 1989, pp. 630-631).

Positing the notion as the truth of the judgement

Given that categorial differentiated unity is the essence of the notion's identity and that the goal of the notion in the form of the
judgement is to posit its categorial differentiated unity, in order to
achieve this goal immanently the notion must detect its own self
rather than sheer otherness in the form of the judgement. This
is the task of positing the truth of the judgement form as the differentiated unity of subject and predicate. It is accomplished in
the movement from the judgement of existence though the judgement of reflection to the judgement of necessity.

Judgement of existence As the U moment of this phase, the judgement of existence constitutes the first of three stages of this cycle
of development. The developmental process of the judgement begins with the judgement of existence since this is the immediate
judgement. The beginning is at first immediate because of the absence of internal reflection. This absence renders the judgement
as the absolute other of the self-determined reflective individual
notion. According to the *Science of Logic* (1989, p. 630), in its immediacy the subject of the judgement 'simply is'; it is the self-subsistent or 'abstract individual'. Similarly, its predicate is one of the
subject's properties taken as an abstract universal.

The judgement of existence exhibits a subject that is immediately united with a predicate yet the unity in question does not also
exhibit essential differentiation since the predicate is connected to
the subject as one of its properties (positive judgement) or as not
all its properties (negative judgement). Subjective reflection initi-
ates a movement which results in the transcendence of this form
and with it the transcendence of reflection as external connection.
In trying to think the categories as immediate we reach a point at

which determinate connection is revealed to be their essence. The initial immediacy of the categories exhibited by the judgement of existence is sublated into their unity, the copula, when in the infinite form of the judgement, the most advanced form of the judgement of existence, it is shown that the difference between subject and predicate cannot be retained in the way required by the form of the judgement.

Judgement of reflection   The categories are reformulated in the judgement of reflection, the P moment of this first phase, so that 'the determination of one is *reflected* ... in the other' (Hegel, 1989, p. 630). A judgement of this form exhibits the essential determinate content of the terms given that the predicate is not limited to one of the subject's properties.

The most advanced form of the judgement of reflection is the universal judgement. It shows that its unity is accidental, even if it reveals the essential determinateness of the terms. The unfolding of the judgement of reflection reveals that the difference of the categories is also sublated into the copula.

Having appropriated both the unity characterising the abstract individual of the judgement of existence and the reflecting being of the categories exhibited by the judgement of reflection the form of the judgement is reconstructed so as to incorporate both these elements. This reconstruction is worked out in the judgement of necessity, the I moment of the judgement's first phase.

Judgement of necessity   According to the *Science of Logic* (1989, p. 657), the development of the judgement of necessity renders explicit the copula's determining role. When the copula becomes the explicit unity of the terms of a judgement it is thereby identified with the notion and posited. This is expressed by the result of the disjunctive judgement, the most advanced form of the judgement of necessity. The disjunctive judgement takes the general form 'A is either B or C or D' and expresses the relation between genus and species. The genus as subject 'contains within it the *determinateness* which constitutes the *principle* of its particularisation into species' (Hegel, 1989, p. 656). In the position of the subject we have the abstract universal (genus) and in that of the predicate we have the universal particularised into its species. As stated in the *Science of Logic* (1989, p. 657) 'the *simple determinateness* of the subject is sundered into the *difference of the species*'. Here the notion is posited due to the presence, firstly, of the differentiation of the subject into its predicate and, secondly, of the unity of the subject with the predicate that is expressed by the copula.

Hegel's inclusion of a fourth judgement form

Hegel's analysis of the judgement is not confined to three main forms. According to the *Science of Logic*, the judgement of necessity gives rise to a fourth form, 'the judgement of the notion'. At this point the *Logic* appears to give rise to the anomaly of having diverged from the system's usual tripartite division within developmental cycles. The question of why Hegel should think this necessary has been addressed in different ways. For example, Johnson (1988, p. 177) suggests that 'Hegel's treatment of the judgement ought to end ... with the judgement of necessity, since ... the identity of subject and predicate has been "explicitly posited"'. For E.E. Harris (1983, pp. 230-231) the diversion from the tripartite division is only 'apparent'. He suggests that the judgements of reflection and necessity correspond to the twofold categories of 'The Doctrine of Essence' and so reads 'The Judgement' as effectively comprising three stages.

Despite their obvious differences, these readings share a failure to appreciate the rationale behind the notion's movement in the sphere of the judgement. While it is correct that the completion of the judgement of necessity marks the explicit positing of the identity of subject and predicate, as Johnson notes, the question that the notion's anticipatoriness raises at the beginning of 'The Judgement', that of the doubling of the object in the form of the judgement, has not been fully addressed at this point. This is because what has been posited as the truth of the judgement has not yet been developed as this truth and, so, still remains relative to this positedness. The development of this truth is the work of the judgment of the notion.

The development of the notion as the truth of the judgement

We have already explained that the disjunctive form of the judgement of necessity marks the point at which the notion has reclaimed itself in the judgement by determining itself as the essence of the judgement form. For this reason it is ready to realise its essence through the further development of the form of the judgement. We indicated above that the truth of the notion as judgement is reflection upon itself as the self-determined essence of the reality of the object. Since the relation between subject and predicate is not yet a concrete differentiated categorial unity, given that the unity is affirmed in the predicate by the abstract copula, the notion is this truth as what Hegel (1989, p. 657) calls an 'ought-to-be' in relation to which 'the reality may or may not be adequate'.

The apodeictic judgement Developing the form of the judgement from the perspective of the 'ought-to-be' eventually reveals that the 'judgement ... has its *ground* in the constitution of the subject and thereby is *apodeictic*' (Hegel, 1989, p. 662). The subject of the apodeictic form of the judgement, the most advanced form of the judgement, contains the universal, that which the subject ought to be, as well as 'its *constitution*', the reason for the subject's accordance or failure to accord with the predicate. In the case of the accordance of subject and predicate:

> we have the universal which is *itself* and continues itself through *its opposite* and is a universal only as *unity* with this opposite (Hegel, 1989, p. 662).

The subject so constituted by the predicate is objectively universal because it is mediated by the determinate reality that it is. This determinateness is its 'opposite' in so far as it is the notion's externality, that to which the essence is to accord. When the notion reaches the form of the apodeictic judgement

> we now have before us the *determinate* and *fulfilled* copula, which formerly consisted in the abstract 'is', but has now further developed itself into *ground* in general (Hegel, 1989, p. 662).

The notion fully reclaims its inner identity in the apodeictic judgement because in it

> the concrete identity of the Notion which was the *result* of the disjunctive judgement and which constitutes the *inner* basis of the Notion judgement—which identity was at first posited only in the predicate—is now restored *in the whole* (Hegel, 1989, p. 663).

At the end of the unfolding of the judgement the truth of the judgement is shown to be the '*determinate* relation of subject and predicate' (Hegel, 1989, p. 663). The abstractness of the copula's being is transcended and

> the *copula pregnant with content*, the unity of the Notion ... has re-emerged from the *judgement* in which it was lost in the extremes (Hegel, 1989, p. 663).

This restoration of the notion's identity does not amount to a regressive return to the condition of the U moment of the notion

('The Notion of the Notion'). At the completion of the developmental process through the judgement the notion has determined its identity to be the identity of its externality. This is the sense in which the notion has returned to its inner identity.

At the same time, the identity thus far determined by the notion is not the absolute categorial differentiated unity given that its concrete determination is merely that of a being whose categories manifest both difference and mediating unity. Considered retrospectively, the apodeictic judgement is the notion's developed identity as the essence of externality where 'externality' is that in which the notion has a presence that may or may not accord with the reality. In other words, the relation of essence (notion) to externality (reality) as it is so far determined is the result of a process that shows the notion to be present in externality given that this process begins with the notion's radical self-loss.

As the P moment of a cycle of development at a broader level, the apodeictic judgement can also be understood as supplying the notion's truth in otherness. In so far as the judgement is the developed inner essence of the notion in externality it passes over into the reflective development of this innerness. That is, the judgement results in the emergence of the notion's determinateness as opposition to its externality. As already suggested, this element of opposition emerges in the apodeictic judgement as the opposite of the universal predicate that acts as the ground through which the predicate is united with the subject. This ground exhibits the re-emergence of the notion's unity and the content filled copula. It, therefore, marks the transition to the syllogism.

THE SYLLOGISM

The syllogism is 'the notion posited in its completeness' in so far as it exhibits, not only the categories as 'self-subsistent extremes', but also the determinate mediating unity of the notion's moments (Hegel, 1989, p. 599). The syllogism initially expresses the determinate being of intercategorial relation as distinct from that of the categorial differentiated unity. The notion's identity is reclaimed in the syllogism, not because the categorial differentiated unity of the notion has emerged as the truth of the categories, but because relating as such, the essential mediating unity of the categories, has been posited at the conclusion of the notion's development through the judgement. The syllogism is the truth of the judgement in the sense that it makes explicit the mediating unity of the notion which the judgement excludes (Hegel, 1989, pp. 664-665).

As the truth of the judgement, the syllogism exhibits the notion's reality in terms of the opposition between the notion's mediating unity and the externality manifested by the self-subsistence of the categories. Having shown itself to be the notion in externality (in the form of the judgement) the notion must now show its mediating unity to be the immanent absolute essence of this externality. In order for this to be achieved the syllogistic development must determine the mediating unity as being in accordance with, rather than opposed to, reality. In this way the notion shows itself to be the essence of its externality in the terms required for the appropriation by the notion of the determinate being of externality.

The form of the syllogism initially takes a shape which accords with the explicit emergence of the determinateness of mediation out of the form of the judgement. The previously absent determinateness of mediation is introduced into the judgement's abstract form, 'the individual is a universal', by introducing the particular ground of the unity. The form thus becomes 'I-P-U' where P represents the particular ground supporting the extremes, 'I' represents the individual and 'U' represents the universal.

The syllogisms of existence, reflection and necessity

The notion's syllogistic self-determination takes place in three stages that progressively make the middle term's determination more concrete. The first of these is the syllogism of existence. In this form mediation is not effective given the self-subsistence of all the terms. The syllogism of existence results in the sublation of the abstractness of the terms and the emergence of their relation. The most advanced form of the syllogism of existence posits their relation as necessary and mediated so that the middle term obtains the determinateness of having the terms posited in it. The mediatedness of the categories is developed in the syllogism of reflection in which the middle term becomes a totality in the sense of a concrete integrated categorial unity. The general form of this syllogism is P-I-U given that the individual plays the role of the mediating unity explicitly. However, the essential relatedness of the categories developed by the syllogism of reflection is not also the notion's absolute identity since the differentiation of the terms is external. The most advanced form of the syllogism of reflection, the syllogism of analogy, gives rise to the mediating unity of the objective universal totality and marks the transition to the most complete syllogism, the syllogism of necessity which takes the form I-U-P. This syllogism develops a structure of relations that produces the concrete absolute identity of the notion in its most advanced form, the disjunctive syllogism. In the next chapter we will return to the analysis of the various syllogistic forms when discussing their connection with real philosophical categories.

FROM SYLLOGISM TO OBJECTIVITY

As we suggested above, the overall aim of the notion in developing its syllogistic form is to exhibit the subjective notion in its 'completeness'. The form of the syllogism renders the subjective notion complete in the sense that it makes explicit the determinate being of the categorial unity and thus gives rise to determinate being that exhibits both moments of the notion, categorial unity as well as the categorial differentiation developed through the judgement. The developmental process through the subjective notion's 'first reality' takes the notion that has arrived at its self-determined, yet abstract, truth (the absolutely indeterminate categorial differentiated unity) through a progressive development of the determinate being of its differentiated categories and of the mediating categorial unity.

In this way the syllogism marks the completion of the process of the subjective notion's development toward the establishment of its objective reality. We will briefly examine the outcome of the syllogistic process in order to clarify the rationale underlying the transition to 'objectivity' in the *Science of Logic* and the task of the notion once it has determined itself into objectivity.

According to the *Science of Logic*, (1989, p. 703), as a result of the subjective notion's development

> the Notion as such has been realized; more exactly, it has obtained a reality that is *objectivity* ... the outcome of the course of the syllogisms is that this externality [the determinations posited in a 'determinate and indifferent difference' to which the Notion 'sets itself in opposition' and is thus 'the inwardness of this its externality'] is equated with the inner unity; the various determinations return into this unity through the mediation ... and thus the externality exhibits in its own self the Notion, which therefore is no longer distinguished from it as an inner unity.

Prior to this moment in its logical development the 'notion as such' is not realised given that its unity is 'only inner' in the sense that its truth as the categorial differentiated unity has been developed in purely formal terms and thus lacks any other determinate being. It, therefore, fails to exhibit itself as the notion or essence

of determinate being. In order to posit itself as the essence of determinate being the notion has to develop its determinate being
in the shape of being which accords with its essence. In the process of constructing such determinate being in and through its
externality the notion arrives at a construction of determinate being that exhibits the unity of determinate being with its essence
in a way that makes it suitable for the realisation of the notion's
inner unity. This kind of determinate being is thus 'externality ...
equated with the inner unity' of the notion in that it is otherness
that 'exhibits in its own self' the inner unity which was previously confined to the subjective notion. In exhibiting the notion's inner unity as its own the determinate being that is suited to the full
realisation of the notion's inner unity (a realisation that is not yet
achieved with the completion of the notion's syllogistic development), nevertheless, realises the notion only in so far as the notion
is an inner unity and the determinate being's own. This is what
we take Hegel to be claiming when he says that at the conclusion
of the analysis of the syllogism that the 'notion as such has been
realized' and that as a result 'externality is equated with the inner
unity' of the notion.

If the above reading is correct, then the movement of the notion through the syllogism should conclude by exhibiting the two
sides of the notion: we should expect to see exhibited, on the one
hand, the subjective notion, the notion as inner categorial differentiated unity, characteristic of its 'first reality', and, on the other, the notion's second reality as objectivity. As the conclusion of
the syllogistic process, the disjunctive syllogism should accordingly exhibit the notion as a realised totality, as the inner (categorial
differentiated) unity that has been posited as the inner unity of a
being whose determinateness is suited to the realisation of this
unity. The notion must show itself as the essence of such a determinate being while the determinate being should also exhibit itself as the externality or other of the notion.

Both these conditions are met when the middle term of the
disjunctive syllogism makes explicit the notion's self-determination. The middle term realises its self-determining power when
it is 'perfectly determinate' and 'contains itself the two extremes
in their complete determinateness' (Hegel, 1989, p. 703). In this
kind of relation to its extremes, the middle term posits objective
universality by exhibiting comprehensive categorial differentiated
unity in its complete determinateness through its differentiation
into the totality of its species. In this way

the whole form determination of the Notion is posited in its
determinate difference and at the same time in the simple
identity of the Notion (Hegel, 1989, p. 702).

All the species together constitute the totality as a whole and each
of the species exhibits the totality in that it is the form as 'determinate difference' in accordance with its essence. This essence is 'the
simple identity of the Notion' in that it is a comprehensive categorial unity. The disjunctive syllogism also exhibits determinate being as the externality or other of the notion given that the totality
appears from the perspective of the particular individual, rather
than from that of the whole, the unity of the totality itself.

At the same time, however, when the notion is realised as a
totality in and through its other in the way just indicated, it simultaneously achieves the transcendence of this stage into otherness. According to the *Science of Logic* (1989, p. 702), the very
'consummation of the syllogism' produces its dissolution. Since
the disjunctive syllogism posits the unity of mediated and mediating by positing objective universality as the totality of the species
it is 'equally *no longer a syllogism at all*'. The completion of the syllogistic process results in the 'disappearance' of the distinction between mediating and mediated in the completely determinate being of the comprehensive categorial differentiated unity (Hegel,
1989, p. 703).

In this way then the *formalism of the syllogistic process*, and with
it the subjectivity of the syllogism and of the Notion in general,
has sublated itself (Hegel, 1989, pp. 702-703).

The sublation of the subjectivity exhibited by the syllogistic
form marks the transition from the subjective notion to the objective notion.

OBJECTIVITY

The syllogism is *mediation*, the complete Notion in its *positedness*. Its movement is the sublating of this mediation. ... The
result is therefore an *immediacy* which has issued from the
sublating of the mediation, a being which is no less identical
with the mediation, and which is the Notion that has restored
itself out of, and in, its otherness. This *being* is therefore a *fact*
that is in *and for itself—objectivity* (Hegel, 1989, p. 704).

Prior to becoming objective the notion's reality involved mediation, as distinct from the achieved immediacy of objectivity, since
its task was the pursuit of its objectification through its subjectivity. The mediating unity of its categories needed to be given

determinate being along with their differentiatedness. Having fully realised this task the notion becomes objective by detecting its own self (its inner unity) in its other. Because the subjective (the notion's inner unity) and the objective (the notion's externality) have been equated, the notion thus becomes its other, the object.

Having thus 'restored itself out of, and in, its otherness' the notion is now in a position justifiably to construct its objective being in accordance with the principle of objectivity which principle is, itself, the notion. This is what Hegel signals when in his overview of the process of development through 'The Doctrine of the Notion' he claims that

> the *identity* of the Notion, which is precisely their [the externally related Notion determinations manifesting externality in their *fixed being*] *inner* or *subjective* essence, sets them dialectically in movement , with the result that their separatedness vanishes and with it the separation of the Notion from the object, and there emerges as their truth the *totality* which is the *objective Notion* (Hegel, 1989, p. 597).

The question of the identity of notion and object is made explicit and gives rise to the objective notion through the sublated mediation of a being that is now immediately 'in and for itself'. Hegel (1989, p. 710) refers to such a being as 'the absolute being of the Notion'. It is 'in and for itself' in that it is, as a whole, self-determined and 'free from limitation and opposition' (Hegel, 1989, p. 709). But it is so only immediately given that with the sublation of mediation (as a result of the syllogistic process) the subjectivity of the notion is also sublated.

According to the *Science of Logic* (1989, p. 597),

> [a]s one with the object, the Notion is *submerged* in it; its distinct moments are objective existences in which it is itself again only the *inner*. As the soul of objective reality it must *give itself* the form of *subjectivity* which, as formal Notion, belonged to it immediately.

Due to its sublation the subjective notion is submerged in the object; it has become 'the soul of objectivity'. The objective notion faces the task of developing its self-determining subjective form in and through objectivity, that is, in and through its absolute being. This further process of development will achieve the identity of the objective notion and the subjective notion.

As we indicated earlier 'objectivity signifies in the first instance *the absolute being of the Notion*' and as objectivity the notion's aim is 'to restore the free-being-for-itself of its subjectivity' (Hegel,

1989, p. 710). The notion is absolute being because it is not just the essence of reality but the reality of its essence. In 'Objectivity' we have the abstract identity of notion and object and, as a result, the appropriate setting within which to realise this identity. The notion which until now was 'being-for-self', that is, absolute self-determination abstractly, is now the material, so to speak, required to realise its self-determination. This realisation amounts to a 'restoration' given that the notion's subjectivity, which has been shown to be the essence of the object, is initially 'submerged in the object'. In coming to know itself as the essence of the object the notion does not also determine the object's determinate being and so does not exhibit what it is, namely a self-determining determination. If this analysis is correct then the objective notion which 'passes over into its *in-itself*' has to achieve the 'reappearance' in objectivity 'of the negativity of the Notion's being-for-self' (Hegel, 1989, p. 753). In other words, the notion has to move beyond its 'immediate freedom' to 'negative freedom', to the activity in which the notion makes explicit that it is also the object's determining essence; 'as the soul of objective reality the Notion must *give itself* the form of *subjectivity*' (Hegel, 1989, p. 597).

The notion will have established its self-determining nature when, by developing itself through objectivity, it reaches the point at which it is its own end. To put it differently, the object must be constructed in a way that shows it also to be the self-determining activity towards its own actualisation. According to the *Science of Logic* this process of construction is developed in three stages: 'Mechanism', 'Chemism' and 'Teleology'.

Mechanical objectivity

The mechanical object is the immediate object, the moments of which

> exist in a self-subsistent indifference as *objects outside one another*, and in their relationship possess the *subjective unity* of the Notion only as an *inner* or an *outer* unity (Hegel, 1989, p. 710).

The mechanical object's development from its immediate existence gives rise to the increasing thematisation of its externality until the notion's essential unity (the comprehensive categorial differentiated unity) becomes the object's explicit principle of self-determination . This unity, the unity of the mechanical object, is 'only inner' in the sense that it is still the unity of the subjective notion that is submerged in the object, even at the most advanced stage of the mechanical object's development, 'absolute mechanism'.

Absolute mechanism, the explicitly organised mechanical object, establishes the object's essential unity as what Hegel calls 'free mechanism', the mechanical object's principle of self-determination which is located in its absolute centre towards which its moments 'strive' thereby exhibiting the object's continued externality. Because the principle of self-determination and, with it, the essential difference of the object are concentrated in the (absolute) mechanical centre, the object's essential difference is also shown to be immediately existent and in this way the mechanical object is only an 'outer unity'.

The mechanical object thereby manifests (a) its essence abstractly as internally organised through its principle of self-determination (inner unity) and (b) its individuality as external relation to other objects from which it is distinguished (outer unity). At this stage of immediacy the notion is a differentiated unity but only internally or in its ideality and not yet explicitly in its reality. As such it fully develops its differentiated unity in order, firstly, to establish that it is ideal. Reflection on its differentiated unity as ideality (its innerness) shows that the two moments of its essential unity, unity and difference, are externally related. The result of the emergence of the mechanical object's principle of self-determination is thus the positing of the immanence of the object's difference. This difference is expressed as the relation of one object toward '*its own other*' (Hegel, 1975, §199), that is, as the relatedness of objects specifically distinguished as (a) opposed in virtue of their differentiated essence and (b) indifferent to the essence of each other.

Chemical objectivity

This leads to the second stage of the object's development, 'Chemism'. This stage consists of the activity of relating objects that are themselves related in the mechanical terms described above. Here the object's relationship 'becomes a relation in which their determinate self-subsistence sublates itself' (Hegel, 1989, p. 710). Chemically interacting objects are objects in virtue of their difference and so are explicitly related to other objects toward which they are drawn. This process produces the repeated sublation of the specific determinateness of objects which combine and the differentiation of objects so combined.

The movement in chemical interaction results in the positing of the distinctness of the essential unity of the objects (manifested in their combination which sublates their self-subsistence) from their externality and immediate independence (manifested in their differentiation).

Teleological objectivity

The object thus advances to the final stage of its development, 'Teleology'. The teleological object 'is the subjective Notion, but posited as in and for itself related to objectivity, as *end*' (Hegel, 1989, p. 710). Teleology gives rise to the explicitly subjective notion as a self-determining relation to objectivity. The notion is thus the object's own end or purpose.

In the emergence of the notion as objective purpose the essential unity of the object becomes the object's end in the sense that the notion engages in an explicitly purposive on going process towards its realisation. At the lower mechanical and chemical levels of objectivity the notion's existence is implicit (Hegel, 1975, §200A). We want to suggest here that in 'Mechanism' this implicit existence of the notion should be understood as essence in abstraction from purposive process. In 'Chemism', the 'reflectional nexus of objectivity' (Hegel, 1975, §202), the notion becomes process explicitly in abstraction from its purposiveness. If this way of understanding the relationship between these levels of objectivity is correct, it follows also that the essential differentiated unity of the object becomes the object's end. Because what is initially only essence and then only process has its true dimensions in the unity of this essence and process, the object becomes essence as end or purposive process. The teleological development of the notion will achieve the notion's 'restoration' in the object since

> the Notion is therefore [as a result of 'the movement of the end'] essentially this: to be distinct as an explicit identity from its *implicit* objectivity, and thereby to possess externality, yet in this external totality to be the totality's self-determining identity (Hegel, 1989, p. 754).

As such the notion completes the process of the development of its subjectivity through the object. When it does so it attains the status of a justifiably retrospective notion. That is, when the notion is in a position to look back on itself and reflectively to know itself as the self-determining object, it will have thereby become one with its object. This unity of notion and object gives rise to 'The Idea'.

6. THE CATEGORIES OF LOGIC AND REAL PHILOSOPHY

On our systemic approach the categorial progression of the *Logic* strictly organises the subject matter of the *Philosophy of Mind*. The development of this subject matter, in turn, proceeds as the work of the idea understood as that which the logical idea becomes as a result of its categorial progression. We can refer to these two claims as 'the strict organisation thesis'.

In our view the strict organisation thesis enables a systemic approach to make sense of many of Hegel's otherwise confusing statements. Hegel's references to 'the Idea' in the *Philosophy of Right* (Hegel, 1981, §32; §142) are a case in point. For example, without regard to the proper systemic significance of the idea it is difficult to see how Hegel can consistently relate ethical life to the idea (Hegel, 1981, §142) at the same time as relating the ethical state to logical objectivity (Hegel, 1991, §198) given that, as we noted in the previous chapter, the category of objectivity precedes that of the idea in the logical categorial progression. We need to understand that the idea that is referred to in the *Philosophy of Mind* is not merely the logical concept that is elaborated at the end of the *Science of Logic*. It is just as much the logical idea in its anticipatory readiness to actualise its notion through the process of organising the concepts of empirical reality. Indeed, as Hegel explains in the *Philosophy of Right* (Hegel, 1981, §1R), in the course of its actualisation the idea has two essential moments: the first is 'its form, ... its mode of being as concept alone' and the second consists of 'the shapes which the concept assumes in the course of its actualisation [that] are indispensable for the knowledge of the concept itself'. The first of these moments is realised in the *Logic* with the emergence and development of what we have called the logical idea. The second is progressively realised in the rest of the

Hegelian philosophical system with the aid of the already developed logical categories and, in the case of the *Philosophy of Mind*, the categories' systemic progression.

An adequate defence of the strict organisation thesis would require much more than we can offer in this chapter. What we hope to do is to take a first step in the direction of such a defence by giving a more specific shape to the two claims of the strict organisation thesis that we introduced above. To this end, we will draw attention to the links between the categories of Hegel's *Logic* and his *Philosophy of Mind* that we believe would be supported by a comprehensive exposition.

HEGEL'S PHILOSOPHY OF MIND

As is to be expected, according to Hegel, mind must manifest itself to itself through a three stage developmental process from 'Mind Subjective' through 'Mind Objective' to 'Mind Absolute ' (Hegel, 1985, §385). On the reading we propose these three stages should be taken to be worked out in the light of the logical idea's progressive development through the *Science of Logic*. 'Mind Subjective' corresponds to the development from 'The Doctrine of Being' to the completion of 'The Judgement' (Hegel, 1989, pp. 67-663). 'Mind Objective' corresponds to the structure of relations developed in 'The Syllogism' and 'Objectivity' (Hegel, 1989, pp. 664-754) whilst 'Mind Absolute' should be understood in the light of the logical development of 'The Idea' (Hegel, 1989, pp. 755-844).

This way of correlating the logical progression with the idea's real categorial development seems to us to accord with Hegel's philosophical texts and, in particular, with the characteristics of the various stages of mind's actualisation. By way of a brief argument in support of it we will give some consideration to the nature of 'Mind Subjective' and 'Mind Objective'. Before doing so, however, it is worth noting that a proposal, such as this one, is worth investigating despite the fact that it obviously does not reflect a neat set of parallels between the headings and sub-headings of the texts of the *Science of Logic* and the *Philosophy of Mind*. After all, Hegel (1989, pp. 54-55) introduces his system of logic by noting that the work's divisions and headings 'are made to facilitate a preliminary survey and strictly are only of historical value. They do not belong to the content and body of the science' or speculative philosophy. This content and body must, instead, be 'brought forward by the subject matter itself.' It follows from this that the divisions proposed in Hegel's text as they are highlighted in his list of contents and headings are not necessarily the correct ones when judged by this last criterion. This, together with the reasons that we have already given for insisting that a sensitivity to the rationale underlying the various phases and stages through which the idea passes is the only way to make sense of the Hegelian system, lead us to conclude that any proposed correlation of logical and real philosophical categories must focus on 'the content and body of the science' as Hegel puts it. We turn now to a brief consideration of 'Mind Subjective'.

Mind Subjective

Mind subjective is the first reality of mind and as such is abstract, immediate and 'unspiritual'. This is mind's 'most inappropriate reality' from which it must begin in order to develop itself unconditionally. The task of mind subjective is to come to know its being as its notion. To achieve this self-knowledge is to realise its notion or essence (Hegel, 1985, §385A). Subjective mind unfolds in three phases that deal with the respective objects of 'Anthropology', 'Phenomenology of Mind' and 'Psychology'. These are respectively 'soul' in nature, 'consciousness' and the being of 'an independent subject' (Hegel, 1985, §387). We suggest that the unreflective subjectivity of soul is organised in accordance with the logic of the undifferentiated unity encountered in 'The Doctrine of Being' (Hegel, 1989). The process that leads to the transcendence of soul, as described in the section entitled 'Anthropology' (Hegel, 1985, §387-§412), aims to differentiate the subjective and the objective. This differentiation results in the liberation of mind from its absorption in nature and the emergence of mind as reflection.

Reflective mind is aware of its subjectivity in being aware of the objective world as that which is different from it. This is the stage in which the unity involved in subjectivity is subordinated to the differentiation between the subjective and the objective. What we have here is a real categorial organisation in accordance with the relation between differentiation and unity as the notion encounters this in 'The Doctrine of Essence' (Hegel, 1989).

A possible objection   One might object to our proposed correlation of the 'Phenomenology of Mind' (Hegel, 1985) with 'The Doctrine of Essence' (Hegel, 1989) that this is inconsistent with Hegel's characterisation of the concept of the ego in the former. Here, Hegel refers to the ego as the 'existent' and 'pure' notion. On the face of it this would appear to link the 'Phenomenology of Mind' (Hegel, 1985) to a logical category belonging to 'The Doctrine of the Notion', a later developmental phase of the *Science of Logic*. If this is correct, then we must be mistaken in our view that the 'Phenomenology of Mind' (Hegel, 1985) corresponds to 'The Doctrine of Essence' (Hegel, 1989).[1]

The above objection fails to take into account that the 'Phenomenology of Mind' (Hegel, 1985) embodies logical categories whose structuring role is fundamentally a matter of a developmental process. Recall from our discussion of the notion's logical development in Chapter 4 that the notion is characterised as 'existent' and 'pure'. This happens on completion of the developmental process through the doctrines of 'Being' and 'Essence'. We pointed out how its main characteristic, differentiated unity, first becomes explicit once unity in the absence of differentiation ('Being') and differentiatedness that is the sphere of external relation ('Essence') have been superseded. Once this process has been completed the notion is 'pure' in that it is a self-determining differentiated unity and 'existent' in that it has completed the process through which it shows itself to be the truth of its moments (the truth of unity and differentiation). Only having justified its principle in this process does the notion become ready, for the first time in its logical development, to examine the implications of having determined itself as this differentiated unity. It follows from this analysis that, even though the notion is not 'pure' and 'existent' prior to the developmental process undergone in 'The Doctrine of Essence' (Hegel, 1989), it is so as the result of the completion of this process.

When we extend our analysis to the concept of the ego (the self-consciousness treated in the 'Phenomenology of Mind', 1985) we can see that it embodies the existent, pure notion only at the end of the phenomenological process. This is the point at which universal consciousness is achieved (Hegel, 1985, §436) and it gives rise to the transition to the concept of reason (Hegel, 1985, §438). We will consider these aspects of the development of reason in a moment. For present purposes what we need to bear in mind is that the section on 'Reason' (Hegel, 1985, §438-§439) constitutes the first elaboration of mind as mind. We would argue that mind as mind is the real category that is organised in accordance with the notion. To be sure, the existent pure notion is not to be found in the earlier phenomenological process simply because this process is structured in accordance with the external relatedness of consciousness to its object. But, as we have already explained, the logic of this kind of

---

1. This concern was raised by G. Marcus.

relationship is abstractly worked out in 'The Doctrine of Essence' (Hegel, 1989). This, then, is the sense in which 'The Doctrine of Essence' (Hegel, 1989) organises the 'Phenomenology of Mind' (Hegel, 1985) and gives rise to the notion as ego.

Reason We have already suggested that the idea arrives at 'Reason' (Hegel, 1985, §436) as a result of the development of reflection into universal self-consciousness. Here, the object of the subject is another subject, the differentiated unity of intersubjectivity. Reason is thus shown, in 'Mind Subjective', to be the notion of consciousness. In this way reason is mind subjective's achieved self-knowledge. Reason is the actuality of 'the simple identity of the subjectivity of the notion with its objectivity and universality' (Hegel, 1985, §438). As the notion of mind, reason is the actualisation of the logical 'notion of the notion' that the *Science of Logic* elaborates in the section on 'The Notion'. The category of reason is organised in accordance with the subjectivity of objective being in that it identifies the objective, 'the very being of things' with the subject, 'its own thoughts'.

Reason which is thus an identity is not only the absolute substance, but the truth that knows it. For truth here has, as its peculiar mode and immanent form, the self-centred pure notion, ego, the certitude of self as infinite universality. Truth, aware of what it is, is mind (spirit) (Hegel, 1985, §439).

This transition to mind in 'Psychology' marks the transition to an awareness of the object as a 'substantial totality' that is 'neither subjective nor objective'. For this reason mind starts only from its own being and is in correlation only with its own features (Hegel, 1985, §440).

Psychology mind Reason's identity of subjectivity and objectivity gives rise to mind which is only immediately mind. Being 'neither subjective nor objective' it manifests a kind of self-loss. This initial awareness of mind is an awareness which, like the reflective structure of the notion, is immediately also its self-loss due to its complete abstractness. Recall from our discussion in Chapter 4 that the notion's self-loss marks the notion's movement to 'The Judgement' (Hegel, 1989), the sphere of the development of determinate difference in which the notion's lost identity eventually re-emerges as the inner identity of its externality.

The above mentioned 'correlation' of mind 'with its own features' that is worked out in the section entitled 'Psychology Mind' aims to develop the knowledge of mind's truth since mind does not initially know this to be its proper form. Even though it is this truth, mind

> is still abstract, the formal identity of subjectivity and objectivity. Only when this identity has developed into an actual difference and has made itself into the identity of itself and its difference ... not till then has that certainty established itself as truth (Hegel, 1985, §440A).

Though we cannot go into it here, an examination of the process by which the form of inward mind becomes an actual difference would show that this real categorial developmental process is organised in accordance with the notion's development as the judgement (Hegel, 1989, pp. 623-663).

At its completion mind achieves the form of the free will and becomes a 'self-determining universality'.

> In having universality, of itself *qua* infinite form, for its object, content and aim, the will is free not only *in* itself but *for* itself also; it is the idea in its truth (Hegel, 1981, §21).

Free mind takes a shape like that of the notion in the logical structure of the apodeictic form of the judgement (Hegel, 1989, p. 661). Like the subject of the apodeictic judgement, the free will is the universal that is identical with its opposite (objective externality) and is itself its own object. Its essence is, therefore, in complete agreement with its object (Hegel, 1981, §§22-24).[2]

Further, just as the apodeictic judgement makes explicit the notion's mediating unity and thereby marks the transition to the syllogism, the structure of relations in which the notion determines the inner unity of its essence to be the essence of its externality, so too

> the absolute goal, or, if you like, the absolute impulse of free mind is to make its freedom its object, i.e. to make freedom objective as much in the sense that freedom shall be the rational system of mind, as in the sense that this system shall be the world of immediate actuality. In making freedom its object, mind's purpose is to be explicitly, as Idea, what the will is implicitly (Hegel, 1981, §27)

Mind objective

Even though free mind returns to its identity its essential unity is still only implicitly the identity of its essence and externality. As

---

2. Passages 4-28 of the 'Introduction' to the *Philosophy of Right* cover the same aspects of mind subjective as those which the *Philosophy of Mind* treats in the section entitled 'Psychology Mind'.

mind objective, the purpose of free mind is (a) to develop its inner unity as a rational system and (b) to actualise this system, that is, to elaborate the absolute unity of the essence of mind with its existence or reality. This goal is pursued through the development of the rational element of existents that embody free will and thereby constitute (progressively more complex) kinds of 'right' (Hegel, 1981, §§29-30).

The development of the idea of right as 'the rational system of mind' or, as Hegel (1981, §2) puts it, of the 'rational factor' in the concept of right, follows the notion's syllogistic development through to objectivity. If we are correct in claiming that the form of the judgement corresponds to the development of mind subjective as outlined above, then we should expect the next stage in the logical progression to correspond to the development of mind objective. But this is not our only reason for proposing this correlation of logical and real categories. In addition, we take into account Hegel's (1989, p. 664) claims that *everything rational is a syllogism*' and that 'no content can be rational except through the rational form' which is the syllogism. Syllogistic reasoning is that which, according to Hegel (1989, p. 665), accounts for the rationality in rational cognition of objects. So, we maintain, the logical form of the syllogism and its truth, namely logical objectivity, play a determining role in the organisation of the categories belonging to the sphere of objective mind, the spiritual world of everything that is existent.

According to the Hegelian system, the sphere of objective mind consists of three progressively more advanced moments, which the *Philosophy of Right* identifies under the headings, 'Abstract Right', 'Morality' and 'Ethical Life'.[3] The third, most complex moment consists of a further three moments, 'The Family', 'Civil Society' (including its differentiated moments, 'The System of Needs', 'The Administration of Justice', 'The Police' and 'The Corporation') and 'The State' (including the individual state's 'Constitution', 'International Law' and 'World History').

On the reading we propose, a detailed examination of 'Abstract Right' (Hegel, 1981, §34-§104) and 'Morality' (Hegel, 1981, §105-§141) in the light of the forms of the syllogisms of existence and

---

3. The sections of the *Philosophy of Right* cover the same ground as 'Mind Objective' in the *Philosophy of Mind*. Whilst we will also draw on relevant passages from the latter for ease of reference we will use only the (sub)titles which appear in the *Philosophy of Right* to refer to the developmental stages and spheres of activity which are the subject of both texts.

reflection (Hegel, 1989, pp. 666-695) would show that the former are constructed respectively in accordance with the categorial interplay of the latter. Similarly, the analysis of the first two moments of 'Ethical Life' (Hegel, 1981, §158-§256) in the light of the syllogism of necessity (Hegel, 1989, pp. 695-704) would show that the Hegelian system constructs (a) the abstract concept of the family in accordance with the logical categorial interplay defining the categorical form of the syllogism of necessity; (b) the abstract concept of civil society in accordance with the logical categorial interplay defining the hypothetical form of the syllogism of necessity; and (c) civil society's differentiated moments in accordance with the logical categorial interplay defining the disjunctive form of the syllogism of necessity.

If this position is correct, the entire process from 'Abstract Right' to the end of 'Civil Society' as marked by 'The Corporation' (Hegel, 1981, §250-§256) should be treated as the process through which the idea determines itself as the essence of its externality in the sense of the inner unity of a being whose determinateness is suited to the realisation of a categorial differentiated unity.

Furthermore, the final moment of 'Ethical Life', 'The State' (Hegel, 1981, §257-§360), should be analysed in the light of logical objectivity (Hegel, 1989, pp. 705-754). It can thus be treated as the process through which the idea determines itself as a self-determining object. That is, having successfully pursued its objectification through the syllogistic development of its abstract moments, the idea of the ethical state becomes the concrete object that develops its subjectivity and essential categorial differentiated unity out of its own determinate being.

In our view this correlation of (a) the syllogistic forms with the abstract categories of objective mind and (b) of the truth of syllogistic reason, namely objectivity, with the most comprehensive categories of objective mind enables a very precise reading of the distinctive characteristics of each of these stages of real categorial interrelations without undermining the dynamism of their developmental nature. Indeed, the ultimate significance of the final stage of ethical life is rendered visible only within the specifics of this logical categorial framework. It is because the organisation of the categories of ethical life rely on both the most advanced form of syllogistic reason and on the sublation of the syllogism's formalism within the domain of self-determining objectivity that the idea of ethical life emerges as the self-determining process of the realisation of the notion's unity with its object.

Such a dynamic unity encompasses the social world as a whole but it also recognises its systematic differentiatedness. Because ethical life is necessarily lived in connection with the world as a whole, this world must, in turn, be socially instituted so as to give appropriate shape to the necessary interdependence of all its differentiated substantive dimensions. In the broad terms of the *Logic* this is to say that where notion and object accord with each other the particular is revealed in the universal, and vice versa, in ways that show them to make up the individual's reflective identity.

At the heart of this view of ethical life is the idea of a socially integrated and instituted ethical intersubjectivity, something which is progressively developed into its more complex modes of being. In line with the developmental logic of the syllogistic process underlying it, ethical intersubjectivity embodies a conception of differentiated unity whose objectivity rests on its having surpassed the limits of conceiving the interrelationship of unity and difference in terms that privilege one of these moments at the expense of the other. These restricted modes of relating unity and difference are embodied in the concepts of property owning personality and Kantian moral agency whose syllogistic organisation is more abstract by comparison. Due to this relative abstractness the mutual recognition characterising these kinds of identities is confined to the mere confirmation by another subject of that which is antecedently affirmed by the individual subject. The moments of unity and difference are therefore merely oppositionally or externally related. In contrast, in both its differentiating and mediating processes, ethical intersubjectivity presupposes the mutually informing relationship of the moments of unity and difference and these are constructed as codependent aspects of their one objective universal essence.

For this reason an intersubjective identity that forms part of ethical life can be understood as one that necessarily incorporates its other into its own dynamic structure. We will examine this idea more carefully when we consider the concept of ethical intersubjectivity as familial love. Here we note that our account is in a position to appreciate how and why the realisation of the full potential of ethical intersubjectivity to embody its substantial universality depends on the possibility of overcoming the mere formality of its universality.

Although a comprehensive elaboration and defence of the above claims is beyond the scope of our present discussion, we will try to give a general outline of how we would proceed. Our purpose here is to supply the reader with an appropriate conceptual framework within which to consider the detail of the logical underpinnings of the concept of the family that will be our focus in Part III of the book.

Alternative correlations Before proceeding with our general outline, it is worth noting that Hegel's theory of right has been correlated with his *Logic* in a number of other ways which we find unsatisfactory. For example, contrary to the implications of the systemic analysis we offered in Chapter 4, Pinkard (1991, pp. 310-312) suggests that 'Abstract Right' corresponds to 'The Doctrine of Being', 'Morality corresponds to the Doctrine of Essence' and 'Ethical Life' 'corresponds to the Doctrine of the Concept' (or notion). Ilting (1984, p. 214) correlates the three stages of 'Ethical life' to the three stages of the logical idea and argues for the plausibility of this reading on the ground that 'both in the *Philosophy of Right* and at the corresponding point in the *Logic*, on Hegel's view, there takes place a liberation of the moments which were not yet released into independence in the preceding stage of development'. Note, however, that Ilting's description of the movement in question is general enough to apply to any movement from immediate universality to the moment of particularity. He does no more in support of his claim than to cite the Hegel (1981, §161) which talks of 'life' as does the relevant section in the *Logic*.

On the other hand, Kolb (1988, pp. 57-117) proposes a reading of Hegel's 'Civil Society' and 'The State' in the light of the general development of the logical categories belonging to 'The Notion' and 'The syllogism'. Whilst useful in some respects, Kolb's reading leaves many questions about the relationship of the logical and real philosophical categories unexplained (cf. Vassilacopoulos, 1994, pp. 196, f.8; p. 255, f.13).

Theunissen (1991, p. 14) presents a much more complex account of the correlation of the theory of right with the *Logic* which emphasises the significance of the notion's logical development and presents the correlation in terms much like the U, P, I progression we discussed in Chapter 4. However, his substantive account of this progression in the case of the theory of right correlates 'Abstract Right' to what we have taken to be the U moment, 'Morality' to the P moment and 'Ethical life' to the I-moment. He argues further that 'Hegel copies the movement of abstract right from the judgement of existence' (Theunissen, 1991, p. 23-24). However, Theunissen's way of presenting the correlation leaves unexplained the place of 'Absolute Mind' (Hegel, 1985) in the wider scheme of the system.

The proposal by Richardson (1989, pp. 68-73) comes closest to our own. However, Richardson puts together his account by detecting points of similarity and difference between Hegel's elaboration of the relevant logical and real philosophical categories. For this reason he ultimately fails to appreciate the role played by logical objectivity in the construction of the idea of the ethical state.[4]

THE SYLLOGISM OF EXISTENCE AND ABSTRACT RIGHT

As we suggested in Chapter 5, the syllogism of existence does not exhibit effective mediation since the notion's mediating unity is present but not self-determining in this syllogistic form. The task of the notion in the syllogism's developmental process is progressively to posit the mediatedness of terms that are initially only immediately united in the middle term. The terms are thus 'abstract determinatenesses ... not yet developed by mediation into *concretion*, but are only *single* determinatenesses'. In the syllogism's first figure, I-P-U, the abstractness of its self-subsistent moments makes them 'merely self-related determinatenesses, and one and all a *single content*' (Hegel, 1989, p. 666).

As we might expect to find on the basis of this structure of formal categorial relations, 'the sphere of Abstract or Formal Right' is the immediate stage of the idea of the free will. This is the stage in which the will is initially 'the inherently single will of a subject' (Hegel, 1981, §34). As such, it does not contain its determinations within it explicitly since initially 'there is no advance and no mediation'. This indeterminacy of the will that contains its determinations only implicitly gives it the determinacy of being the single will, the person as such (Hegel, 1981, §34A).

Personality, to begin with, has no other content except self-consciousness of its 'simple relation of itself to itself in its individuality'. As such its universal element, which is awareness of its infinity and freedom, is also abstract (Hegel, 1981, §35). Universality is, therefore, not incorporated in the 'mere being' of the individual

---

4. Richardson (1989, pp. 77-78, f.10 & f.14) also cites a number of German papers which correlate other parts of the Logic with the theory of right and one which correlates 'Absolute Mechanism' with 'The State'. For extensive critical discussions of the alternative views see Vassilacopoulos, 1994, pp. 188-274.

person (Hegel, 1981, §34A). Nor does this abstract personality contain the will's particularity (Hegel, 1981, §36).

Accordingly, the self-subsistent categories constituting the first figure of the syllogism of existence organise the real categories of personality. Just as the notion's development in the syllogism of existence unfolds in the activity of immediate individuality so too the decision making person relates to the external world of nature through the self-subsistence of an 'immediate individuality' that renders the person's will 'something subjective'. Because this restriction contradicts the potential universality or infinite self-relatedness of personality, personality struggles to lift itself above this restriction and to give itself reality, or in other words to claim that external world as its own (Hegel, 1981, §39). The 'struggle' of personality to claim the external world as its own is organised pursuant to the dynamics of the logical task of overcoming the oppositional relationship between immediate individuality and the notion's mediating unity in particularity. As we pointed out in Chapter 5, this opposition is exhibited in the structure of relations in which, although it is present as particularity, the mediating unity is ineffective due to the self-subsistence of the categories. As immediate individuality, personality gives expression to the discord between the subjectivity characteristic of the categories in their opposition to each other and subjectivity as the notion has constructed it. Recall that this latter is the individual of the notion of the notion that shapes mind's absolute identity. On the other hand, the category of particularity is the medium by which personality 'gives itself reality'. Particularity, therefore, organises the world of self-less nature which is here to be understood broadly as whatever falls outside the simple self-relation of the will.[5] This too is consistent with the formal categorial requirement that the mediating unity itself be an immediate existent.

The syllogism's first figure and property ownership

According to Hegel, the 'general significance' of the first figure of the syllogism of existence is that

> the individual, which as such is infinite self-relation and therefore would be merely *inward*, emerges by means of particularity into *existence* as into universality, in which it no longer belongs merely to itself but stands in an *external relationship*;

---

5. In our present discussion we make no effort to defend Hegel against the charge that this amounts to an objectionable transformation of nature into a self-less 'thing' so that it can then be humanised.

conversely the individual, in separating itself into its determinateness as a particularity, is in this separation a concrete individual and, as the relation of the determinateness to itself, a *universal*, self-related individual, and consequently is also truly an individual; in the extreme of universality it has withdrawn from externality *into itself* (Hegel, 1989, p. 667).

Property ownership expresses this relation in which the category of individuality is immediately united with universality in particularity. The Hegelian system takes the external sphere in which the person translates his or her freedom to be 'what is immediately different and separable from him' or her. This is 'the external pure and simple, a thing' (Hegel, 1981, §41 & §42) and it extends to the person's own body and labour power in so far as the person is an 'immediate existent' (Hegel, 1981, §43R; §47-§48). The act of taking possession of such a 'thing' transforms the latter into an embodied will (Hegel, 1981, §45). Still, the person's relation to the particular thing that embodies his or her will is not completed with possession but involves the further 'modifications' of property: 'use', 'the thing as something to be negated' and 'alienation, the reflection of the will back from the thing into itself' (Hegel, 1981, §53).[6] These three aspects of the relation of the person to the external world are respectively expressions of the premises and conclusion of the syllogism's first figure, I-P, P-U and I-U. In use the property item (including the person's labour power and its products) is shown to be the embodiment of the particular will (Hegel, 1981, §59) in something which has universal value (Hegel, 1981, §63) whilst alienation marks the return of the will out of its particularity to its universal infinite self-relation.

Through the category of the property item, which has thus been defined as the particular embodied will, the person manifests his or her external relationship. That is, he or she objectifies his or her otherwise subjective will and becomes a concrete individual to this extent. However, this concretion does not thereby manifest the person's essential unity given that any one of an indefinite number of 'things' can become the will's embodiment and the content of the individual's unity with a specific particular is contingent and arbitrary (Hegel, 1981, §49). As regards the content of the terms of the first figure of the syllogism of existence, Hegel (1989, p. 670) explains that because the

---

6. For an argument against the view that 'talk of the embodiment of the will' is not reducible to the claim that the will of the owner is expressed in the use of the thing, see Knowles.

terms are immediate determinatenesses and, therefore, qualitative they cannot capture the notion's essential determination. As a result, one syllogism can at best contingently and arbitrarily unite a subject with only one of its particular properties the universality of which is in turn only an abstract determinateness. Because an indefinite number of such syllogisms may concern the same subject they 'must also pass over into contradiction'. Applied to the idea of property ownership taken in the form of a syllogism of this kind, this analysis suggests that the essence of personality cannot be captured adequately by the idea of the property owning identity understood as the embodiment of the single will in a thing.

Indeed, if we draw further on the analysis in the *Science of Logic* of the first figure, we can say that the failure of the idea of property ownership to manifest the person's essential unity is not simply due to the arbitrariness of the content of the particular relationship established, the fact that the property owner is related to externality by contingently putting his or her will in any one of an indefinite number of what would otherwise be mere 'things'. It is instead due to the very form of this relationship since the arbitrariness of the content derives from this form. In the form of property relations the person can only return to his or her infinite self-relation by withdrawing from the externality that is organised in accordance with the moment of particularity. This is revealed in the form of the syllogism's conclusion. The conclusion of the first figure, I-U, shows that the determinateness of the abstract particular that is related to the individual (I-P) cannot also be characterised as a totality in the sense of the three moments' essential unity with their reality. Since the conclusion does not incorporate particularity into the individual's infinite self-relation true individuality is secured only in the relation of the embodied (P) individual to the universal (P-U).

The conclusion also shows that in abstracting from the specificity of its embodiment the individual treats the whole of externality as if it were its potential embodiment but this conclusion cannot be substantiated in this structure of relations given that each moment can only ever express a single determinateness. In other words, the determinateness of particularity can only be expressed as the negativity of the individual's universal infinite self-relation, the separation of the individual's infinite self-relation from its particular being whose universality is itself merely an infinite abstract multiplicity of determinatenesses.

Property ownership exhibits the same limits. Alienation of the property item returns the person to his or her abstract self-relation. This is a condition that does not involve the embodiment of the will in the particular. At the same time, the implication of this structure of relations is that the external world amounts to the potential embodiment of the person's will but this cannot be substantiated since any particular act of taking possession of a thing merely relates the person to that single property item and control over the universal value of a property item through its use merely creates a potential relation between the embodied will and comparable items; it does not relate the person to every other 'thing'.

Reply to two objections Two rather obvious objections to the above analysis are worth considering here. The first argues that Hegel's treatment of labour power as property is internally inconsistent whereas the second focuses on an apparent inconsistency between our claim that 'Abstract Right' corresponds to the logical form of the syllogism and the references to various judgements in 'Abstract Right' (Hegel, 1981, §53, §85, §88, §95). Though we cannot presently undertake an exhaustive discussion of these two issues we hope to say enough to illustrate the explanatory power of our interpretive approach. This, in turn, reinforces our view of the merits of the kind of systemic reading of Hegel's speculative thought that we have been advancing.

The alienability of labour power In his Marxist materialist inspired critique of Hegel's accounts of personality, property and labour power Arthur (1980) argues against Hegel that the account of labour power as (alienable) property lacks coherence. He thinks that this is because alienation requires, but cannot supply, a process through which human talents 'achieve "a mode of externality" on the basis of which they are alienable on a par with "things" yet without estranging personality from itself' (Arthur, 1980, p. 10). So, he thinks that there is some tension between Hegel's claim regarding the alienability of labour power and the view that the 'substantive characteristics, which constitute one's own private personality and the universal essence of one's self-consciousness are inalienable' (Arthur, 1980, p. 10).

This objection fails to take into account considerations that come into focus with an analysis of property ownership based on the categorial interplay of the syllogism of existence. Firstly, on the Hegelian account an 'external thing' is alienable and does not thereby require alienation of one's 'universal essence' because the relevant categorial relations have not given rise to this possibility. As we indicated above, in the relation I-U of the first figure, the category of individuality unites with universality but this unity concerns only an abstract determinateness since universality has not been determined as the essential nature of individuality. Because the relationships between the real categories at issue are organised in accordance with this relation of individuality and universality. The return to the person's abstract self-relation through alienation of the property item does not affect the 'substantive characteristics' of 'personality as such, one's universal freedom of will, one's ethical life, one's religion' (Hegel, 1981, §66).

Secondly, if Hegel were committed to a once and for all reduction of labour power to the class of 'external things' that have the potential to become persons' property, then his account would involve an unacceptable treatment of labour power, not only for the Marxist reasons given by Arthur, but also for reasons within Hegel's own account of 'Civil Society' (Hegel, 1981). To see why Hegel is not committed to this sort of reduction even though he treats the abstract idea of labour power as potentially alienable we need to bear in mind the implications of the fact that in the logical categorial progression the syllogism of existence is positioned as an incomplete syllogistic form. Note, firstly, that when it takes the form of the syllogism of existence 'the notion is at the very height of self-estrangement' (Hegel, 1975, §183A). In a similar vein, Hegel describes personality that is organised in accordance with the self-estranged notion as the abstract will which is 'itself at bottom external' (Hegel, 1985, §530). So, the conception of the person's body and powers as alienable property can be understood as itself being an expression of the will's externality in the above sense. If this is correct, then, like the abstractness of the syllogism of existence as a whole, this rather narrow conception of the will may eventually be transcended. Indeed, in our brief discussion of 'Ethical Life' below we will indicate how various aspects of the ideas of 'Abstract Right' and 'Morality' must in fact be transcended consistently with the logical progression from the formalism of the syllogism to logical objectivity. For present purposes it suffices to suggest that a detailed analysis of the relevant logical categorial interplay can show why the idea of the property owner that is elaborated in 'Abstract Right' cannot be straightforwardly added to Hegel's account of regulated market relations in 'Civil Society'. It needs instead to be appropriately reconceptualised when it is taken to be part of the Hegelian idea of the ethical state. Such a logically grounded reconceptualisation would also suggest that labour power need not be conceived merely as alienable property.[7]

The judgements of abstract right Like Theunissen (1991), one may think that because Hegel (1981, §53) describes possession, use and alienation as 'respectively the positive, negative, and infinite judgements of the will on the thing' the categorial analysis of property should be based on the logical form of the judgement of existence rather than on that of the syllogism as we have maintained. Quite apart from the explanatory power of our proposed correlation between the syllogism and abstract right there is textual support for the view that we should not simply take it for granted that Hegel's references to judgements in 'Abstract Right' are proof that this stage of objective mind is organised in accordance with the judgement's logical form. This support is to be found in Hegel's discussion of the relationship between the logical forms of judgement and syllogism in the *Science of Logic*.

To begin with, note that the judgements to which Hegel refers in the *Philosophy of Right* are all brought together into a unity. They are the will's judgements and through them the will expresses its unity with its reality. Theunissen's position fails to appreciate that in forming a unity the judgements thereby become a syllogism. When we introduced the syllogistic form in Chapter 5 we noted that in the logical categorial progression the syllogism is presented as the truth of the judgement. The syllogism is, as Hegel says, the judgement with its 'ground'. Moreover, the rational and, in the present context, spiritual element is to be found in its unity.

Notice also that there is nothing inappropriate about the attempt to understand a (number of) judgement(s) in terms of one of the syllogistic forms that belongs to the system. Hegel himself talks in such terms. For example, he refers to the categorical judgements that make up the categorical syllogism (Hegel, 1989 p. 696). He also makes the point that

> everything is a syllogism, a universal that through particularity is united with individuality; but it is certainly not a whole consisting of three propositions (Hegel, 1989, p. 669).

That is,

> to regard the syllogism merely as consisting of three judgements is a formal view that ignores the relationship of the terms .... It is altogether a merely subjective reflection that

---

7. This position is defended in G. Vassilacopoulos, 1994.

splits the relation of the terms into separate premises and a conclusion distinct from them (Hegel, 1989, p. 669).

At least two things follow from all the above for our discussion of Hegel's concept of property. First, the logic of property must be syllogistic in form rather than simply given in the form of a set of judgements. The important thing about these judgements is the relations between them and the way in which their unity is expressed. Secondly, since, according to Hegel, the analysis of the syllogistic form cannot properly be reduced to the analysis of its isolated judgements the corresponding real categorial analysis of the distinct modifications of property must pay attention to Hegel's account of the way that the judgements are related in the form of the syllogism of existence.

The transition to the second and third syllogistic figures, contract and wrongdoing

According to Hegel (Hegel, 1989, p. 671), given the abstractness of the moments and the unity of the individual with only one of its determinatenesses, from the viewpoint of speculative philosophy the conclusion of the first figure of the syllogism of existence does not carry any weight even though it may be formally valid. This is because the opposite conclusion could be drawn with equal force from a syllogism with a different content. Applied to the syllogistic organisation of the idea of property ownership this suggests that the same subject can be correctly taken to be a property owner on the basis of the syllogism we have been discussing (possession, use and alienation of property) even though the opposite conclusion, that the subject is not a property owner, is equally derivable from a syllogism having the same form and an entirely different content. This is why formal property relations are an inadequate embodiment of the will's freedom albeit the first of its embodiments.

The limits of the form of this figure derive from the fact that the immediacy of the terms contradicts the essential nature of the syllogism which is mediation. Mediation is, after all, manifested in the relations of the terms. That is, the simple determinateness of particularity is posited as the relation of the terms and, so, as the mediatedness of the conclusion qua conclusion of the syllogism (Hegel, 1989, p. 672).

This gives rise to the demand that each of the premises of any particular syllogism themselves be proved. This, demand, in turn, results in (a) the sublation of this form of ineffective

mediation and (b) the immanent emergence of forms of mediation that function as demonstrations of the truth of the premises
of the first figure.

> For the mediation of P-U, we have *I;* accordingly the media-
> tion must take the form P-I-U. To mediate I-P, we have U; this
> mediation therefore becomes the syllogism I-U-P' (Hegel,
> 1989, p. 673).

The first figure presupposes the other two while it is also presupposed by them. The extraction of two more figures from the
first figure of the syllogism of existence is still related specifically
to the activity of immediate individuality. In fact the transition to
the second figure, P-I-U, makes explicit the previously unacknowl-
edged mediating activity of the individual of the first figure.

> As regards the *form* [of the first figure], the *mediation* likewise
> has for its *presupposition* the *immediacy of the relation*; therefore
> the mediation is itself mediated, and mediated by the *immedi-
> ate*, that is, the *individual* (Hegel, 1989, p. 674).

The immediate individual is placed in the position of the middle
term in the second figure in order to give expression to the unity effected through its opposition to particularity. This opposition
marks the transition to the figure P-I-U.

The process of this immanent construction of the second and
third figures of the syllogism of existence out of the first figure organises the real categorial development from property ownership
to contractual relations and wrongdoing as the second and third
forms of 'Abstract Right' (Hegel, 1981, §72-§103).

According to the *Philosophy of Right* 'by distinguishing himself from himself [a person] relates himself to another person' and
this differentiation of the will as 'being contrasted with another
person' underlies the contractual relation. This amounts to the realisation of the implicit identity of two persons who 'really exist for
each other' 'only as owners' through 'the transference of property
from one to the other'. At the same time, the differentiation of the
will into the particular will that is 'opposed to itself as an absolute
will' constitutes wrongdoing (Hegel, 1981, §40).

Hegel (1981, §71) explains the transition from property to contract in terms of the existence of property 'as an embodiment of
the will'. He notes that 'from this point of view the "other" for
which it exists can only be the will of another person'. Just as the
transition from the first figure of the syllogism of existence to the
second is rooted in the demand for the demonstration of the truth
of the premise, P-U, which truth is its mediation by the moment

of individuality, so too the transition from property ownership to contractual relations indicates that the truth of the particularity of the will and its universality has to do with their mediation by individuality. The alienation of a property item to another individual shows that the universal will is not merely related to an external 'thing' but to that formerly external thing that has become the will's embodiment. This conclusion marks the transcendence of the single will and the movement to the actuality of mutual recognition and participation in a 'common will' (Hegel, 1981, §71-§72) as distinct from the mere 'anticipated relation to others' that characterises the form of property ownership (Hegel, 1981, §51).

Notice, here, that property owners' mutual recognition is, as Raymond Plant (1980, p. 73) maintains, the necessary social dimension of the right of property. However, Plant also suggests that this social dimension is indicative of a communitarian rather than individualistic vision of modern commercial relations. Although we cannot go into this point in any detail we think that this does not follow from the social dimension of property since, as a vision of social relations, individualism need not deny the social aspect of these relations. It merely qualifies them in accordance with a view of the rights of the individual not to be interfered with.[8] Our syllogistic analysis of the Hegelian account of property ownership indicates that the necessary social dimension of property is restricted to the property owner's purely formal recognition that the other person equally has a property owning identity.

The existence of another property owner is rendered explicit by the alienated property item. As an embodied will that is also alienated, the alienated property item presupposes the presence of another property owning identity to whom the alienated property item must belong (Hegel, 1981, §72-§73). Accordingly, contractual relations make explicit the contradiction anticipated by the structure of relations characterising property ownership. As Hegel (1981, §72) puts it, the contractual process mediates the contradiction that I am a property owner only in so far as I cease to be one.

The concept of contract also makes explicit the limited way in which the will's essential unity can come into existence as the unity of particular wills in the sphere of 'Abstract Right' (Hegel, 1981, §73-§75). Significantly, this kind of unity does not manifest an absolute universality. This is why in the speculative system the

---

8. Compare an earlier discussion of property by Plant, 1983, p. 154. Here, he discusses its social dimension without implying that property is related to a distinctively communitarian redescription of commercial relations.

form of contractual relations is limited to the treatment of persons' property relations and cannot properly be extended to ethical ties such as marriage and citizenship. [9]

The syllogism's fourth figure and justice as punishment

The development of the categories of abstract right to their rational conclusion gives rise to the emergence of the demand for 'justice as punishment' (Hegel, 1981, §103). Critical discussions of Hegel's views on the question of the nature and justification of punishment tend to read Hegel as if he were primarily proposing a justification of the social practice, as distinct from identifying the rational element in the conditions which give rise to crime and, consequently, revenge and the demand for punishment (cf. Cooper, 1984, pp. 151-167; Wood, 1990, pp. 108-124).

In contrast to these writers Hinchman (1984) attempts to situate Hegel's defence of the necessity of punishment within the broader context of his writings. So, he places emphasis on the significance of identifying the universal element in the criminal will. We believe that our syllogistic analysis of 'Abstract Right' has the potential to show why Hinchman's focus on the concept of the universal is correct. Although, we cannot defend our position here, we note that a detailed discussion would show that the demand for 'justice as punishment' is logically grounded in the categorial progression which gives rise to the fourth figure of the syllogism of existence, U-U-U. This figure renders explicit the eliminative power of an abstracted formal universal. Through the systemic elaboration of this developmental logic the categories of abstract right establish the right of particular persons to commodity productions, exchange relations and criminal justice understood as justice that is necessarily mediated by the authority of the universal.

The logical ground of the transition to morality

An examination of the way in which the fourth syllogistic figure effects the necessary transition to the syllogism of reflection (Hegel, 1989, p. 679-681) would assist in the understanding of the categorial interplay underlying the emergence of the concept of morality out of the demand for justice as punishment. This latter question does not seem to us to have been adequately resolved in the critical literature. Consider as an example the explanation for the transition from 'Abstract Right' to 'Morality' that Stillman (1980a,

---

9. For further discussion of Hegel's relationship to the social contract tradition see Benhabib, 1984, pp. 159-177.

pp. 103-115) proposes. He points to Hegel's acknowledgment that, although necessary for individuality and freedom, property may also be in tension or conflict with these, due to its externality. 'What a person can and cannot do with his property ... is partially determined ... by nature and society ... by putting his will in such a thing, (1980a, p. 107). A concern for morality is introduced supposedly in order that the conflict may be mitigated.

> Through the understanding of morality ... the individual comes to be merely a property owning person ... he has a concrete set of characteristics and attitudes which shape and express, indeed which are, his life' (Stillman, 1980a, p. 108).

To explain the transition Stillman appeals to what Hegel would call the natural admissions of consciousness. These are conditions that do not carry any weight when the elaboration of the idea's real categories is at issue. Stillman (1980a, p. 108) also suggests that in order to live a fuller life one ought to be concerned with those aspects of human life that are not self-directed or directed exclusively to one's property.[10] The problem with this reading is that it leaves unexplained Hegel's claims regarding the relational necessity for both the move and the precise direction that it takes. Why should the Hegelian system hold that the categories of abstract right necessarily give rise to those of morality? Although this is not the place to pursue this issue further, the answer, we would submit, must have to do with the character of the fourth figure and the grounds it reveals for the transition to the syllogism of reflection.

THE SYLLOGISM OF REFLECTION AND MORALITY

Just as the syllogism of reflection develops the reflective relation of the categories, so too morality is the sphere in which the moral subject reflectively develops its particular subjectivity. In line with our syllogistic analysis the moral subject is, here, to be understood as the infinitely self-related will that has become an object to itself. A detailed examination of 'Morality' (Hegel, 1981, §105-141) in the light of the syllogism of reflection (Hegel, 1989, pp. 686-695) would show that the three aspects of the moral will are respectively developed in accordance with the categorial progression from

---

10. See also the comparison of Hegel and Marx on property and individuality by Stillman, 1980b, pp. 130-167. This analysis presents the transition from the concept of the person of abstract right, the 'logical construct', to 'the man of civil society' (Stillman, 1980b, pp. 133-134). While Stillman describes this process it is left effectively unexplained.

the syllogism of allness through the syllogism of induction to the syllogism of analogy. For present purposes, however, it is important to note that once the particularity of the subject has been established in terms of the individual's right of desire satisfaction in accordance with the form of the syllogism of induction, the sphere of morality treats the particular moral subject's truth as the truth of his or her universal essence (Hegel, 1981, §128). This universal essence is developed in accordance with the logical categorial relations exhibited by the form of the syllogism of analogy.

The syllogism of analogy

According to Hegel (1989, p. 692) the abstract schema of the syllogism of analogy is I-U-P. That is, its middle term has been determined as 'an individual taken in its universal nature' and

> another individual forms an extreme possessing the same universal nature with the former. For example:
> The *earth* is inhabited,
> The moon is *an earth*,
> Therefore the moon is inhabited (Hegel, 1989, p. 692).

The objective significance of this form is that the middle term is shown to be the moment of universality in which individuality and particularity are indeed incorporated. It, therefore, constitutes a totality. The individual is, on the one hand, immediately united with its essence (in the position of the middle term) while the presence of another individual (in the position of an extreme) shows that the middle term is also a particular. The mediation of the individual in the position of the extreme with the essential nature (universality) with which the first mentioned individual is immediately united simultaneously affirms the universality of the immediate individual.

However, in this structure of relations

> it is undetermined whether the determinateness which is inferred for the second subject belongs to the first by virtue of its *nature* or by virtue of its *particularity*.... . analogy is still a syllogism of reflection in as much as individuality and universality are *immediately* united in its middle term. On account of this immediacy, the *externality* of the unity of reflection is still with us; the individual is only *implicitly* the genus (Hegel, 1989, p. 694).

The form of analogy makes explicit the problem with the syllogism of analogy. Although universality is treated as the essential nature of the individual, and not merely as one of its contingent properties, this nature is only implicit given that the terms are immediately united. For this reason the form leaves open the possibility that the predicate that the conclusion attributes to a second individual as the determinateness of its universal nature may belong solely to the first in virtue of its particularity. Accordingly, the correctness of the conclusion of the syllogism of analogy must already be presupposed in so far as the syllogism takes for granted the immediate relation between universality and individuality that is exhibited by the middle term.

It follows from the above that the determinateness of the individual subject's universal nature which is supposedly given in the conclusion is unsubstantiated. Nor is it capable of being substantiated in this form. All that the syllogism of analogy can genuinely express is the abstractness of the individual's universal nature. According to Hegel (1989, p. 694), 'this syllogism is in its own self the demand for itself to counter the immediacy which it contains' in order that the conclusion it purports to give be a genuine conclusion. Since the immediacy in question is that of individuality 'it is the moment of *individuality* whose sublation it demands'.

Moral subjectivity, good and conscience

The logical categorial relations that define the syllogism of analogy organise the real categories of 'good' and 'conscience' as they relate to the moral subject (Hegel, 1981, §129-140). The good is the universal essence of the individual qua moral subject whose 'particularity is distinct from the good and falls within the subjective will' so that 'the good is characterised to begin with only as the universal abstract essentiality of the will, i.e., as duty' (Hegel, 1981, §133). Duty for duty's sake cannot, however, justifiably produce the content of specific duties so as to give the moral subject's universal essence its determinateness, even though this particular content is required for the purposes of realising the good (Hegel, 1981, §133-135). While the good remains the abstract universal essence of the moral subject, his or her 'true conscience', 'the disposition to will what is absolutely good' is the immediate universality which 'establishes the particular and is the determining and decisive element in him' or her (Hegel, 1981, §136-137).

The category of the conscience bound moral subject is organised in accordance with the form taken by the middle term of the syllogism of analogy. This category constitutes an individual whose immediate relation to his universal nature generates the determinateness of specific duties as duties required by the good.

The subject's reasoning concerning the duty to do the good takes the following form.

The moral subject who is bound by conscience, A, has the specific duty, X.

B is a moral subject who is bound by conscience.

Therefore, B has the specific duty, X.

The discussion of the syllogism of analogy shows the unjustifiedness of extending to one particular a determinate universal essence (good as specific duty) on the basis of an identification of an immediate universal essence (conscience) belonging to another individual.

This is the sort of reasoning that underlies the potential for evil and hypocrisy (Hegel, 1981, §139-§140). At the same time, however, the categorial relations permitting it also ground the potential of self-consciousness to make 'the absolutely universal its principle' (Hegel, 1981, §139). According to the *Philosophy of Right* (1981, §141) the integration of good and conscience 'into an absolute identity has already been implicitly achieved'. The requirement that conscience and the good be mediated calls for the transcendence of the element of immediacy that conscience manifests.

The transition to the syllogism of necessity

The transcendence of the immediacy that defines the moral subject's conscience results in the transition to the absolute universality of 'Ethical Life' in which the substantial universality of the good and its determining principle are united. This transition process, we contend, is governed by the logic necessitating the transition from the syllogism of analogy to the syllogism of necessity. The syllogism of analogy results in the negation of individuality that is simultaneously the positing of universality. It thus marks the transition to the syllogism that has 'objective universality, the genus, purged of immediacy' for its middle term (Hegel, 1989, p. 694). This is the syllogism of necessity which, as already indicated, comes under the general schema I-U-P (Hegel, 1989, p. 695).

THE SYLLOGISM OF NECESSITY AND THE ABSTRACT MOMENTS OF ETHICAL LIFE

The syllogism of necessity

As we explained in Chapter 5, the emergence of the form of unity belonging to the syllogism of necessity marks the transition to a structure of categorial relations in which the notion's task is to realise the middle term's self-determining power. The middle term must, itself, posit its self-determining power as a prerequisite for realising the absolute identity of the notion with its object. Having emerged as the totality which is an objective universality, the middle term of the syllogism of necessity exhibits the characteristics of (a) the notion's non-contingent correspondence with reality; and (b) its categorial differentiated unity (the unity of the universal, particular and individual). According to the *Science of Logic*, at this point in the logical progression the terms of the syllogism have been determined as 'moments of a *necessary* existence' and the

> middle term is not some alien immediate content, but the reflection-into-self of the determinateness of the extremes. These possess in the middle term their inner identity, the determinations of whose content are the form determinations of the extremes (1989, pp. 695-696).

The middle term of the syllogism of necessity no longer manifests a self-subsistent identity. Since the necessity of relatedness has been established, the mediating unity no longer appears to be merely superficial or external, as is respectively the case with the syllogisms of existence and reflection.

Even so, the self-determining character of the middle term does not yet extend to the other terms of the syllogism. For this reason the middle term must undergo a process of fully realising its implicit self-determining power. This gives rise to the first form of the syllogism of necessity, the categorical syllogism, which is described as 'immediate and thus formal' (Hegel, 1989, p. 696). The categorical syllogism expresses the U moment of this cycle of development and so exhibits the abstractness of the notion in the position of the middle term. Because the absolute unity is initially immediate due to its implicitness its determinate other, the P moment in the cycle, is expressed as the hypothetical syllogism in which form and content are posited as having come apart (Hegel, 1989, p. 699). That which mediates and that which is mediated acquire the diverse form of 'immediacy of being' (Hegel, 1989 p. 698). Finally, in the disjunctive syllogism we have the formulation of the unity of the moments from the perspective of the I moment. This is the explicit form of the notion's fully self-determining categorial differentiated unity.

The abstract moments of ethical life

As already suggested, a detailed consideration of the forms of the syllogism of necessity would show that they determine the rational character and structure of the abstract moments of 'Ethical Life', 'The Family' (Hegel, 1981, §158-§181) and 'Civil Society' (Hegel, 1981, §182-§256). In Part III we will try to show that, aside from Hegel's support for a model of the male dominated heterosexual family, the exposition of familial love in the *Philosophy of Right* mirrors the mode of categorial interrelations that we attribute to the form of the categorical syllogism. We will examine this form in suitable detail in the next chapter. Here we will outline our understanding of the logical underpinnings of 'Civil Society'.

As one of the abstract moments of 'Ethical Life', 'Civil Society' establishes the right of particularity to satisfaction through productive and exchange relations. It does this by uniting the forms of intersubjective relation previously established as embodying freedom with the equally already established freedom of subjective particularity. Recall that 'Abstract Right' establishes the right of commodity production and exchange relations while 'Morality' establishes subjective particularity in terms of the right of desire satisfaction. These relations of production and exchange for the purposes of desire satisfaction take the form of 'an association of members' in an 'abstract universality'. In other words, civil society takes the shape of a formal association that, at best, involves cooperation for mutual benefit given that its members exist as 'self-subsistent individuals'. Such individuals do not recognise the necessary place of others, whether individuals or institutions, in the definition of their identity as individuals. As units within civil society, individuals are thus 'externally' related in that they do not take each other or their social organisations to be integral to the identity of each. Even their *common* interests' are initially to be understood in this light as an aggregation of their 'particular' interests.

More specifically, according to the *Philosophy of Right* (1981, §182), the abstract idea of civil society consists of an interplay between the principles of particularity and universality understood in the following terms. On the one hand, we have the particular concrete person who forms a self-interested 'totality of wants and a mixture of caprice and physical necessity'. Such a person relates to all else merely instrumentally. On the other hand, there is the form of universality, that is, the institutions by which society is organised into a formal association of private persons who thus meet their interests, needs and desires. Because the interplay between these two principles of particularity and universality is organised in accordance with the hypothetical form of the syllogism, they take the contradictory form of 'mediating and mediated immedia-cies'. This contradictory form shapes the reality in which the 'in-ner substantial identity' of the two principles is held together out of necessity whilst they manifest an outward appearance of mutu-al indifference. In other words, whereas the being of each neces-sarily depends on the being of the other they nevertheless relate to each other as being incidental to their own ends. Their substantial content and the form of their being have come apart in this sense.

The hypothetical syllogism exhibits a kind of a negative unity in which relatedness is treated as the lack of any necessary unity of form. For this reason the idea of civil society is elaborated as a sphere of activity in which each of the two principles appears to be what it is irrespective of the other whilst this very process gives ef-fect to 'a system of complete interdependence' (Hegel, 1981, §183). That is, in so far as there is indeed a mediation of particularity and universality, in so far as the concrete person 'thinks, wills and acts universally' in the process of satisfying his or her needs, the neces-sary interrelatedness of the moments is rendered explicit.

An extensive analysis of 'Civil Society' in the light of the hypo-thetical form of the syllogism would first draw attention to the spe-cific features of each principle from the point of view of their ap-parent self-subsistence. This appearance exhibits and reveals the limits of their contradictory form as mediating and mediated im-mediacies. Neither the particular concrete person's use of self-in-terested means-ends rationality nor the reasoning of the formal universal can adequately express their relation given that, contrary to the standpoint of each, neither principle shapes this interrela-tion exclusively. Furthermore, a detailed analysis would show pre-cisely why this contradictory interrelation of particularity and uni-versality incorporates an ethical dimension, namely, the 'process whereby particularity is educated up to subjectivity' (Hegel, 1981, §187). This process gives rise to the conditions that permit the emergence of social institutions that represent the formal embodi-ment of subjects that are aware of themselves as free individuals.[11]

The transition to the disjunctive syllogism and the differentiation of civil society

The hypothetical form of the syllogism shows that the necessary interdependence of the moments of universality and particularity is grounded in the fact that the being of each one of them is no less

---

11. Cf. Vassilacopoulos, 1994, pp. 195-207.

the being of the other. This recognition allows their substantial differentiated unity to emerge as their absolute form. The disjunctive syllogism renders this form explicit given that it reveals all the possible ways of uniting the moments of universality, particularity and individuality within the constraints of syllogistic reasoning (Hegel, 1989, pp. 701-703). These constraints are given by the logic of exclusive individuality whose mode of being is ultimately that of the formal universality of particularity that we analysed in Chapter 3 of the book.

The differentiation of civil society into its three moments amounts to the kind of limited systemic differentiating activity just sketched. On this reading, the ideas making up the externally combined system of economic, legal and political units are not merely to be understood as different aspects of the one social system; they also exhibit particular ways of viewing the social system taken as a whole. Accordingly, the idea of differentiated civil society incorporates economistic, legalistic, governmental and corporate understandings of the social system that are respectively based on different individual forms of uniting the universal and the particular to the exclusion of the other forms of unity.[12]

The transition from the syllogism and civil society to objectivity and the ethical state

When we analyse 'Civil Society' in the above terms we can make sense of the relationship between this idea and the Hegelian idea of 'The State'. This relationship has been typically understood in terms of the differentiated civil and political aspects of social life. That is, whereas 'Civil Society' is taken to elaborate the real categories constituting non-political relations, 'The State' is supposed to complete the social picture by elaborating the role of government and its various agencies. Our syllogistic analysis of the Hegelian idea of ethical life suggests that such an understanding conflates the dichotomised categorial interrelations found in 'Civil Society' with the idea of the fully integrated ethical system constituted by the categories belonging to 'The State'. As previously indicated, in the *Logic* 'The Syllogism' marks the completion of the subjective notion's development of its determinate being in order to determine itself into 'Objectivity'. Just as the transition in the *Logic* to 'Objectivity' establishes objectivity as the truth of the syllogism, so too the move from 'Civil Society'

---

12. Cf. Vassilacopoulos, 1994, pp. 208-227.

to 'The State' shows the latter to be the truth of its abstract moments, 'Civil Society' and 'The Family'.

While the idea of the state emerges as their truth out of the logical progression of the categories toward the development of their determinate being as a comprehensive unity, in this way it also shows itself to be the 'beginning' or framework within which the abstract moments of family and civil society are developed (Hegel. 1981, §256R). The nature of this framework is supplied by the nature of logical objectivity given that the syllogistic process results in the idea of the emergence of the object. As a result of the logical categorial progression the object emerges as an organic whole. It follows from this understanding of the system that the categories of 'The State' cannot simply add to and complete the abstract account of civil life. It does not elaborate an exclusively political dimension of social life that is limited to the role of government and state agencies. On the contrary, when we read the categories of the ethical state in accordance with the dynamics of logical objectivity we recognise the idea of a systematically differentiated social whole whose various dimensions are organically interrelated. Indeed understood in this way the idea of the ethical state supplies the fundamentals of the idea that we referred to in Part I of the book as the self-determining essence of modernity once it has overcome the moment of its self-denial. The idea of the ethical state presents a complete system of civil and political relations, albeit one that has yet to emerge historically.

Objectivity and the ethical state

If our systemic approach to the interpretation of Hegel's philosophy is sound, then the idea of the ethical state must be understood as actualising the spiritual sphere in the sense that it elaborates the essential unity of its categories with their being in accordance with the objective notion's process of construction from mechanical through chemical to teleological objectivity. An extensive analysis of these three stages of logical objectivity would show that the notion's movement through them grounds the three stages of the development of the idea of the ethical state in terms of the related ideas of the constitution, international law and world history (Hegel, 1981, §259). Like the mechanical object the 'individual state' develops its internal organisation out of its immediacy, progressively making more explicit its essential unity. On this interpretation the state's essential unity, its constitution, must be equally 'only inner' or 'only outer' in the sense of an (inner) unrealised essence or the (outer) reality of this unrealised essence that we discussed in Chapter 5. The *Philosophy of Right* (1981, §271) attributes two sides to the state's constitution, its internal organisation and its outward relations. Hegel deals with these two sides of the constitution under the headings: '*The Constitution (on its internal side only)*' (Hegel, 1981, §272-§20) and '*sovereignty* vis a vis foreign states' (Hegel, 1981, §321-§329), respectively. State sovereignty is presented in terms of relatedness to others because it is the explicit manifestation of the state's essential difference which difference is nevertheless the difference of its ideality or innerness. If we have regard to the 'outer unity' of sovereign states as mechanical objects, we can appreciate their existence in relations of opposition to each other. The main characteristic of these relations is that they are characterised by mutual indifference to the other's essential difference.

If the internal organisation of the state and its sovereignty do indeed respectively express the 'inner' and 'outer unity' of the organised object as we maintain, then it follows (from the relevant development of the notion in the *Logic*) that the individuality of the state is manifested exclusively in the sovereign state's outer unity. This is the reality of its unrealised essence which it manifests irrespective of its precise internal organisation. What is required at this level of immediate actuality is that the sovereign state be essentially a state. That is, it must have some internal organisation which differentiates it but this internal organisation need not be fully developed (in the terms of the internal unity that the *Philosophy of Right* presents in some detail).[13] This follows from the analysis of the mechanical object's unity as only inner or only outer.

The transition to 'International Law' (Hegel, 1981, §330) should then be understood in the light of the logical transition to 'Chemism' (Hegel, 1989, p. 727) and the idea of international relations must be seen as rationally grounded in chemical interaction. Finally, 'World History' (Hegel, 1981, §341) brings to the actuality of the idea of the state its explicit teleological dimension as is the case with the logical object (Hegel, 1989, p. 735).

How are these different aspects of the logically organised ethical state connected to each other? On the interpretation we are proposing Hegel's elaboration of the much discussed constitution 'on its internal side' should be understood as an account of the state's

---

13. For a detailed exposition of the individual state's internal organisation as a unity of three syllogisms see Vassilacopoulos, 1994, pp. 251-274.

essence taken in abstraction from its purposive process. The development of the internal organisation of the idea of the constitution amounts to the full elaboration of this essence as an abstract moment that is properly the end or purpose of the idea of world history, that is, of the state understood as a teleological object.

The process of world history is purposive because in it is made explicit the unity of notion and object in so far as the world historical process is the process of objective development towards the realisation of its own essence or self-determining end. In this way world history constitutes the unity of (a) the essence in abstraction from its purposive process (constitutional law) and (b) the process in abstraction from purposiveness (international law). As 'mind which gives itself its actuality' world history exhibits the restoration of the notion in the object.

Reply to an objection Even though this is not the place to pursue this task in any comprehensive way, we will respond to an obvious type of objection to the position we have been advancing about the relationship between the logic of objectivity and the ethical state. In doing so, our purpose is to reinforce the claim we made at the beginning of this chapter that our systemic approach has much to offer by way of settling the meaning of a number of Hegel's rather puzzling claims about the logical underpinnings of his social philosophy.

If one lists Hegel's references to concepts haphazardly and without the aid of some basic understanding of the organising principle that explains the relations between them, one can come up with a seemingly chaotic picture. So, we might ask, for example, how Hegel (Hegel, 1985, §541) can be understood consistently to associate the state's internal organisation with the notion's 'subjectivity' if the individual state's organisation follows that logic of mechanical objectivity for the systemic reasons we have claimed. After all, given that (a) the subjective notion's logical categories (judgement and syllogism) precede those of logical objectivity, and (b) mechanism belongs to the latter group of categories, is this not textual support against our proposed method of correlating the categories of the system's logic and social philosophy? Indeed, if we compile, as we can do, a number of such pieces of textual evidence, ought we not to conclude that any strict organisation thesis of the kind we have advanced must be mistaken?[14]

---

14. This objection has been raised by G. Marcus.

If we take the developmental character of the categorial progression seriously we can see why this conclusion relies on a much too simple understanding of the meaning of 'the notion's subjectivity'. As we explained in Chapter 5, in the *Logic* and, in particular, in the part that deals with the doctrine of the notion (Hegel, 1989, pp. 575-844), the notion starts off as (a) 'subjective' in the sense of being merely formal. Through its activity as such it sublates its subjectivity and becomes (b) the objective notion whose subjectivity is 'submerged ' in the object. As this kind of objective notion it develops itself to the point where it (c) regains its subjectivity as the self-determining principle of its own object. Thus at the end of the logical categorial progression the notion as 'Idea' is subjective in this latter sense.

The nature of the notion's movement from (a) formal subjectivity to (b) objectivity to (c) the self-determining subjectivity of its own object is critical for a systemic reading of the correlation between logical objectivity and the ethical state. Because what is presented in the *Philosophy of Right* is the work of the idea and because the idea is the subjective notion that has passed through the process of objectification, in the above sense, the idea is the subjective notion in the sense of (c) above; it knows itself as the self-determining organising principle of its categorial reality.

THE CRITIQUE OF HEGEL'S SOCIAL PHILOSOPHY

As the above comments suggest, we believe that an extensive reading of 'Ethical Life' by reference to the logical forms we have proposed has the potential to shed light on some of the most puzzling claims in the *Philosophy of Right* about the character of the spheres of ethical life and their relationship to each other and to the logical categories.[15] But we also believe that such a reading supplies a sound basis for assessing the adequacy of Hegel's own exposition of ethical life. Granted that the *Logic* can and should function as the legitimate immanent perspective from which to engage critically with the claims of the *Philosophy of Right*, what would such a role involve?

Raymond Plant (1983, pp. 185-196) has also addressed the question of how one might evaluate Hegel's basic principles. Plant suggests that 'Hegel's own practice generates three particular criteria which are conjointly necessary and sufficient conditions for a rational test of the adequacy of his explanations' (Plant, 1983, p.

---

15. For further work in this direction see Vassilacopoulos,1994, pp. 188-274.

185). The first is drawn from Hegel's 'insistence that philosophical explanations must exhibit necessary connections between those things, practices or forms of experience which are explained' (Plant, 1983, p. 186). The second criterion is derived from the nature of the dialectic, one of the features of which is the 'preserving at the more developed level patterns of experience or notions developed further back' (Plant, 1983, p. 191) and the third calls for the coherence of philosophical explanation of a mode of experience with relevant empirical knowledge (Plant, 1983, p. 192).

Plant (1983, p. 144) bases his argument that Hegel's social philosophy fails to satisfy all three criteria of adequacy on a reading which, unlike our own, takes Hegel to be proposing a reconciliation of ordinary man with his existing social world through the practice of philosophy. For this reason he takes seriously the charge from an empiricist point of view that Hegel cannot satisfy his first criterion because to operate with a notion of necessity in his explanations is ultimately to provide tautological explanations which have no claim on the (empirically discernible) facts (Plant, 1983, p. 186). Plant (1983, pp. 187-189) argues further that Hegel's theory cannot be rescued from a criticism along these lines by relying on a conception of 'contextual necessity or loose entailment' since the developments that Hegel presents do not just take place within contexts with a shared pattern of behaviour, as the application of such a conception presupposes, but between contexts as well.

Plant (1983, p. 196) concludes that 'Hegel's philosophy is to be rejected on the grounds of its failure to survive his own implied tests of adequacy' but this need not be accepted. Hegel's speculative notion of the categorial progression's logical necessity suggests that the criteria Plant identifies are too general to play the role he attributes to them.

Furthermore, although Plant (1983, p. 166) correctly emphasises that the rationality and necessity of the process of social development is 'secured through the structuring of the Idea' in that this structuring reveals the pattern of relationships generated from what appears to be fragmentary at each stage of development he does not explain why the idea's structuring should develop concepts relating to social relations in one specific direction and not some other.

Our detailed exposition of the Hegelian concept of the family in Part III of the book will attempt to demonstrate the precise way in which our systemic approach can fill these sorts of gaps. Indeed, in criticising Hegel for his failure to make the right kind of move from the logical categories at a critical point in his elaboration of the idea of the family, we hope to correct an important error in his elaboration of the Hegelian system's social philosophy.[16]

---

16. Interestingly, Flay (1980, p. 171) suspects 'that a lacuna exists between ... parts of the system of the philosophical sciences and that, therefore until we ascertain precisely the nature of this break in the system of sciences, we shall not be able to judge forcefully the validity of the analysis given in the philosophical sciences of nature and spirit'.

PART III

7. THE CATEGORICAL SYLLOGISM AND THE CONCEPTS OF FAMILY, LOVE AND INTERSUBJECTIVE IDENTITY

In this chapter we will begin presenting our argument that the logical structure of the categorical syllogism (Hegel, 1989, pp. 696-698) strictly organises the Hegelian concept of the family and the related concepts of love, marriage, sexuality, family property, parenting and the law.[1]

---

1. We use the phrase 'Hegelian' throughout our discussion to distinguish between the approach that we believe to be consistent with Hegel's system of logic and Hegel's own elaboration of the real categories in his *Philosophy of Mind*. It is also worth noting here that in the *Science of Logic* (1989, p. 727) Hegel mentions love as one of the spiritual relations for which the chemically organised 'sex relation' is taken to be the formal basis. This indirect association of love with the logical structure of 'chemism' might be seen as textual evidence for the view that the Hegelian system correlates the real category of love with the logical category of chemical objectivity and not with that of the categorical form of the syllogism as we propose. This, however, would be mistakenly to assume that the Hegelian system allows for one correlation to the exclusion of the other. We suggest that in its entirety familial love is an ethically integrated relationship between individuals qua chemically related bodies who also realise the form of their loving being as this is internally organised by the categorical form of the syllogism. Thus the chemical nature (Hegel, 1989, pp. 728-733) of such relationships can be seen as determining the substance or content of relevant processes of interaction when we focus attention on the ethically integrated realisation of love as elaborated in the Hegelian idea of the ethical state. As we will see later, it does not follow from this that chemism also defines the internal form of familial love. Its internal organisation must be based on the notion's formality (Hegel, 1989, p. 597) given that familial love involves an element of recognition by outsiders. Our discussion will focus on the aspect of the Hegelian account of familial love that elaborates the internal structure of the concept taken in abstraction from the further features of its ethically integrated realisation within the Hegelian idea of the ethical state.

As we saw in Part II, the *Logic* constitutes the systematic and comprehensive elaboration of the fundamental formal categories of philosophical thought. This process involves a cyclical progression from the most abstract to the most concrete of forms. The demand, as Hegel puts it, that thought verify itself to itself governs the progression of the categories. This means that no point of the process can rest on mere assertion. Thought must create its concepts immanently. Thought acquires the status of objectivity by determining its content as the mediated result of the thinking process. The outcome of this categorial progression establishes thought as the unity of its two aspects, unity and difference. Thought thus determines itself as the concrete unity of subject and object through the unity of form and content. Thought acquires this status pursuant to the full investigation of the formal categories and their diverse modes of interrelating. This investigation explores the dynamic of categorial interrelations that exhibit alternative configurations of thought's differentiated unity, that is, of the notions of unity, difference and their relationships.

The 'Doctrine of the Notion', the third part of the *Science of Logic* which includes the treatment of the syllogistic forms, explores thought's differentiated unity. This part elaborates the interplay between the basic categories of universality, particularity and individuality.[2] The form of this cycle of categorial interrelations is produced as the result of a movement through categories that are thought, firstly, in their immediate presence, in abstraction from all relatedness (the categories of being), and, then, as pairs of correlatives exhibiting relatedness externally (the categories of essence). As the truth, in the sense of inevitable presupposition, of these preceding configurations of differentiated unity, the differentiated unity of universality, particularity and individuality emerges in what Hegel conceives as thought's sphere of freedom. This is the sphere in which thought explicitly thematises its 'self-evolved determination' (Hegel, 1989, p. 596).

Thought constructs syllogistic reasoning within the sphere of its freedom. The role of syllogistic reasoning is to unite the abstract categories of universality, particularity and individuality and to overcome their immediacy (unmediatedness). It achieves this by bringing the categories into definite relations that give them

---

2. Since the meaning of these categories shifts in accordance with the categorial progression, to give a fixed definition of them (cf. Kolb, 1988, pp. 60-61) is unavoidably to privilege the meaning they acquire at some particular stage of the categorial progression.

their objective meaning. The most important of these relations are those of differentiation and mediation. In syllogistic reasoning thought's unity takes on the form of explicit mediation as represented by one of three terms that is positioned as a middle term between two extremes. Its difference is exhibited as the middle term's differentiating activity. Both these aspects characterise each of the three categories at various points in the syllogistic process. This process gives rise to forms exhibiting increasingly more adequate ways of conceiving the differentiated unity of the categories. Differentiation and mediation are exhibited to varying degrees, with varying effects and measures of success. All this depends on precisely where and how the categories are positioned both in the complex relation of each to the other two at any given moment, as well as in the whole process of syllogistic development. This latter is the process that begins with the abstract forms that represent mere existence. It moves to the external reflection upon the categories and ends when the categories become necessarily interrelated.

For present purposes, it is enough to bear in mind that, for Hegel, the totality of syllogistic forms, their respective dynamics and limits are rendered fully visible in this elaborate way. His treatment of the syllogism purports to represent all the conceivable modes of differentiating and uniting the three categories. These modes begin with the case in which the categories are in their respective self-subsistence. That is, they are mutually indifferent to their respective determinations and their indifference exhibits various oppositions and external relatedness. The syllogistic cycle culminates in the full integration of the categories that have become necessarily (non-contingently) interrelated. Each category reflects all three within it, as the result of effective differentiation and mediation by the category of universality.

The completed syllogism, in which the middle term determines both aspects of the complex process of differentiation and mediation, is related to its preceding formulations in much the same way as a geometric circle is related to the process of its construction prior to its completion. A full account of the features of the constructive process at any point prior to completion would include reference to two kinds of features. There are those that can be found in the completed construction. There are also those that must be transcended since, were they to be retained, they would undermine the would-be qualities of the completed construction.

The categorical syllogism is an incomplete formulation of the syllogism. It is the first of three modes of the third, most fully developed form of the syllogism, the syllogism of necessity. As such it exhibits two kinds of features. On the one hand, there are those that result from the preceding syllogistic process and characterise the syllogism of necessity in its objectivity. On the other, there are those that derive from the dynamic of the mode in question, a dynamic in which aspects of immediacy, contingency and subjectivity persist. The contingent aspects of the syllogism are its subjectively determined aspects. The presence of degrees of subjectivity is, in turn, due to the middle term's failure effectively to determine differentiation, mediation or both of these.

In this chapter we will offer a rather detailed account of both the objectively and the subjectively determined aspects of the categorical form of the syllogism. Although rather abstract and complex, this discussion is necessary as it will form the basis of our analysis in the remainder of the book. We will elaborate a Hegelian understanding of the ethical significance of family life by returning time and again to the insights that we can draw from the structuring dynamic of the categorical form of the syllogism.

THE CATEGORICAL SYLLOGISM

As it emerges from the syllogistic process that precedes it, the categorical form of the syllogism expresses a certain combination of objectivity and subjectivity due to the character of its middle term. As regards its objective aspect, the middle term has determined itself as a differentiated unity that constitutes a totality, that is, a category the being of which is necessarily (non-contingently) related to the being of the other categories. Accordingly, whereas in the preceding formulations of the syllogism the middle term characteristically lacks any effective power of differentiation or mediation, the categorical syllogism exhibits the middle term's effective power to differentiate itself into its extremes and, hence, to determine their character to this extent. The middle term has the status of objectivity in precisely this respect.

Furthermore, this status of objectivity has been taken up by the category of universality. As objective universality, then, the middle term gives the extremes their essence which is their common content or substantiality.[3] However, in differentiating itself into its

---

3. The notion of essence need not connote properties that are attributed to (some class of) human beings in a fixed and predetermined way. Our characterisation seeks to avoid the charge of essentialism that is targeted to theories which posit some universal human or sex-specific essence in terms of a set of properties. Cf. Grosz, 1992, pp. 332-344; Phelan, 1989. In relation to Hegel's philosophy

extremes the middle term does not merely define the extremes as objective universal essence. Significantly, in doing so it also renders visible the preconditions of its actualisation as a potentially, as distinct from effectively, mediating unity. These preconditions constitute the terms of the middle term's differentiation in accordance with the basic features of its universal essence: qua essence the middle term is the essence of an individual being whereas qua universal essence it is the essence of a plurality of such beings. In this way the middle term differentiates itself into the moments of (individual) unity and (universal) difference respectively. As this differentiated middle term, the middle term is necessarily related to its extremes and thus constitutes an effective differentiating unity. The extremes are, in turn, necessarily related to their middle term in so far as each one of them expresses one aspect of their common essence. This means that, to this extent, the moments of unity and difference are not mutually indifferent or externally related. Since the incompleteness of the substance of one is exhibited in its relationship to the other they are mutually informing.

At the same time, due to the preceding categorial process, the objective universality of the categorical syllogism inheres in the category of particularity. As particularity, the middle term still lacks a reflective relation to itself and retains a degree of immediacy. Due to its immediacy the middle term's universal essence is only an abstract essence in the sense of a simple quality taken apart from its relationship to other individual determinations. This immediacy permeates and affects the conception of the extremes, individuality and universality. They, in turn, retain a degree of immediacy that is exhibited in their self-subsistent form. Due to their persistent self-subsistence, the extremes retain a degree of externality: they are indifferent to the middle term qua mediating unity and thus exceed the grasp of its unifying potential or power. So, the defining characteristic of this mode of categorial interrelations is that, whilst the particular middle term effectively determines the differentiation of the categories into individual unity and universal difference, it does not effectively bring them back into a unity.

The indifference of the extremes to the unifying potential of the middle term is exhibited by the fact that mediation is effected by the extremes rather than by the middle term. In other words, effective mediation depends on the independent character of the extremes. In effecting mediation themselves, the extremes form a unity

see also Redding, 1996, pp. 156-158.

through their objective universal essence in so far as it is presupposed but not as the result of that which necessarily relates them. Instead, mediation by the extremes depends upon that which exceeds the common abstract essence attributed to them by the middle term. In the case of the individual this common abstract essence is accompanied by a specific nature, a concrete content consisting of diverse properties belonging to the individual being irrespective of the precise determination of its objective essence.[4] Not having been determined in any particular way, the content and internal organisation of these properties is taken to be open ended and fluid. The universal, in turn, exceeds its abstract essence in virtue of the concrete differences that characterise individuals involved in the unification of the moments of unity and difference.

Rather than forming a fully concrete unity, the mediation effected by the extremes exhibits the abstractness of their essence; what comes into concrete being is a relationship that involves a unity of abstract unity and abstract difference. This mode of interrelating has important implications regarding the character of the extremes' concrete being. Because the unity in question is only a unity as regards an abstract essence it does not extend to the whole being of that which is brought into the unity. Accordingly, the necessary relatedness of the categories that, as already explained, is brought about by the middle term's differentiating activity does not also characterise the mediation that is brought about on the basis of the excess characterising the being of individuality and universality. It follows that in this mode of interrelations the concrete being of individuality is constituted by a contingent excess. The excess in question is contingent relative to the extremes' objective essence in the sense that the excess plays no role in the necessary relationship constituted by the differentiating activity of the middle term.

Further, the presence of the element of contingency just referred to is not itself contingent. On the contrary, since the individual in question is a concrete being constituted by a universal essence as well as a specific nature that exceeds the grasp of this essence, this specificity must be exhibited in the categorial interplay. In addition, the contingent excess that characterises the being of the extremes is not merely present in the extremes' differentiatedness; the contingency in question is not overcome in the relevant process of unification. Rather, the concrete being of individuality remains

---

4. The notion of a specific nature is not to be understood here as invoking a fixed and inescapable condition. Rather, it refers to whatever makes a specific being that specific being.

a necessarily contingent excess even as mediation is effected. This condition constitutes what we can refer to as 'the necessity of contingency'. The necessity of contingency is a relation of difference, not only in relation to the unity of individuality and universality in the terms just indicated, but significantly, in relation to the unity of content exhibited by the objective universality of the middle term. The latter relation is rendered visible with the availability of a multiplicity of forms in which the middle term's abstract essence might be expressed. The availability of multiple forms is necessary since the abstractness of the middle term's essential determination means that form and content are not identical.

With the identity formed as a result of the mediation, the position of the extremes is, nevertheless, transformed. In their identity, individuality and universality are not merely indifferent to the middle term's power of mediation in the way indicated earlier. On the contrary, in effecting mediation they appropriate their common essence and establish a reflective relationship to it, though not to the power of mediation itself. This enables individuals to relate reflectively to the specifics of their unity from within their established unity. Even so, they do not reflectively relate to the source of their unity's existence as a unity. The latter reflection is an aspect of the unity that retains a degree of immediacy. It, therefore, remains within the power of merely subjective reflection.

The extremes continue to retain a degree of immediacy due to the fact that their formed identity remains a particular unity. Their objective universality is still limited in so far as it inheres in the category of particularity that occupies the position of middle term. Furthermore, because the identity formed is still only a particular unity, its persistent immediacy must also be exhibited by its external relationship to whatever falls beyond this unity. Being externally related to that which falls beyond its unity constitutes the way in which a unity that exhibits the necessity of relatedness does so qua particular.

Accordingly, the objective meaning of the syllogistic form is further enhanced by the categorical syllogism in a very precise way. It is a mode of relating the moments of unity and difference that surpasses the notion of a common essence in the sense of a property or properties belonging to each of a number of different individuals. The categorical syllogism exhibits the form of being as a common or universal essence where 'universal essence' is given the more refined sense of a necessary interrelationship through a quality that frames the activity taking place within it. A universal essence in

this sense functions as the field in which different individual beings relate and through which the necessarily contingent aspects of
their beings are rendered capable of attaining a rational character
(in Hegel's sense of being reflectively grounded) and being transformed accordingly. At the same time, due to the role played by the
necessity of contingency in this mode of interrelations, the exercise
of this transformative element remains within the power of subjective reflection. The mediation effected due to the contingent excess
of the extremes remains subjective or, conversely, lacks objectivity
to this extent.[5]

THE CONCEPTS OF LOVE, FAMILY AND INTERSUBJECTIVE IDENTITY

We turn now to consider Hegel's initial characterisation of the family in the light of the above analysis of the categorical form of the
syllogism. As is well known, in the *Philosophy of Right* (§158-§160)
Hegel introduces the family as an ethical unit that consists of three
aspects, marriage, family property and parenting that culminates
in the family's ethical dissolution. At this point he draws upon a
certain understanding of the relationship between the concepts of
family, love and individuality. From the outset (Hegel, 1981, §158),
the family is presented as the 'immediate substantiality' of spirit
that is specifically characterised by love. However, love is described
as spirit's 'feeling of its own unity'. Furthermore, within the spiritual unity that is created by familial love one is self-conscious of
one's individuality as a self-determined essence so that one is as a
family member rather than as an independent person. These three
basic ideas organise the sphere of intimate life in its spiritual or
ethical dimension when this is reflected upon in abstraction from
its place in the comprehensive idea of an ethically integrated social
whole. As we explained in Chapter 6, Hegel refers to the idea of an
ethically integrated social whole as 'the ethical state'.[6] Once we out-

---

5. Cf. Burbridge, 1995, pp. 181-183.

6. The discussion that follows focuses on the modern idea or concept of the
family as a social unit that has a spiritual or ethical dimension in the Hegelian
sense discussed in the previous chapter. This is a modern concept in the sense
sometimes attributed to the ideal of the so-called 'sentimental family'. That is, in
contrast to the family of traditional society, the modern family is founded on love,
is based on affect and psychological attachment and it is located in the private
sphere of intimacy (cf. Robinson et. al., 1997, p. 90; Midgely and Hughes, 1997,
pp. 60-62). For reasons that will become evident in the course of our discussion
the Hegelian idea of the family needs to be distinguished from conservative and
liberal-communitarian 'family values' discourses that link the ethics of familial

line the logical structure underlying these conceptual relations it will be possible to see precisely how they relate to other aspects of intimate life of which Hegel makes no mention.

Familial love

We will begin by indicating how Hegel's description of familial love follows the pattern of relationships that is given by the categorical form of the syllogism. In our earlier discussion of the reflective process that is captured by the syllogistic progression we explained that the objective significance of the categorical form of the syllogism initially lies with the fact that the category in the position of the middle term (that which is supposed to bring together two other categories that are positioned as extremes) has determined itself into a differentiated unity that is a totality. This means that it necessarily relates to the other categories in the light of its effective power to differentiate itself into its extremes. Consequently, it defines them to this extent. The concept of familial love plays precisely this role. Its essence is an objectively universal differentiating power which determines the identity of each family member as that of a loving being. Ethical love is thus necessarily intersubjective in the sense that it constitutes an objective universal essence that functions as loving beings' substantive field of interaction. Within this substantive field the loving bond embodies the moments of unity and difference. The first, the moment of unity, takes the form of individual self-unity as this structures the identity of the loving self. The second, the moment of difference, takes the form of the universal difference that defines family members as a plurality.

In being a simple quality familial love also exhibits the immediacy (unmediatedness) characteristic of the categorical syllogism's middle term. Love is at once an objective condition, in the above mentioned sense of a field of interaction within which loving beings relate to each other, and no less a feeling. In this way it conforms to the self-determination of a concept that is positioned as the middle term of a categorical syllogism. The idea of

---

life to an idealised type (cf. Moller Okin, 1997, pp. 22-25; Midgely and Hughes, 1997). It also needs to be disassociated from attempts, like that by Virginia Held (1993), to construct a non-contractual morality out of an analysis of ethical bonds within families. Finally, note that we will leave aside another two areas of discourse on the family. The first concerns the social and political practices of families within specific types of historical communities (cf. Nicholson, 1997) and the second concerns the family as a biological unit (cf. Firestone, 1970).

the family unit is itself grounded in the feeling of unity created by love. This is an immediate sharing of the experience of love within which each family member feels the interconnectedness of his or her loving essence. In other words, family members affirm their loving essence immediately even though this is necessarily secured intersubjectively, that is, in the practice of sharing the experience. This is what we take to be the significance of Hegel's references, firstly, to the family as the 'immediate' substantiality of spirit and, secondly, to familial love as 'ethical life in the form of something natural' (Hegel, 1981, §158A). The naturalness of this first moment of ethical life derives from its connection to love as an unmediated feeling.

Family membership as dynamic individuality

Just as love is necessarily related to its differentiated moments, they too are necessarily interrelated and mutually informing. The loving self is a kind of pure awareness that seeks the recognition of an other pure awareness as a constitutive aspect of its own identity. This means that within the field of love there are two preconditions for ethical intersubjectivity that derive from the precise differentiation of the moments of individual unity, as embodied by the loving self, and universal difference that is expressed in the plurality of loving selves. The first condition is that ethical subjectivity be conceived as a dynamic process; a loving self is ethically self-related in so far as one conceives of oneself in terms of a process to be realised. The second precondition for ethical subjectivity is that the mutual recognition that ethical subjects give each other must be incorporated into the identity of each. In being recognised, the self-unity characterising each loving self is transformed through an incorporation of difference as represented by the other self. Being necessarily intersubjective in this sense allows one's loving essence to transcend the subjective boundaries of individuality. It is in the dynamic potential of this kind of mutual recognition, in which a mutual informing of the pure being of selves is achieved, that differentiated unity is intersubjectively realisable as an objective essence.[7]

OTHER KINDS OF INTIMATE AND LOVING RELATIONSHIPS

The Hegelian association of love and dynamic individuality with the concept of the family raises some questions about other kinds

---

7. Compare Redding, 1996, p. 185.

of loving and intimate relationships that we need to address before proceeding with our exploration of the Hegelian concept. The kinds of relationship we have in mind here fall into three general groups: (1) loving relationships in the absence of family ties; (2) sexual relations in the absence of love where love is understood as an on going relationship; and (3) the single parent family that arises from the decision of only one person to raise a child or children.[8] To be sure, an investigation of these sorts of relationships would reveal important similarities between each of them and the kind of familial love that is defined by the Hegelian account. However, a comprehensive investigation of the sphere of intimate life must be left to another occasion. For present purposes we want to make three points about these other sorts of relationships in order to explain why it is that we will not deal with them any further.

First, whatever the points of overlap, there are some significant differences between them and the Hegelian concept of familial love. To begin with, whilst the unity characterising familial love is, of course, not restricted to family ties, its distinctive features need not be present in other kinds of necessarily intersubjective relationships. For example, what we referred to above as the objectively universal essence of familial love need not define the friendship relationship. The idea that love functions as the objective field within which friendly interaction takes place might characterise a friendship derived from the participants' good natured being, but it need not. As Aristotle explains, aside from this form of 'perfect friendship,' friendship might instead be grounded solely in participants' desires for utility or pleasure. The feeling that friends have for each other in these latter types of instance cannot be said to give expression to their loving beings in the same way that this is secured with the determination of family members as loving beings.

Similarly, the feeling of unity that is generated by familial love differs in a crucial respect from the feeling characterising solidarity with strangers. The necessarily intersubjective identities that define ethical solidarity cannot remain at a similar level of immediacy since such identities come into being as a result of being reflectively endorsed by individuals. Unlike the bonds of solidarity with strangers, the creation of family ties does not depend on some kind of reflective endorsement of the bond (even though

8. The cases of single parenting that result from a couple's decision to separate or from the death of one parent fall within the framework of the Hegelian concept and will be discussed in Chapter 9.

a decision to formalise such relations by marrying involves such reflection). The immediacy of the origin of familial love is most clearly demonstrated by the case of children's' unreflective love for their parents but it is also captured by the idea of falling in love.

Furthermore, the features of the dynamic individuality that is at the heart of familial love need not be present in other kinds of loving interaction. Thus the process of incorporating difference into one's identity as a loving being is altogether lacking in universalistic or 'cosmopolitan' altruism, as it is sometimes referred to (Galston, 1993, p. 123). This is altruism directed to humanity at large. The very abstractness of the idea of humanity that renders any particular person a suitable object of universalistic altruism leaves out of the altruistic interaction the element of incorporating difference into the altruist's loving identity. When one person acts altruistically towards another in virtue of the latter's humanity, the first person relates himself or herself to that which they share in common rather than to their specific difference. This kind of altruistic act denies any place to the process of incorporating difference into an individual's identity because it presupposes a static conception of the individual's identity that is given prior to the interaction. That which renders any specific individual a suitable object of universalistic altruistic love is his or her capacity to invoke in the altruist the latter's pre-determined identification with the abstract quality, humanity.[9]

If this brief analysis is correct, then the dynamic individuality that is presupposed by the concept of familial love cannot come into play in altruistic love because the particularity of the individual with whom the altruist interacts is not recognised. Dynamic individuality also does not come into play in the case of single parenting but for a different reason. Here, it is not that the individual to whom the loving activity is directed, namely the child, is recognised in one way rather than some other. It is rather that the asymmetry involved in the parenting relationship altogether excludes the kind of mutual recognition that dynamic individuality

---

9. These comments are explicitly restricted to universalistic or cosmopolitan altruism. Our analysis clearly does not apply to so-called 'personal' altruism (cf. Galston, 1993, p. 123), that is , altruism directed to family members and friends for reasons having to do with the special nature of these kinds of relationships. Since our objective here is limited to identifying fundamental differences in the structure of different kinds of relationships, we do not need to isolate for special consideration sub-classes of friendships or family ties that include acts of altruism. We, therefore, leave aside comparisons between such 'conditional altruism' and universalistic altruism and their respective moral weight (cf. Blum, 1980, pp. 77-81).

presupposes. The parenting relationship not only lacks the presence of two selves who are both capable of recognising their own self-unity in the other, but it typically begins from a relationship of undifferentiated unity (Fromm, 1985, pp. 30-32; Kristeva, 1989, pp. 160-186) and progresses towards the child's attainment of his or her atomic individuality. Accordingly, single parenting does not involve the mutuality that makes the realisation of dynamic individuality possible in other familial ties.

Indeed, outside the parental bond, a single parent may remain atomically related to all others. This is also the case with intimate relations based on the mutual satisfaction of individuals' desires. Thus, those who relate to each other primarily through the desire for good sex or, what is sometimes referred to as 'sex without love', can be said to affirm each others' atomic individuality. This constitutes a fundamental structural difference between good sex and sex as one aspect of an on going loving relationship.

This brings us to the second point we want to make about the sorts of relationships we have been outlining above. In our view the structural differences that we have highlighted signify differences of kind. If this is correct, then it would be inappropriate to evaluate and rank relationships belonging to one kind by reference to criteria that are simply drawn from the preferred characteristics of another kind of relationship. Indeed, comparisons that overlook the structural differences are apt to create unnecessary confusion about the relative value of relationships that share largely superficial similarities. As an example, take the comparison of sex without love and sex in a loving relationship. Russell Vannoy (1990) disagrees with Rollo May that sex with love is better than sex without it. First he draws attention to the ways in which May's arguments ignore differences between sex with and without love (Vannoy, 1990, pp. 20-22). Then he puts forward a case for the superiority of sex without love by drawing attention to qualities that can only be found in the absence of an on going loving relationship. Vannoy cites the uniqueness and freshness of a new encounter, the excitement generated by the unknown, the freedom from obligations generated within on going relationships and so on (Vannoy, 1990, pp. 23-28). However, he does not explain why the presence of such qualities amounts to a better kind of relationship as distinct from a merely different one. Vannoy takes for granted that the operative evaluative criteria for good sexual relations, whether between strangers or as part of an on going loving relationship, must be the same. But this mistakenly presupposes that the sexual aspect of an on going loving relationship must only ever be externally related to the structure of the loving bond. We will argue in Chapter 8 that on our Hegelian account the value of sex within a loving union cannot be fixed (in the way that an analysis like Vannoy's supposes).

For present purposes we need to note simply that were we to begin from the contrary assumption, that sex within a loving relationship has the potential to generate what we might call 'acquired pleasures', that is, pleasures of a kind that derive from familiarity over time, then we could just as well find forceful arguments for the view that sex with love is superior. Such comparisons seem pointless when we have regard to the view that sex with and without love are different in kind. In our view this has to do with the fact that, whereas the former engages our dynamic individuality, the latter engages our atomic individuality. To conflate these two distinct aspects of individuality is to misunderstand the kinds of relationship each makes possible and meaningful.

This said, note that the necessarily intersubjective identity at the heart of the Hegelian concept of dynamic individuality does not cancel out atomic individuality. This means that one and the same human being can simultaneously engage in and be recognised as an atomic and as a dynamic individual in respect of different relationships.

The final point that we want to make concerns the implications of not including the above mentioned sorts of relationships in the Hegelian account of ethical life. So far, we explained, firstly, what we take to be fundamental differences in these kinds of relationships and, secondly, our reasons for thinking that differences of kind render unhelpful the simple comparison of similarities and differences in their characteristics. Even so, one might think that the exclusion of these other kinds of relationship from the Hegelian account of ethical life signals their presumed relative inferiority. To appreciate why this is not the case we should note that the Hegelian elaboration of the system of ethical life does indeed focus on the systemically instituted aspects of intimate ethical life. As we will see in the course of our discussion, the concept of the family forms part of this account because, like the concepts of civil society and the ethical state, it involves a necessarily objective dimension, namely public recognition. This is what sets the concept of the family apart from other equally important ethical concepts like friendship that does not depend on any form of recognition by outsiders.[10] So, by focusing on the Hegelian concept of the family we will not be presuming its ethical superiority over the kinds of relationships that we have mentioned above. We will instead set them to one side on the ground that their respective structures call for a different kind of treatment.

---

10. The above remarks need to be qualified to take account of the view that single parent families, in the limited sense referred to at the outset, can and should be publicly recognised. From the standpoint of the Hegelian account, the single parent family gives selective expression to the idea of familial love for the reason we have already explained. This kind of selectivity, however, merely puts it on a par with relationships like the childless marriage.

8. THE FAMILY AND PERSONALITY: MARRIAGE AND INTERSUBJECTIVE IDENTITIES

In the previous chapter we suggested that the relationship between the Hegelian concepts of family, love and intersubjective identity is organised by the categorial interrelations that the categorical syllogism's middle term makes possible. We put forward the idea that because Hegel's concept of love is positioned as the middle term between the concepts of the family and that of individuality the idea of familial love functions as a field within which family members interact as loving beings. The reciprocal love of family members, in turn, gives rise to the situation in which individuals bring into the fullness of being their necessarily intersubjective identities. The family member is defined by a dynamic, mutually recognising individuality.

Now we want to consider in some detail the internal dynamics of the Hegelian concept of familial love.[1] Hegel's analysis focuses on monogamous, male dominated, heterosexual marriage, collective family property, parenting and the ethical dissolution of the family. It is worth noting that marriage, family property and parenting are not presented as necessary and sufficient conditions for the existence of families. Instead, they constitute the potential ethical dimensions of a long term coupled relationship based on love. This said, our objective is to show, firstly, how a suitably modified and refined elaboration of these ideas follows the pattern of categorial interrelations defining the categorical form of the syllogism; and secondly, how our Hegelian approach can be used to reconceptualise and resolve issues within contemporary theoretical debates about the sphere of intimate life. We will start

---

1. Unless otherwise indicated, in the remainder of our discussion all references to love are intended as references to familial love.

our discussion in this chapter by drawing attention to the logical structure that underpins Hegel's elaboration of the idea of monogamous marriage leaving to one side his claims about the significance of sexual difference and about the role of the law. The next chapter will focus on family property, parenting and the family's dissolution. Our critical discussion of Hegel's sexist and heterosexist views and his claims about the family and the law will be left to the last two chapters.

The marriage union embodies both the objective and subjective aspects that respectively define the rational and non-rational aspects of the syllogism's form. The former, as previously explained, are expressed in the ethical or spiritual dimensions of love. The latter reveal the contingency and immediacy that the form retains due to its relative incompleteness. They are found in the various specificities of marriage unions based on love. Nevertheless, together, the objective and subjective aspects of marriage consist of familial love's formal embodiment in the sense that marriage gives love its precise shape.

THE SUBJECTIVE SIDE OF MARRIAGE

The 'subjective side' of the marriage union is initially to be found in the particularistic, even unique, ways in which people are attracted to each other or come to choose their marriage partners (Hegel, 1981, §162). Let us begin by explaining how the categorical syllogism supplies the logical basis of this claim. As we explained in the previous chapter, the defining characteristic of this syllogistic form is that the category in the position of the middle term does not effectively mediate between its differentiated categories so that the extremes must secure their unity. This suggests that even though loving beings necessarily presuppose their universal loving essence, they must, nonetheless, invoke a variety of contingent factors to make their decisions to marry and/or to remain in a particular marriage.

Understanding the logical ground of the subjective side of marriage in the above terms allows us to draw upon the precise character of the syllogism's form to elaborate the precise role that is played by the contingent factors associated with the marriage relation. Recall that the categorical syllogism's middle term is a universal essence that, nevertheless, inheres in the particular. Due to this limit on its effective power of determination, the extremes exceed the grasp of the middle term's differentiating power and thus retain a degree of contingency that is evident in their self-subsistent form. This, in turn, means that effective mediation depends, in part, upon the independent character of the extremes relative to their middle term. This independent character is constituted by individuals' specific natures and the concrete differences between united individuals, namely their different specific natures (as distinct from their objective universal essence). Accordingly, even though it is differentiated individuals' common abstract essence that is brought into a unity, the mediation is nevertheless initiated and effected by individuals qua common abstract essence and the different specific natures that constitute the contingent excess of their essential determination. Correspondingly, though a loving individual's union with another individual is the union of a loving essence that they do not determine, their union is, nevertheless, dependent for its initiation and actualisation upon the difference of their specific natures that exceeds their loving essence.

The above analysis explains why Hegel (1981, §176) claims that because of the 'fundamental contingency of marriage' people cannot justifiably be compelled to marry or to remain married to someone they do not want. The marriage union must be (re)created and maintained by willing participants. This willingness extends beyond the objective aspect of each participant's intersubjective identity to their different specific natures.

Eros born of chaos

In the context of our present discussion, individuals' different specific natures are embodied in the diverse needs, interests, values, desires and pleasures that constitute each loving being as the specific being that he or she is. In line with the open endedness and fluidity of the contingent excess characterising this aspect of individuals' concrete being, the character of the diverse aspects of individuals' different specific natures is taken to be neither fixed nor organised in any particular way. This is what is meant by the contingent excess that co-defines the concrete identities of loving beings who form a marriage union. The role played by the contingent excess of loving beings' concrete identities reveals the immediacy and self-subsistence characterising the differentiated extremes of this syllogistic form.

This role is not limited to the formation of a marriage union. The contingent excess of loving beings continues to inform their relationship throughout the process of its actualisation. This is because, as we argued in the previous chapter, the contingent excess of the concrete being of individuals is itself necessary in the sense that the contingency following from the limits of the middle term's objectivity must be exhibited in the categorial interplay.

Furthermore, the syllogism's form gives rise to the possibility of transforming the specifics of individuals' contingent beings. Recall that within their unity individuals establish a reflective relationship to their universal essence. This empowers them to relate reflectively to their differentiatedness (although the loving relation, itself, comes into being without the aid of this kind of reflectiveness). This is the conceptual source of a union's transformative power. Loving beings who have formed a marriage union thus have the power to transform their contingent excess through the practice of love.

The transformative power of a marriage union does not inevitably give rise to the suppression or reduction of differences. Within a loving relationship the transformation of specific aspects of lovers' contingent beings enables, though it does not require, such specifics to acquire a spiritual significance. In so far as two individuals come together in a loving union the syllogism's form shows why their interaction as beings with specific natures cannot be primarily instrumental or strategic. Effecting mediation, or being willing members of an ethical relationship in the terms already outlined, empowers them with the spiritual and emotional energy characteristic of love, an energy that makes possible and meaningful the process of creating an ethically integrated self out of the chaotic character of atomic needs and desires.[2] In this on going creative process of a self-affirming becoming, rather than compromising the fluidity of desires and pleasures, the blindness of their atomic character is transcended. This is a blindness that on its own would give rise to the valorisation of diverse, uncompromised and, ultimately, competing satisfactions. Still, the scope of creative love is, here, unlimited, but not shapeless, given that the shape of creative love is defined by the operative mode of intersubjectivity that we outlined in the previous chapter.

It follows from the unlimited scope of creative love and the defining role of ethical intersubjectivity that the full exploration of a loving couple's creative potential, and indeed the question of what is to remain beyond its scope, is entirely a matter for the participants themselves. For this reason the Hegelian concept of marriage is consistent with the practice whereby married couples

---

2. We believe that Lorde's characterisation of women's erotic energy can be analysed in the terms of this logic even though she expressly denies the value of associating the erotic power of love with marriage. Lorde, 1993, esp. pp. 341-342.

determine their own marriage vows. For example, the Hegelian concept of marriage does not presuppose that sexual desire be taken as exclusively satisfiable within the confines of what a couple, whether heterosexual or homosexual, might have to offer each other. It requires instead that this sort of issue be a matter for them to explore and determine as a couple. Later we will argue that the Hegelian approach, not only has the conceptual resources to accommodate 'open marriages', but it also does not need to limit these to heterosexual relations. Indeed, on the Hegelian approach the participants of a loving relationship need not even identify as heterosexual or homosexual. It is left up to them to determine the significance of a marriage partner's bisexuality or 'queer pleasures'. In order to show that the Hegelian approach makes this openness possible, we need to explain how the subjective side of the Hegelian concept of marriage relates to its objective side.

THE OBJECTIVE SIDE OF MARRIAGE

As Hegel (1981, §161) puts it, marriage is a union of 'self-conscious love'. Familial love that is reflectively given the form of marriage is neither purely natural, in the sense of being unmediated, nor merely instrumental as is a merely contractual relationship. Furthermore, it is not merely a feeling (Hegel, 1981, §161A). This is because lovers' free consent to marry gives expression to the objective significance of the loving relationship (Hegel, 1981, §162). What matters from this point of view is that lovers do indeed share in a loving feeling and, so, in marrying freely, they can manifest their common essence.

In creating a union their aim is to 'make themselves one person' in the precise sense of actualising their intersubjective identity or bringing into full being the unity of their existence with their universal essence. In Hegel's (1981, §163) words,

> [t]he ethical aspect of marriage consists in the parties' consciousness of this unity as their substantive aim, and so in their love, trust, and common sharing of their entire existence as individuals.

When the parties to a marriage are in the frame of mind just described, their marriage union becomes spiritual in the sense that it rises 'to a plane ... above the contingency of passion and the transience of caprice' (Hegel, 1981, §163). In other words, irrespective of the contingent factors that bring two persons together to form a marriage, when their interaction is a loving one their love cannot be reduced to the presence of these subjective factors. For, this would be to ignore the essential nature of love, the fact that each person necessarily finds his or her abstract essence in the other person. Marriage thus embodies the objectivity that characterises the middle term of a categorical syllogism.

Objections to the idea of marrying to become one person

The idea of becoming one person through marriage has been subject to criticism by feminist political theorists. One objection concerns its supposed reductionism. For example, Susan Moller Okin (1979, p. 341) suggests that with his reference to marriage partners' willingness to renounce their individual personalities 'Hegel is the clearest example of a theorist who assumes total altruism to govern intra-familial relationships'. After all, he takes women not to have 'any distinct life or interests at all' (Moller Okin, 1979, p. 285).

Note, firstly, that Hegel implies that the renunciation of individual personality involves a kind of struggle on the part of willing individuals. They must give their 'free consent' 'to renounce their natural and individual personality to this unity of one with the other' (Hegel, 1981, §162). On a psychological level, this can be understood as a willingness to engage in the process of what E. S. Person (1990) describes as 'loving merger' as distinct from either 'mere bonding' or 'fusion'. According to Person (1990, p. 125), loving merger is not reducible to the mere satisfaction of mutual interests, as is the case in mere bonding. Instead, this process of becoming one

> connotes an interpenetration of selves .... There is a quality, simultaneously, both of mingling with the beloved and expansion of the self.

Person (1990, p. 127) adds that merger

> may most readily be expressed through physical means, but its actual locus is within the psyche. It is here that the fluidity of ego enables the kind of interpenetration of selves that constitutes merger. The repository of meaning is located in the merger itself, in the lovers' internal psychic process. Merger is in part surrender to a person, but primarily it is surrender to love's powers.

We should not confuse this process with fusion where the latter is understood as an unsustainable state in which lovers' egos merge completely (Person, 1990, p. 127).

On the conceptual level, the process of becoming one person is a mark of free intersubjectively constituted dynamic individuality in the sense explained in the previous chapter. In other words, one does not renounce individual personality per se (in favour of 'total altruism' in intrafamilial relations) but only one mode of personality, namely that which takes it for granted that exclusive atomic individuality is exhaustive of individuality. The renunciation of 'natural and individual personality' thus involves the reconstitution of personality in line with its necessarily intersubjective dimensions and the dynamic individuality associated with this.

We will have more to say about the precise embodiment of the form of this intersubjective personality in the next chapter. For the moment, we want to point out that by insisting on the common sharing of their entire existence as individuals the Hegelian approach need not be understood as calling upon marriage partners to give up all concern for the pursuit of their several interests. On the contrary, as we suggested when considering the subjective side of marriage, all that is required is that the very identification of these kinds of interests and needs be thematised within the framework created by a loving union. After all, as we explained in the previous chapter, the actualisation of an individual's dynamic individuality does not cancel out appropriate expressions of atomic individuality. Within such a framework personal autonomy is not sacrificed but refigured in terms of its necessarily intersubjective dimensions. This is a point which contemporary feminist relational theories of metaphysics and epistemology have sought to develop. [3] This said, the Hegelian claim that partners to a heterosexual marriage become 'one person' would, of course, be problematic if the category woman were overtly or covertly subordinated to that of man, as it is in Hegel's *Philosophy of Right*. In chapter 10 we will argue that the Hegelian approach we favour does not suffer from this limitation.

The critic may still object that even if the Hegelian approach does not imply the elimination of individual personality, still marriage partners give up a significant degree of privacy they would otherwise enjoy as separate individuals. Relatedly, vulnerable individuals lose state protection from spousal abuse. A version of this general objection has recently been formulated by Claudia Card (1996). Her position is worth considering here because it focuses on the formal structure of the marriage relationship.

Card (1996, pp. 12-13) observes correctly that, unlike typical contractual arrangements that specify the obligations of parties in a formalised way, a marriage contract creates very loosely defined

---

3. See, for example, Fox Keller's (1985) account of dynamic autonomy.

obligations. Further, by meeting their obligations, the parties to a marriage usually strengthen, rather than discharge, their obligations to each other as is the case in contractual relations. She suggests that spousal arrangements conform better to an unacceptable mutual guardianship or trustee paradigm.

> The obligations of a trustee, or guardian, are relatively abstractly defined. A trustee or guardian is expected to exercise judgement and discretion in carrying out the obligations to care, protect, or maintain. The trustee *status* may be relatively formal .... But consequences of failing to do this or that specific thing may not be specified or specifiable, because what is required to fulfill duties of caring, safekeeping, protection, or maintenance can be expected to vary with circumstances, changes in which may not be readily foreseeable. A large element of discretion seems ineliminable. This makes it difficult *to hold the trustee accountable for abuses* (Card, 1996, p. 13).

If we leave to one side the question of the source of the inadequacy of legal protections against spousal abuse we can focus attention on the very structure of marriage relations that Card's mutual trustee paradigm presupposes. Two points are especially noteworthy.

Firstly, a mutual trustee relationship permits unilateral decisions and actions on behalf of a beneficiary. In the relationship between trustee and beneficiary all effective power, for example, to determine what is in the beneficiary's interests and to act on this determination, may reside with the trustee. Thus the identities of the parties to such a relationship may remain atomically constituted. Of course, this need not be the case. For example, the trustee relationship of parent and child may well involve (a) a parent whose identity internally incorporates his or her relationship to her child and (b) a child whose necessarily intersubjective identity is not yet fully differentiated from his or her parent. Nevertheless, what has significance for the purposes of our discussion is that the necessarily intersubjective aspect of a marriage relationship is not a necessary feature of the trustee paradigm.

Card could respond that a necessarily intersubjective aspect of the marriage relationship is equally incapable of consistently being recognised within the contract model of marriage. We would point out that, whilst the Hegelian approach recognises the marriage contract, it restricts the idea of a marriage contract to the mutual and freely entered into commitment to become one person. Such a mutual commitment is not the actuality (the unity of this existence with the essence) of a marriage union but only what we might call the anticipation of its actuality. The contract paradigm is unsuited to capturing the essence of marriage. The reason is that the essence of marriage is given by the interplay of its objective and subjective aspects whereas contract concerns only the objective aspect of marriage in its initial emergence. As Hegel (1981, §163R) points out, even though a contract marks the beginning of a marriage, 'it is precisely a contract to transcend the standpoint of contract, the standpoint from which persons are regarded in their individuality as self-subsistent units.' (Cf. Hegel, 1981, §75R.)

Secondly, a trustee's relationship to a beneficiary is unavoidably hierarchical given the way in which it invests the power of decision and action. A mutual trustee and beneficiary relationship merely duplicates this hierarchical structure with the parties' role reversal. Yet, Card offers no reasons for thinking that a hierarchy is inherent to the structure of a marriage union. On the contrary, if we are correct in our view that the concept of marriage conforms to the structure that defines the categorical form of the syllogism then, as we will argue in the next section, it cannot consistently conform to a hierarchical structure of relations.

We do not mean to deny that many actual marriages are hierarchically ordered. We also do not mean to deny that when they are hierarchically ordered to the detriment of vulnerable parties existing marriages might conform to a trustee paradigm. This kind of observation could prove useful as part of an adequate sociological explanation for the historical failure of legal and other social institutions to protect against spousal abuse. Still, we should not conflate (a) this kind of sociological argument for avoiding marriage under certain cultural conditions and (b) the philosophical argument to the conclusion that the institution of marriage as such is irreparably flawed due to the very structure of the relations that the concept invokes. When a symmetrical structure of relations is taken to be an indispensable feature of the concept of marriage the requirement that marriage partners be willing to become one person cannot be reduced to vulnerable partners' unreasonable exposure to others' uncontrollable abuses. This said, we can now turn to explain why it is that the Hegelian concept of marriage presupposes a dyadic structure of relations between symmetrically related partners.

The dyadic and symmetrical structure of marriage

The formal structure of the marriage relationship is necessarily dyadic in the sense that Nel Noddings (1984) attributes to the care relationship in general. Noddings analyses the relationship of ethical care in terms of repeatable and reversible reciprocal dyadic relations. She outlines the formal structure of the care relation as follows.

> (W,X) is a caring relation if and only if
> (i) W cares for X (as described in the one-caring) and
> (ii) X recognizes that W cares for X.
> When we say that 'X recognizes that W cares for X' we mean that X receives the caring honestly .... Hence, its reception becomes part of what the one-caring feels when she receives the cared-for.
> ... the relationship can be mutually (or doubly) caring if we can interchange W and X and retain true expressions (Noddings, 1984, p. 69).

Care 'as described in the one-caring' refers to 'engrossment' and 'motivational displacement' in the 'cared-for'. In Noddings' (1984, p. 30) words, 'caring involves for the one-caring, a "feeling with" the other'. This does not call for the projection of one person's personality onto an object of contemplation. Rather, it calls for 'receiving the other', 'seeing and feeling with the other'. Engrossment in the other is achieved by making oneself available to the other through one's commitment to this kind of receptivity.

In addition, caring requires a 'motivational shift' in which one allows one's 'motive energy' to be shared and 'put in the service of the other' (Noddings, 1984, p. 33). This is to be distinguished from merely responding emotionally or non-rationally (Noddings, 1984, p. 34). Indeed,

> in caring, my rational powers are not diminished but they are enrolled in the service of my engrossment in the other. What I will do is subordinate to my commitment to do something' (Noddings, 1984, p. 36).

The process of caring involves a lateral shift from a mode of consciousness that is receptive in the above terms to one that is reflexive in the sense of being directed towards oneself and what one has received. At this point one reflects upon the received subject matter and the demands generated by one's commitment. Noddings' account acknowledges that one may engage in instrumental and object-related thinking in this process. However, her account of care requires that the one-caring 'move back to the concrete and the personal' in order to 'keep [one's] objective thinking tied to a relational stake at the heart of caring'. Failure to do this transforms the situation into caring about (an abstractly constructed) problem rather than for a person (Noddings, 1984, pp. 35-36). Engrossment and motivational displacement in the other effectively involve a commitment to the other as the subject and not the mere object of one's attentions. A conceptual continuity between caring and cared for subjects is presupposed for the possibility of the realisation of this kind of receptivity.

The kind of interaction just described (the attentiveness, the responsiveness to, and recognition of, the attentiveness and the receptivity of the recognition of care) is entirely dependent upon the presence of dyadic relations since the caring process must flow to and from participants for its actualisation. This dyadic structure also defines the formal framework of marriage partners' loving actions towards each other. The reason for the necessity of such a symmetrical dyadic structure is to be found in the way in which the moments of unity and difference come together in the idea of the marriage union. Recall that because it is organised in accordance with the categorical syllogism's middle term, love is an abstract essence. Its differentiating activity produces the individual self's abstract self-unity and abstract universal difference. We earlier made the point that due to the middle term's objectivity the individual's abstract unity is not self-subsistent but is, instead, internally related to the moment of difference. This internalisation of difference is made explicit when the extremes come together through their universal essence. To the extent that this universal difference, the abstract difference of individuals, is internally related to the moment of individual unity it must be symmetrical. This is implied by its relative abstractness that does not depend on this or that specific difference that might be hierarchically ordered.

The necessity of a dyadic structure derives from the character of the difference that must be internalised in order that it be brought into a unity of the syllogism's categorical form. To overcome the self-subsistence of the individual's abstract self-unity this self-unity cannot merely be internally related to (some) specific differences. Instead the individual's abstract self-unity must be internally related to that which expresses the very idea of excluded difference because it is this idea that is presupposed by the self-subsistence of the individual's abstract self-unity.

Now, the idea of excluded difference is expressed by the copresence of two atomically related individuals. This is because they stand in an external relation to each other where (a) the other represents the difference that is excluded by the self-subsistent self-unity of the first and (b) this self-unity excludes difference by being indifferent to it. Individuals who restrict their mutual recognition to their respective abstract property owning identities are the paradigm instance of this type of interrelation. Accordingly, in reciprocally internally relating themselves to what they previously excluded, namely another atomic individual, the difference that atomic individuals would otherwise exclude can play a constitutive role in the intersubjective identity that they thereby form. It follows from the above analysis that the structure of the marriage union is necessarily dyadic in the sense that any and every expression of the (relevant kind of) loving potential of one loving being must be completed through a second loving being whose responsiveness and recognition, in turn, enable the first to respond receptively.

So far we have been arguing that the categorical form of the syllogism supplies a basis for thinking that we should understand the objective side of the concept of the marriage union in terms of marriage partners' symmetrical and dyadic relatedness pursuant to their reciprocal willingness to become one. This is not to deny the existence of spousal abuse or inequalities in actual marriages. It is also not to deny that, historically, the legally sanctioned heterosexualisation of the sphere of intimate life has been premised on a culturally reinforced dimorphism. What we have been trying to do is to draw out the conceptual basis for recognising the ethical significance of marriage, understood as an on going coupled relationship, without implying that the long term coupled relationship represents the paradigm ethical unit to which other kinds of intimate relationship should conform.

This position raises a number of questions. In particular, if we grant the ethical significance of marriage, what should we make of Hegel's claim that it must also be monogamous and what are the implications of our analysis for communal and other living arrangements? Critics of Hegel, such as P. J. Steinberger (1988, p. 187), suggest that even though Hegel convincingly argues that *something like* marriage is necessary to the unfolding of Objective Spirit, [he] has failed to prove that *only* [monogamous] marriage can do the job'. This is because the demands of familial life can also be otherwise met. For example, communal living arrangements could just as well 'satisfy procreative and other social urges and 'provide children with sound moral instruction' (Steinberger, 1988, p. 187). We will examine these issues in turn.

THE OBJECTIVE SIGNIFICANCE OF MONOGAMY

Here is how Hegel (1981, §167) presents the rationale behind his claim that marriage is essentially monogamy.

> In essence marriage is monogamy because it is personality—immediate exclusive individuality—which enters into this tie and surrenders itself to it; and hence the tie's truth and inwardness (i.e. the subjective form of its substantiality) proceeds only from the mutual, wholehearted, surrender of this personality. Personality attains its right of being conscious of itself in another only insofar as this other is in this identical relationship as a person, i.e. as an atomic individual.

The first thing to note about this passage is that, rather than merely being linked to the demands of procreative and child rearing functions, Hegel's association of marriage with monogamy invokes the conceptual necessity for two individuals reciprocally to renunciate their atomic individuality. In our discussion so far we have attempted to explain why it is that at least two symmetrically and atomically related individuals must be involved in this process. Now, we also need to appreciate Hegel's reason for thinking that only two such individuals can be involved in creating a particular marriage union at any one time. Of course, in addition to being understood as the practice of being in a long term coupled relationship with only one other individual at a time, monogamy can also be understood as being in a sexually exclusive long term coupled relationship. We will return to this narrower sense of monogamy once we have explored the question of the rational ground of monogamy in the first of these two senses.

In our view the key to an adequate understanding of the Hegelian concept of monogamy is the conceptual significance of Hegel's reference, in the above cited passage, to 'immediate exclusive individuality'. The immediacy and exclusiveness characteristic of personality as atomic individuality also characterises personality that has been reconstituted as an intersubjective identity in the terms we discussed in the previous section. Monogamy, the on going coupled relationship, embodies the immediate exclusiveness of an intersubjectively constituted identity. This is because when two hitherto atomic individuals come together to form a couple based on their love for each other (a) they bring into being a mutual immediate responsiveness to each other's being as lovable and (b) they recognise the lovable in each other as belonging exclusively to that other.

We can best explain this notion of immediate exclusiveness by drawing on a comment that Giorgio Agamben (1993) makes about the lovable. In discussing a certain view of the interrelation-ship of the concepts of the universal, the singular (particular) and the individual in 'the intelligence of an intelligibility', Agamben draws attention to a being's 'being-such'. This is found in the very condition of belonging to the being in question (Agamben, 1993, pp. 1-2). He illustrates the significance of belongingness to 'being-such' with reference to the idea of loving the lovable because this idea cannot be reduced either to the love of the loved one's particu-lar properties or to the love of the abstract universal that he or she is taken to instantiate.

> Love is never directed to this or that property of the loved one (being blond, being small, being tender, being lame), but nei-ther does it neglect the properties in favour of an insipid gen-erality (universal love): The lover wants the loved one *with all of its predicates*, its being such as it is. The lover desires the *as* only insofar as it is *such* (Agamben, 1993, p. 2).

We want to suggest that this kind of link between love, the beloved, his or her particular loved properties and their belongingness to the beloved in the lover's experience of the lovable does not merely ensure the beloved's irreplacability for the lover. It also accounts for the kind of exclusiveness that the Hegelian approach takes to be in-dispensable to the idea of the marriage union that is based on love.

The non-necessity of sexual exclusiveness

So far, we have suggested that the immediate exclusive individual-ity that the idea of monogamy is called upon to embody should be understood in terms of the exclusiveness generated by the 'being-such' of the lovable. The 'being-such' is rendered intelligible in the lover's experience of an immediate feeling of love toward the particular beloved. If this analysis is correct, then the Hegelian approach does not also need to rely on the concept of monoga-mous marriage understood narrowly as being in a sexually exclu-sive long term coupled relationship. As Richard Mohr (1994, pp. 49-50) concludes on the basis of moral argument, the idea of mar-riage to one person at a time need not involve sexual exclusiveness.

Plural marriages

As part of her attack on the idea of marriage, Claudia Card makes the point that in order to accommodate the plural on going in-timate relationships of many lesbians the marriage institution would need to recognise plural marriages. Card thinks that it would not be enough to recognise open marriages (marriages that do not demand sexual fidelity), since people who have more than one on going intimate relationship might wish to accord to intimate non-spouses the same material benefits that they provide to their spouse. She concludes that even though plural, as distinct from open, marriages would be required to give expression to many lesbian relationships this option is dubious because it has unknown economic implications (Card, 1996, p. 8; p. 10).

A Hegelian response to Card's plural marriages objection would begin by pointing out that, although our conceptual analysis of monogamy provides no normative basis for denying plural marriages, it renders a concept of plural marriages unnecessary from the point of view of the *Logic*. This is because the immediate exclusive individuality of symmetrically related marriage partners' intersubjective identity would merely be repeated in each of their several marriages.

This said, a Hegelian approach would also need to point out that whilst it is correct that the concept of marriage does not accommodate the case of being in more than one on going intimate relationship at a time, this need not be seen as a problem. This is because the concept can be suitably disconnected from the heteronormativity of the institution as we currently know it. We will defend this latter claim in Chapter 10. For now, let us assume that the concept can be disconnected from the institutional practices that historically have contributed to the marginalisation of other kinds of intimate loving relationships. Once we have put this issue to one side we can see that the Hegelian concept of marriage does not need to accommodate the kind of relationship that Card has in mind. After all, Card's preferred relationships need have nothing to do with the creation of a necessarily intersubjective identity of the kind that we have argued is at the heart of the marriage union. Consider by way of illustration Card's references to a long term intimate relationship of her own. She states,

> my partner of the past decade is not a domestic partner. She and I form some kind of fairly social unit .... We do not share a domicile (she has her house; I have mine). Nor do we form an economic unity (she pays her bills; I pay mine). Although we certainly have fun together our relationship is not based simply on fun .... We know a whole lot about each other's lives that the neighbours and our other friends will never know. In times of trouble, we are each other's first line of defence, and in times of need we are each other's main support. Still, we are not married. Nor do we yearn to marry (Card, 1996, p. 8).

Although the participants to the relationship just described obviously share much that is meaningful and worthwhile for them, Card makes it clear that the creation of a necessarily intersubjective identity is not at issue and that she and her partner continue to relate to each other as atomic individuals. This is reflected in Card's representation of their economic relations. Their relationship has no need for the creation of communal property or what Hegel (1981, §170) calls labour and care for common possessions. For reasons that we will explain in the next chapter, the Hegelian approach takes collective property to be part of the process of actualising the marriage union.

Of course, the above observations are not meant to be critical of the kind of relationship Card describes. (On the contrary, though we cannot demonstrate the point here, it could be argued that the form of this relationship conforms more closely to the categorial interrelations that define the disjunctive form of the syllogism. This is a later, more advanced stage in the categorial progression of the Hegelian system of logic.) For the purposes of our present discussion we want to draw attention to the differences in orientation towards partners' economic relations in the two kinds of relationship in order to support our contention that such differences are indeed indicative of relationships that are different in kind. Because of the character of the intersubjectively constituted identity at the heart of the concept of marriage, on the Hegelian approach, marriage partners' economic relations cannot be understood exclusively in terms of the distribution of benefits and burdens to atomically related individuals. Since Card's discussion presupposes precisely this kind of interrelationship, her objection to marriage (that marriage would need to, but cannot easily, be understood in terms of plural marriages if it were to capture many lesbians' experiences of their intimate relations) is misplaced.

Furthermore, Card should not complain that whereas the Hegelian approach recognises the marriage union it fails to do the same for the kind of relationship she describes. As we suggested in the previous chapter, the inclusion of marriage in the elaboration of Hegel's system of ethical life reflects the view that instituted marriage has a necessarily public dimension.

MARRIAGE AND COMMUNAL LIVING ARRANGEMENTS

We turn, finally, to consider the implications of including the idea of marriage in the Hegelian concept of the family for our understanding of communal living arrangements. More specifically, does the Hegelian approach fail to have regard to the benefits of communal living? Let us begin to answer this question by indicating what we consider such benefits to be. On a practical level, they may involve everything that we might need to enjoy, or to cope with, life given our circumstances. Communal living arrangements have the tendency to enrich (as well as tax) the stock of emotional, material and economic resources that we can devote to the sphere of intimate life. Sharing resources with networks that include friendship and/or kinship ties spanning over generations may be people's preferred way of life or, in conditions of economic hardship, this may be the only available way of life.[4]

On a more theoretical level, John Hardwig (1997) has recently restated the case for pluralistic communal living, in preference to living in coupled relationships, on the ground that the former type of arrangement gives its participants an epistemic advantage. Hardwig maintains that the potential for self-knowledge within coupled families is restricted by the way it creates shared intimate space. Although we must rely on others' observations and evaluations of us in order to learn about ourselves, the coupled family's creation of shared intimate space corresponds to the exclusion of all outsiders. This, in turn, restricts the observation and evaluation of us to two mutually exclusive and exhaustive classes of individual. There are 'those who are *very* close or *very* distant and removed' (Hardwig, 1997, p. 112).

Hardwig (1997, p. 112) envisages an alternative that constitutes an 'intermediate position' pursuant to which our self-reflection can draw upon others who are 'close but not too close'. He thinks that pluralistic communes can provide such an intermediate position because they allow for 'outsiders within'. He makes the point that, instead of preserving the space that couples usually keep to themselves, communes try 'to make the private public' without giving up privacy. The creation of a 'private public' space is the creation of a space that (a) is open to people who are outsiders from the perspective of the intimate couple but (b) still excludes strangers who have not earned participants' trust and approval (Hardwig, 1997, p. 113).

So, Hardwig's theoretical objection to the coupled relationship is based on his view that it cannot create the sort of private public space that is available to the members of a pluralistic commune. This inability, he believes, explains why the intimate

---

4. Cf. Stack, 1974; Nicholson, 1997, p. 38. We will discuss the specific question of the significance of communal child care in the next chapter.

couple cannot enjoy the epistemic advantages of communal living. Let us grant that pluralistic communal and, indeed, other non-coupled living arrangements may be worthwhile and beneficial on a practical level. Let us also grant that on a conceptual level, the private public space that Hardwig associates with pluralistic communal living has the potential to situate its participants in a richer epistemic and, we would add, ontological context. By this we mean that participants in a private public realm would be exposed to relatively more comprehensive ways of knowing and being than those available in a restricted exclusively private social sphere. Now, we want to argue that the Hegelian concept of marriage is not necessarily in conflict with ideals of communal and other non-coupled living arrangements.

Firstly, we have already given our reasons for thinking that it does not follow from the inclusion of a certain kind of ethical relationship in the Hegelian elaboration of ethical life that other kinds of relationship might implicitly be treated as less worthwhile or as lacking value altogether. We should add here that it does not follow from the understanding of the concept of marriage as the family's formal embodiment that the Hegelian concept of the family cannot recognise people living in non-coupled households as belonging to families. On the contrary, according to the Hegelian concept, alternative living arrangements such as communes, extended kinship networks and single parent households constitute families insofar as participants' interactions invoke their necessarily intersubjective loving being.

Secondly, there is no reason to think that the Hegelian concept of marriage requires couples to choose between living alone and living in a pluralistic commune. To begin with, the objective side of the concept of marriage does not necessitate any particular household living arrangements. Instead, the determination of this question is left to couples to work out pursuant to the subjective side of the marriage relationship. For reasons that we will discuss in the next chapter, although the Hegelian approach takes the concept of family property to be an important aspect of the family's actualisation, this concept need not be embodied in a (single) family home. It follows that the concept of marriage does not support marriage partners' pre-given right to live with each other, let alone to live with each other to the exclusion of all other adults pursuant to a general right to family privacy. Any ethical rights to share a household and to privacy against outside interference must derive from the specific ways in which they collectively determine what is definitive of their sphere of intimacy. So, for example, a couple may or may not choose to share different aspects of their daily lives with each other, or with other adults, as part of the on going creative process of their self-affirming becoming that we discussed earlier.

We have been arguing that the Hegelian concepts of marriage and family do not preclude flexibility in married couple's choices regarding living arrangements. Our suggestion is that their openness to being associated with a range of living arrangements enables the Hegelian concepts of marriage and family to be capable of embodiment in communal living arrangements. But, what is it that enables these concepts to accommodate the possibility of creating an epistemically and ontologically enriching private public space? Our answer is that this power derives from the way in which the concepts of marriage and family are integrated into the Hegelian idea of the system of ethical life. We have already explained how, in treating the categories that belong to the idea of the family as an abstract moment of ethical life, the Hegelian approach situates the former in a complex network of concepts defining an ethical state. These concepts, we explained, are governed by a triad of different syllogistic interrelations that together give expression to the idea of society as an organically differentiated unity whose social spheres are integrated in ways that admit of degrees of publicness and privateness. The family is thus not inevitably relegated to the private side of a public-private dichotomisation of social spheres. On the contrary, as an integrated part of an ethical state's sphere of civil life, it belongs to precisely the kind of 'private public' sphere that Hardwig identifies, namely one with sufficient ideological dissimilarities and emotional distance between participants who, nevertheless, enjoy each others' trust and care.

Hardwig's discussion fails to acknowledge this possibility because his analysis proceeds from the view that the modern division of social space into mutually exclusive and mutually exhaustive public and private realms inevitably confines the coupled family to the exclusively and exhaustively private domain (cf. Hardwig, 1997, p. 112). However, the brief analysis of modernity that we offered in Part I of our book suggests a rather more complex explanation for the overwhelming tendency to limit our thinking about modern familial relations involving couples in terms that oppose them to wider communal living arrangements. This explanation would have it that we limit ourselves to this oppositional mode of thinking because we fail to have regard to the current condition of modernity as the negative moment in the process of the actualisation of its ideals. When our reflective framework is fixed in a way that presupposes the universal givenness of particularity that we explored in Chapter 2 the ideas of the coupled family and the pluralistic commune can, at best, represent competing ideals for the particularistic organisation of private social space. Similarly, in the current condition of modernity whose institutional organisation recognises the universal givenness of particularity we appear to face either-or choices, like that between living as a couple or living in a commune, precisely because, having been equally relegated to the particularistic private, the coupled family and the commune are forced to compete for space. In the next chapter we will examine this issue further in connection with the conceptualisation of communal child rearing.

9. THE FAMILY AND PERSONALITY: FAMILY CAPITAL, CHILDREN AND THE FAMILY'S DISSOLUTION

The Hegelian approach takes family property and parenting to be the substantial embodiments of love in the sense that these two types of essentially communal activity put into practice and actualise the formal marriage union. Recall from the previous chapter that marriage should be understood as the consent of two people to become one person and to act within a commonly created field of loving interaction. The substantial embodiments of love have their objective and subjective sides. As well as offering an account of these, in this chapter we will try to show how their respective structures accord with the necessary and contingent features of the categorical syllogism's form.

THE OBJECTIVE SIDE OF FAMILY PROPERTY

According to Hegel (1981, §169), the second phase in the completion of the idea of the family concerns its ability to own property. He claims that '[t]he family, as person, has its real external existence in property'. This claim initially seems odd when read alongside his later comment that 'it is only in the children that the unity [of marriage] itself exists externally, objectively, and explicitly as a unity' (Hegel, 1981, §173). If love, the substantiality of the family, is embodied in the practice of raising children why is the family also presented as having to reappropriate personality with its consequent external embodiment in property? Indeed, why should we attribute any ethical significance at all to family property? After all, the unity of family property has been exposed as an instrument of patriarchal domination (Moller Okin, 1979, p. 15). To answer these questions we need to have regard to two issues. The first concerns the way in which Hegel's syllogistic analysis relates the abstract concepts of personality and property. We will draw on our brief discussion of this connection in Chapter 6. The second concerns the way in which these concepts are refined in accordance with the organising power of the categorical syllogism when they are explicitly related to the family.

Substantial personality and property

As we explained in chapter 6, Hegel analyses the abstract concepts of personality and property in terms of the relationships provided by the first abstract form of the syllogism of existence. This analysis suggests that, in its abstract or formal mode, personality begins as the simple self-relation of an immediate individual whose identity is purely inward or merely subjective. Thus constituted, the person overcomes his or her mere subjectivity by relating himself or herself to the external world. This, in turn, is secured by taking possession of some particular (supposedly self-less) thing and thereby adopting the universal identity of a property owner. Private property is thus the first external embodiment or objectification of the atomic individual's will that otherwise remains merely subjective.

The Hegelian concept of property (the idea of contingently placing one's will in a thing through alienable possession of it) plays the role of objectifying an otherwise merely subjective will. This is because the form of this concept is suited to relating personality, through a particular, to the will's externality as such. Hegel reintroduces the concept of property, rather than relying solely on that of parenting, to elaborate the form of the external embodiment of the family's 'substantial personality' (cf. Hegel, 1981, §169) because of this relationship of the concept of property to personality.

Indeed, it is the form of the family's formed substantial personality, as distinct from the substance of the formed substance, that we need to bear in mind when considering the relationship between the concepts of person and property ownership, as distinct from that of person and parenting. As we have already seen, the family's substantial personality is love that has acquired an intersubjective form and this requires an external embodiment that is not reducible to love understood as the substance of personality.

Now, in the case of the family and its property, the categorical form of the syllogism must be called upon to explain the further relationship between the person qua family unit and this unit's common or collective property. According to Hegel (1981,

§171), the family's property is necessarily 'common property, so that while no member of the family has property of his own, each has his right in the common stock'. If family property is the external embodiment and objectification of the family's intersubjective will qua person, then the property in question must itself be collectively held.

The distinguishing feature of collective family property is that in being held by family members in common it cannot be reduced to the private property of any of them. This latter possibility can only be justified when there is a corresponding dissolution of the family's personality. As we saw when discussing the form of the marriage union, in becoming one person the identity of marriage partners is necessarily intersubjective in the sense that each engages in a reciprocal dynamic process of reflectively becoming one. This interactive process has the effect of transforming the internal dynamics of the concept of personality as this concept relates to the family. Whereas formal personality is defined in terms of the individual subject's immediate simple self-relation, the family's substantial personality is, as we have seen, defined in terms of the internal unity of the moments of individual self-unity and the universal difference of family members' specific natures.

We have also already seen how the above mentioned difference between the two conceptions of formal and substantial personality derives from relevant differences in the categorial interrelationships that characterise the first form of the syllogism of existence and the categorical form of the syllogism of necessity. What we need to consider now is the explanation that the categorical form of the syllogism offers regarding two further issues. The first concerns the question of how these concepts of formal and substantial personality are related in the process of actualising the family's substantial personality through the acquisition, use and maintenance of family property. The second concerns the precise form of the embodiment of the family's intersubjective personality in collective family property. In particular, why does Hegel (1981, §169) claim that family property must take the form of capital in order to become the embodiment of the family's substantial personality?

Family property and the process of sublating atomic individuality

Consider first the question of the relationship between the concepts of formal and substantial personality as they relate to individuals who have entered into a marriage union. Here we need to have regard to one of the implications that follows from the fact that the categorical form of the syllogism retains a degree of immediacy and contingency due to its relative incompleteness. We have seen how this immediacy affects the form of the categories in the position of the extremes. It renders them self-susbsistent with the result that their effective mediation turns out to be contingent. Nevertheless, the contingency of mediation, which is due to the fact that it relies upon individuals' different specific natures, shows itself to have been determined as contingent. This is because, in effecting their mediation, the extremes are still dependent upon the middle term in two ways: they presuppose and reflectively relate to its universal essence. This dual dependence relationship gives rise to a process in which individuals' immediate form is sublated. What this means is that the very process of forming a unity within the necessity of relatedness that is determined by an immediate substantiality ultimately produces a mediated result. The result in question is that the form of the extremes is shown not to be wholly independent of the middle term's determining power. To the extent that they come together within their presupposed universal essence that is determined by the middle term's differentiating power, to that extent individual identity is transformed from a self-subsistent category that is immediate to one that is mediated and, in turn, has limited self-determining mediating power.

In the family's substantive actualisation this situation is expressed as follows. As we have already seen, the creation of a marriage union based on love gives rise to the idea of the family's intersubjective personality when the individuals involved are willing to renounce their respective atomic individualities. Because loving beings who are united in this way presuppose the essential nature of their love, they manifest the immediacy characterising their substantial bond. However, we have also seen how within this union they are in a position to exercise the transformative power that comes from being reflectively related to their universal loving essence. To the extent that they exercise the creative power of their love, to that extent they sublate the immediacy of their personality that is grounded in their atomic individuality (hereafter, 'atomic personality'). This means that the process of actualising their love, which is always a matter of some degree, is ultimately responsible for the transformation of individuals' identity. Their identity is transformed from the immediacy of formal atomic persons to the substantially mediated and mediating individuality (albeit within the limits given by their immediate bond) qua members of a substantial intersubjective person, the family.

An important point follows from the above analysis about the relationship between the concepts of atomic and intersubjective personality as they relate to the family. Our analysis suggests that we are concerned with a process that (a) sublates atomic personality to the extent that it succeeds in actualising intersubjective personality; and (b) is itself dependent upon the necessity of the contingent. Accordingly, the sublation of individuals' atomic personalities as a result of their family ties must be an on going struggle whose achievement is always a matter of some degree.

The ethical significance of family capital

Hegel (1981, §170) claims that the family requires capital, that is, 'possessions specifically determined as permanent and secure', because it is 'a universal and enduring person'. Our analysis above offers a way of appreciating what Hegel takes to be the ethical significance of family capital. In characterising the family as a 'universal' person Hegel is indirectly appealing to the idea that the family's substantial personality is grounded in an objective universality which, we have seen, defines both the middle term and one extreme of the categorical form of the syllogism. However, we have also seen that formal personality no less embodies a universality, albeit one that expresses a static moment that cannot permanently secure the objectivity of personality given its reliance on the alienable possession of a particular property item. Hegel's reference to the family as an enduring person implicitly alerts us to the relative stability of the family's substantial personality and, relatedly, to the above mentioned temporal dimension of family life. This must, in turn, find its external embodiment in a form of collective property that is similarly enduring. This, then, is the ethical basis of family capital which is 'permanent and secure' and not just an alienable possession with some use value in so far as it is the means of need satisfaction.

There are two related aspects to this understanding of family capital. In order that its substantial personality have 'real external existence' the family must have capital, firstly, because this form of property has the potential to embody personality understood as an ongoing dynamic process; and, secondly, because it has the potential to embody the moment of universal difference that is manifested in family members' different specific natures throughout this process. As the external embodiment of the family's substantial personality, family capital must reflect the family's continued dependence on its members' different specific natures for its actualisation. Accordingly, it is also available for the satisfaction of

the sorts of needs that family members associate with their respective specific natures.

We have already drawn attention to the openendedness and
fluidity of family members' specific natures in the context of explaining the subjective side of marriage. Here, it is worth noting
further that the very meaning of family members' needs continues to be thematised after the establishment of a loving union, that
is, when formal mediation has been effected through marriage
and is in the process of being substantively actualised. This is why
the meaning of family members' needs is not treated as fixed.

Needs are themselves capable of acquiring an ethical character pursuant to the transformative power of loving beings' reflectiveness that we examined in the previous chapter. The *Philosophy
of Right* reinforces this interpretation with the claim that

> [t]he arbitrariness of a single owner's particular needs is one
> moment in property taken abstractly; but this moment to-
> gether with the selfishness of desire, is here transformed into
> something ethical, into labour and care for a common posses-
> sion (Hegel, 1981, §170).

What we have here is a 'community of personal and private interests' (Hegel, 1985, §519) expressed in the common 'care for the future' (Hegel, 1985, §520). Needs lose their 'natural' or immediate
character in so far as they are reflectively defined and endorsed in
family members' intersubjective practices of creating the means
of their satisfaction. This idea of needs contrasts strongly with the
notion of needs that operates when persons act as atomic individuals (cf. Vassilacopoulos, 1994, pp. 200-201). In the case of this latter notion the expression of a desire for something can be a sufficient ground for deciding to pursue the means of its satisfaction.

When family members cooperatively create, use and maintain
collective family capital ethical need satisfaction, not only tends to
reinforce such practices, but it also encourages family members to
become future oriented. They make sense of themselves not just
by reference to what each one of them is but by reference to what
they might be or become through their communal efforts. In this
way a normative filter is created through which their understanding of their needs is transformed having regard to the communal
character of family capital.

Transforming private property into family capital To recognise family capital as an external embodiment of the family's substantial
personality is to recognise the ethical significance of this kind of

social relationship. But, just as the question of how much property one holds is incidental to the recognition of one's property owning capacity, so too the specific amount of a family's capital is not something about which the Hegelian approach provides instruction. It merely insists that there be family capital of some kind.

Does this imply that individuals' privately held property should be treated as family property upon marriage, whatever this property happens to be? Note, firstly, that the logic governing the objective aspect of family capital leaves open the normative question of precisely how any particular family should create, use and maintain its own capital. Due to the persistent contingency that governs this sphere of ethical life, what property the members of a particular family are prepared to make into their family capital must be a matter for them to work out.

Secondly, since creating a substantial personality does not cancel out atomic individuals' formal personality, the Hegelian approach can admit the possibility that marriage partners might retain their respective privately held property in their capacities as atomic individuals. What the Hegelian approach excludes is the possibility of privately holding property that belongs to the family. This is how we think the Hegelian approach should understand Hegel's (1981, §171) claim that family

> capital is common property so that, while no member of the family has property of his own, each has his right in the common stock.

It follows from these two observations that whether or not individuals' privately held property should be treated as family property upon marriage depends entirely upon the particular way in which a married couple creatively incorporates their different specific natures into the objective side of their loving union. Even where the family's capital is concerned, the transformative power of a marriage union based on love remains within the domain of subjective reflection.

Reply to objections Earlier we noted the feminist objection to the idea of family property on the ground that it functions as an instrument of patriarchal domination. We do not wish to deny that historically family property has been associated with an investment of the power of its administration in the hands of male heads of households. Of course, Hegel (1981, §171) is no exception in this regard. However, our analysis above suggests that the Hegelian concept of family property is at odds with a (gendered) hierarchical family structure that takes for granted the exclusive right of one (male) family member to control family property. This follows from the view that family members cannot rightly hold family property privately, that is, in their capacity as atomic individuals. So, the proper object of the feminist objection is the idea of a gendered hierarchy and not the communal character of family property.

Claudia Card (1996) reveals another source of concern about the idea of family property. She worries that the attainment of economic benefits through marriage can have a corrupting effect on a loving relationship. People who do not really love each other, or who no longer love each other, get and stay married for the financial gain (Card, 1996, pp. 8-9). Card goes on to suggest that the right of one party to receive economic support or 'a share of the other's assets to which they would not otherwise have been entitled' creates 'new economic motives to preserve emotionally disastrous unions' (Card, 1996, p. 9). The corrupting potential of married couple's property interests is one of the grounds upon which Card opposes the idea of marriage.

To be sure, engaging in the communal practice of love and care for common possessions involves taking risks and experiencing pressures to which we might not otherwise be exposed. But, Card's objection presupposes that marriage partners necessarily relate to their own and each other's property only as atomic individuals. This is why in her view one individual's right to receive a share of the family property upon divorce or, indeed, even in the course of a marriage appears as an unjustified intrusion upon the other's private holdings. This position privileges a consideration that is important in analyses of rights to property shares that invoke a contribution principle, namely the individual source of the effort that is put into the generation of property. At the same time, Card's position fails to take into account the possibility that a married couple may be communally oriented toward the creation of the social conditions (that is, the emotional, psychological and cultural conditions) that make possible any such effort. We believe that this possibility ought to be accommodated by a theory of intimate life and it can best be accommodated with the recognition of the ethical significance of family property in something like the terms we have proposed above.

THE OBJECTIVE SIDE OF PARENTING

As we mentioned above, Hegel (1981, §173) says of children in connection with the marriage union that

[i]t is only in the children that the unity itself exists externally, objectively, and explicitly as a unity, because the parents love the children as their love, as the embodiment of their own substance.

The 'addition' to this section of the *Philosophy of Right* gives an idea of the difference between the 'embodying' roles of family capital and children in the family unit.

Such an objectivity [that of the unity of love between a married couple] parents first acquire in their children, in whom they can see objectified the entirety of their union. In the child, the mother loves its father and he its mother. Both have their love objectified for them in the child. While in their goods their unity is embodied only in an external thing, in their children it is embodied in a spiritual one in which the parents are loved and which they love (1981, §173A).

The children of a marriage embody the objectivity of the family's substantial unity, namely love, as distinct from love in the form of substantial personality. In this the role played by the concept of the children of a marriage differs from that played by family capital. This, as already indicated, functions as the external embodiment only of the substantial unity qua intersubjective personality.

Here, Hegel explains that children are peculiarly positioned to embody 'the entirety' of the marriage union because of their spiritual being. So, what is it about children's spirituality that enables them to embody the marriage union's entirety and in what does the entirety of this union consist?

The ethical significance of children and parenting

In response to the first of these questions it is worth noting that what matters, from an ethical point of view, is the practice of parenting rather than maintaining the family as a biological unit by giving birth to or raising one's own offspring. As Hegel (1985) points out elsewhere, the ethically significant relationship between parents and children concerns the 'second or spiritual birth of the children'. This refers to their upbringing and education, as distinct from their 'natural generation', even when people consider procreation to be of 'primary importance in first forming the marriage union'.[1]

---

1. Hegel, 1985, §521. Although, Hegel repeatedly invokes the biological family, on mistaken grounds that we will examine in the next chapter, he does not conflate this with the source of the ethical bond between parents and their children. The conflation of the family as a biological and as an ethical unit led early radical

The Hegelian concept of parental love invokes two features that Erich Fromm (1985) identifies in parental love. On the one hand, there is the immediate or unconditional love of one's children just because they are. On the other, there is the conditional love of children for the expectations they fulfil (Fromm, 1985, pp. 30-36). Whereas the first of these features secures for the child the experience of being loved, the second is linked to the experience of becoming responsive to the demands of one's beloved.

> In respect of his relation to the family, the child's education has the positive aim of instilling ethical principles into him in the form of an immediate feeling for which differences are not yet explicit, so that thus equipped with the foundation of an ethical life, his heart may live its early years in love, trust and obedience (Hegel, 1981, §174).

In being this kind of 'spiritual' embodiment of their parents' love, children are in the special position of being able to realise their power immediately to reciprocate this love as a result of their initial undifferentiated unity with their parents.

The kind of reciprocity that exists between parents and children is particularly important for the external embodiment of the entirety of the marriage union because, as we have already explained, familial love is defined, not only in terms of the necessary interrelatedness of loving beings, but also in terms of the immediacy of this kind of relatedness.

The ethical dissolution of the family and the subjective side of familial love

There is a second reason why children are in a position to embody the entirety of the substantial unity created by familial love. This has to do with the fact that they also give expression to the family's ethical dissolution. Because this is the final phase in the internal dynamics of the Hegelian idea of the family it needs to be incorporated in an adequate appreciation of the marriage union in its entirety. So, what does the family's 'ethical dissolution' refer to and how is this expressed by the children?

> The ethical dissolution of the family consists in this, that once the children have become educated to freedom of personality, and have come of age, they become recognized as persons in

feminists such as Shulamith Firestone (1970) to ignore the value of the latter in calling for the destruction of the former. But see Sidney Callahan (1997) for a recent argument that reproductive technologies should not be used to create arrangements in which biological parents are not given ethical responsibility for parenting.

the eyes of the law and as capable of holding free property of their own and of founding families of their own ... . The old family on the other hand falls into the background as merely their ultimate basis and origin (Hegel, 1981, §177).

Unlike the 'natural dissolution' of the family unit by way of the death of the parents (Hegel, 1981, §178) or marriage breakdown ending in divorce (Hegel, 1981, §176), the ethical dissolution of the family unit manifests the persisting subjectivity, immediacy and contingency of its substantial unity. These features are attributable to the relative incompleteness of the syllogistic form with which the idea of the family accords. This incompleteness, as already explained, derives from the fact that, in that it inheres in the moment of particularity, the objective universality of the categorical syllogism's middle term is limited to the substantial unity of its abstract essence. This universality cannot extend either to the whole concrete being of the categories positioned as its extremes or to the precise form of their effective mediation. It follows from this that the mediation effected is limited in that it is not integral to the being of the category in the position of the middle term. For this reason the concept of the family is not self-sustaining. In contrast to the concept of the ethical state, which is a more comprehensive stage of ethical life and contains the resources to be self-sustaining through the reproduction of its members, the family unit's structure does not allow for its internal reproduction. Instead the ethical activity of the married couple produces the very ground of its own ethical, because necessary, dissolution.

It follows that parents must raise their children, not to remain members of their family, but to become 'self-subsistent persons' (Hegel, 1981, §186). What makes children peculiarly appropriate for this kind of embodiment, once again, is their potentiality. According to Hegel (1981, §175),

> [c]hildren are potentially free and their life directly embodies nothing save potential freedom.... In respect of his relation to the family the child's education ... has the negative aim of raising children out of the instinctive, physical level on which they are originally, to self-subsistence and freedom of personality and so to the level on which they have power to leave the natural unity of the family.

Potentially free personality is presupposed for the immanent ethical dissolution of the family. To this end children must be educated out of their initial undifferentiated unity with their parents to become independent persons qua atomic individuals, as distinct from family members.

Indeed, in being responsible for raising children to attain their formal subjective freedom as atomic individuals, the family unit does not merely produce its own dissolution, but also grounds an immanent transition to 'civil society', the sphere of interaction between persons so formed.[2] It is sometimes suggested that Hegel presents the family as the first moment of the idea of ethical life because it provides the Hegelian state with ethical citizens through the cultivation of substantial ties. For example, according to L. P. Hinchman (1984, p. 220), 'the state must acknowledge its enormous debt to the family, since the latter provides it with ethical citizens rather than persons'. On a similar note, S. Avineri (1980, pp. 133-134) presents the family as 'projecting particular altruism' as its mode of human association while 'universal altruism' is projected as that characterising the state. He, therefore, implies that the altruism, that is, the 'non-moralistic', 'other-regarding' orientation that individuals first experience in relation to their own particular family members is ultimately extended to the members of one's society at large and thereby made universal.

These suggestions fail to justify what appears to be a conceptual leap from the (familiar) substantial or altruistic ties characteristic of interpersonal relationships to the purported similarly substantial or altruistic ties with non-specific others. M. Westphal's (1984, pp. 77-92) elaboration of the structure of the Hegelian state as 'a We of the same sort as the family' raises similar questions about the justifiability of elaborating large scale social phenomena in the light of the characteristics of interpersonal relationships.

In contrast to these interpretations, on the analysis we have proposed above, the ethical significance of parenting has to do with the need to develop atomic individuals who have the potential to pursue their formally free subjectivity and not merely with individuals who are united by substantial ties. A view similar to the one we are proposing has been defended on entirely different grounds by H. Brod (1992, p. 64). Brod (1992, p. 65) observes that

> Hegel argues that when the family is fully philosophically conceptualized and set in a larger context, we can see that there are essential political dimensions to family life in the transmission of capital and in the inculcation of ethical consciousness, what we might today call socialization for citizenship.

2. For an extensive analysis of the logical ground of this transition see Vassilacopoulos, 1994, pp. 184-187.

On our reading it is only when this 'larger context' is supplied by the third moment of ethical life, the ethical state, that familial relations can be appropriately reconceptualised as fully integrated with social and political life more broadly. We must leave the investigation of this reconceptualisation for another occasion.

Reply to an objection

One might object to our treatment of the ethical significance of children and parenting that we have overlooked the significance of communal child rearing practices. One might think that this is due to the fact that the Hegelian concept of the family abstracts the questions of the ethical formation and dissolution of the family from wider cultural practices. Consider for example, parenting practices that share the responsibility for raising children across households and amongst people who are not necessarily biologically connected to the children (cf. hooks, 1984, p. 144; Firestone, 1970).

To respond to this kind of objection we need to draw attention to a couple of distinctions that could be made. In our approach the operative distinction is not between the married couple's exclusive parenting practices and alternative arrangements. On the contrary, the cultural specifics of the parenting practices that the Hegelian approach takes to be of ethical significance may well vary. So, for example, our Hegelian approach can recognise people sharing responsibility for raising children with a wider circle of intimate others. What matters for the ethical significance of parenting is whether or not those raising the children are related to each other and/or to the children through their mutual loving feeling. When they are not such relationships are lived through the opportunities and limits made possible by atomic individuality. For example, the primary basis of a child care giver's relationship to a child and/or to relevant others may be need satisfaction or economic interdependence. In contrast, when they are related through their mutual loving feeling the structure of their relationships holds out the possibility of certain kinds of ethical experience that are not otherwise available to the participants.

10. SEXISM, HETERONORMATIVITY AND PLURAL SEXUALITIES

HEGEL'S SEXIST AND HETERONORMATIVE VIEWS

As is well known, in the *Philosophy of Right* and elsewhere Hegel identifies marriage with a male dominated heterosexual union. In his view, the biological difference of the sexes is transformed, through its 'rational basis', into something that has 'ethical significance' (Hegel, 1981, §165). Hegel also presents ethically significant sexual difference in terms of a rigid sex-role differentiation. This latter confines the wife to the sphere of family life and gives the husband the powers (a) to represent the family in the outside world (Hegel, 1981, §166); and (b) to control the administration of its capital (Hegel, 1981, §171).

Feminist critiques of Hegel's sexism

For obvious reasons, feminist political theorists have subjected Hegel's views about (the place of) women to considerable criticism. An important part of this criticism has been aimed at exposing its contribution to the western intellectual tradition's masculine bias. This bias has sometimes been taken to consist of the uncritical reproduction by men of the misogynist ideas of their own times. However, it has also been understood as involving a deeper, more disturbing problem for western thought. In particular, feminist political theorists have been arguing that there is a conceptual linkage between the category, woman, and the inferior side of a set of hierarchically related dichotomies such as masculine-feminine, reason-feeling, humanity-nature, culture-nature and public-private.

Genevieve Lloyd's *The Man of Reason* (1984) and Jean Bethke Elshtain's *Public Man, Private Woman* (1981) offer two early defences of this general thesis.¹ The authors of these books take Hegel's work to support their thesis (Lloyd, 1984, p. 84; Elshtain, 1981, p. 177). Elshtain (1981, p. 179) suggests that the conceptual linkage of the category woman to categories that are treated as inferior is not central to Hegel's theory. So, her reading of the *Phenomenology of Spirit* allows for a possible reformulation of Hegel's account of familial love in order to remove its masculine bias.

On Lloyd's reading, however, Hegel's conceptual association of woman with categories such as feeling, nature and the private is a necessary one. If this is correct, his masculine bias cannot be corrected within this structure of categorial relations. Woman, according to Lloyd, is defined as that which must be transcended by man. The same view is advanced by Patricia Jagendowicz Mills (1979). Jagentowicz Mills (1979, p. 75) argues that 'Hegel's account of intersubjectivity implies the equal recognition of women even though he himself is tied to a framework that prevents him from actually seeing women as man's equal'. In this 'framework' woman is conceptually aligned to nature, man's other (Jagentowicz Mills, 1979, p. 85).

It is worth noting that these readings draw primarily on Hegel's account of the phenomenology of human consciousness in the *Phenomenology of Spirit*. Some feminists argue that this account is better described as an account of the development of male consciousness towards self-consciousness and that its further implications for the development of female consciousness must somehow be teased out of this.² We do not wish to defend Hegel's account of the phenomenology of consciousness against this attack. However, we think it is important to point out that a simple reading of his statements concerning family life in the *Phenomenology of Spirit* alongside those of the *Philosophy of Right* can give a distorted view of what he is actually claiming. Such an approach hinders an adequate assessment of the contemporary value of his political and ethical thought.

Here it is worth bearing in mind the brief interpretation of the place and role of the *Phenomenology of Spirit* in the Hegelian system that we set out in Chapter 3. On this interpretation it would appear that, whatever the implications of the *Phenomenology of Spirit* for the phenomenological development of female and feminine consciousness, such implications cannot also supply the ground for our internal critical assessment of Hegel's account of relations

---

1. For a more recent and still more comprehensive argument see Plumwood, 1993.
2. See for example, Hayim, 1990, p. 13.

between the sexes that forms part of the idea of ethical life. These relations need to be assessed in the light of relevant developments in Hegel's *Logic,* since this is where he derives his understanding of their supposed 'rational basis'. As we have already argued, the developmental dynamic of the *Logic* proceeds following the demonstration of consciousness' inability adequately to reflect upon itself within the givenness of the subject-object dichotomy. Hegel's references to female/feminine consciousness in the *Phenomenology of Spirit* form part of this demonstration. So, there is no reason to think that within the Hegelian system they must also be taken to have ethical force in the relevant sense of this term.

Note also that an approach to Hegel's theory like the one we have offered is in a position to explain why Hegel seems to identify the category, woman, with her natural, biological difference on some occasions but not on others. Despite the general charge by feminist critics that Hegel defines woman as man's other, or as linked to nature through her reproductive functions, there also exists considerable, otherwise unexplained, textual evidence to suggest that his theory does not amount to a mere reduction of woman to her natural or biological functions.[3]

We have suggested, so far, that feminist critiques of Hegel's sexism can either call for a removal of the theory's sexism or, when they take the problem to be ineliminable, they suggest that to engage with the theory is to study the internal workings of some inherently masculine concepts. If this latter position were correct, it would be reason enough to conclude that Hegel's theory of familial love has no contemporary value from the point of view of the search for a justifiable ethical orientation. However, feminist critics who insist that Hegel's sexism presents an ineliminable structural problem for his theory do not offer convincing explanations for their view that his system needs to relegate women to an inferior social position.

More recently, Seyla Benhabib (1992, p. 243) has advocated a third feminist approach to reading Hegel. She calls this a 'feminist discourse of empowerment' because it aims to read the text in the light of the lived experiences of relevant women. Using this methodology, Benhabib interprets the sexist claims of the *Philosophy of Right* in the light of Hegel's personal interaction with women such as Caroline Schlegel. Benhabib (1992, p. 252) then argues that his views should be understood as a personal reaction against

---

3. For a brief summary of such textual evidence see Easton, 1987, pp. 34-42.

the power of women, like Schlegel, who were, not only the 'early forerunners of the early women's emancipation, but also represented a new model of gender relations, aspiring to equality, free love and reciprocity'.

This response to Hegel's sexism is markedly different from the ones we mentioned above in so far as it moves beyond the published text. Nevertheless, it shares with them the tendency to impose on Hegel's political theory considerations that are external to the logical progression on which the theory claims to be based. For the sorts of reasons we have already mentioned, it seems to us that we should only resort to factors outside the Hegelian system, like his personal dislikes, to explain his views in the event that a systemic reading proves unsatisfactory.

Moreover, despite all the attention that has been given to Hegel's work, his feminist critics have had little to say about the reason that Hegel gives in the *Philosophy of Right* for invoking the notion of sexual difference. We will turn to a consideration of this reason next. In doing so, we will assume that Hegel's reference to the 'rational basis' of sexual difference is an implicit reference to the relevant part of the *Logic* that organises relations within the system of 'Ethical Life' (Hegel, 1981). We will also leave aside the important but separate question of the relationship between the phenomenologies of human, male, female, masculine and feminine consciousness.

Hegel on the ethical significance of sexual difference
According to Hegel (1981, §165),

> [t]he significance [of sexual difference] is determined by the difference into which the ethical substantiality [love], as the concept, internally sunders itself in order that its vitality may become a concrete unity consequent upon this difference.

The claim being made here is that the ethical love that brings the idea of the family into concrete being must take a heterosexual form precisely because the formation of the unity in question depends upon the presence of a difference that can be brought back into a differentiated unity. What we wish to argue is that this is implicitly a reference to the requirement that the category positioned in accordance with the categorical syllogism's middle term must differentiate itself into the moment of a universal difference in order that this moment be unified with that of an individual self-unity. If this is correct, then Hegel would appear to appeal to sexual difference and, through this appeal, to endorse heteronormativity (heterosexuality taken as the ethical norm), in order to locate the element of difference within the idea of the marriage union. Recall that this is the first stage in the development of the concept of the family.

Furthermore, since the element of difference is crucial for the necessity of contingency that shapes the meaning of familial love, this appeal to the notion of sexual difference can ultimately be explained as part of his attempt to expose the necessity of contingency within the family unit. This is the point at which our analysis must part company with the Hegel of the *Philosophy of Right*. However, we are not just taking issue with his sexism and heteronormativity. Significantly, we want to elaborate and defend what we believe to be the genuine import of the categorical syllogism's form. We will argue that if we have proper regard for the requirements of the categorical syllogism's form the idea of family life does not need to invoke a notion of difference that is sexualised. To explain the point at which we think Hegel misunderstood the demands of his own *Logic*, we will need to return to a consideration of the nature and role of the operative concept of difference.

The non-necessity of sexualised difference

The first thing that our analysis must do is to show why Hegel does not need to sexualise his notion of difference. To this end we will argue that the notion of difference is introduced and preserved directly in the constitution of family members' intersubjective personality. This is because the family is necessarily dependent on the concrete being of individuals who are as much constituted by their different specific natures as by their universal essence.

We need to recall, firstly, that the notion of universal difference is positioned as one of the extremes in the categorical form of the syllogism as a result of the middle term's substance differentiation. Secondly, the syllogistic form does not also ensure that the middle term fully determines this notion given the abstractness of its essential determination. This means that when the differentiated moment of difference is brought into a unity with that of individual self-unity this is achieved in the light of the difference that contingently exceeds the middle term's unifying power. This difference, as we have already seen, is to be found in individuals' specific natures (hereafter 'specific difference'). So, the idea of specific difference is already expressed in the being of the concrete individuals involved in the differentiating and unifying processes to which this syllogism gives shape.

This said, we also argued that the limits placed by this mode of interrelations on the middle term's power of determination, not only leaves it to the extremes to effect their mediation, but their unity is produced and maintained thanks to the contingency that defines them, that is, to the role played by their different, open ended and fluid, specific natures. The continued presence of specific difference is, therefore, ensured in this way. For this reason the Hegelian account of the family does not need to sexualise the operative idea of difference. It follows that, even though Hegel is correct to insist that the concept of the family presupposes the continued presence of specific difference, this latter should not be secured by appeal to the idea of sexual difference.

So much for the supposed logical basis of Hegel's claim regarding the ethical significance of sexual difference. How might we make sense of his appeal to different roles for men and women and, in particular, of the exclusion of women from activity outside the sphere of the family? Is there any systemic ground for restricting women in this way?

To be sure, at this first stage in the development of the idea of the family, Hegel needs to explain the relationship between the family's internal life to its 'external' activity. This latter is activity that only needs to be understood in the general terms of the family's life outside its own domain when the idea of the family is elaborated in abstraction from its place in an integrated ethical system. So, Hegel is obliged to say something about the role of family members in 'externality'. Now, we want to suggest that, having mistakenly introduced the rigid idea of sex-based biological difference, he goes one step further and uses an extension of this idea to define the family's relationship to its external world. The family's outside activity becomes the domain of the male head of the household only if sex-role differentiation is mistakenly attributed ethical significance. So, Hegel's insistence on the confinement of women's activities to the internal life of the family is not required by the *Logic*.

THE LOGICAL STRUCTURE OF FAMILIAL ROLES AND SEXUALITIES

So far we have been arguing that the sexism and heteronormativity in the *Philosophy of Right* can be traced back to Hegel's misidentification of the requirements of his own *Logic*. Hegel misunderstood the way in which the relevant notion of difference should be expressed in the Hegelian concept of the family. Now we want to move on to consider what the *Logic* implies about familial roles and sexualities in positive terms. In particular, we will address the following questions. Firstly, since sex-role differentiation cannot be relied on to account for family members' roles, whether within or outside the family, how are these roles to be determined? Secondly, given that sexual difference need not form part of the marriage relationship, how are sexualities to be viewed within the family and, in particular, how might marriage and homosexuality be related? Thirdly, even though sexual difference is not necessitated by the need to preserve the element of specific difference within the concept of the family, might its ethical significance be otherwise grounded? The answers to these questions draw upon our analysis in Chapter 7 of the ontology and necessity of the contingent.

Familial roles within the family's domain
In Chapter 8 our discussion of the marriage union indicated how, due to the necessity of their contingent excess, individuals who are united through their loving being are in a position to exercise their transformative powers in their creative interaction. It is in their unique interaction that married people can define and redefine their roles and work out the nature and meaning of the guidelines of their ethical conduct, such as care, respect, trust and the like. For this reason, family members' reflections upon the question of how to determine their different roles should be understood in terms of the family's way of addressing 'the common task of looking after the family generally' (Hegel, 1981, §174). Hegel puts this criterion forward when explaining different aspects of the relationship between parents and their children. He notes that it is the basis upon which parents can require their childrens' service 'as service' as well as the ground for restricting the demands that parents can justifiably make on their children for their contribution to the family's way of life. What Hegel fails to realise is that the criterion of care for the family as family members' common task must also be the basis upon which to determine all family members' contributions to the maintenance of family life, including the generation of its capital.

Familial roles in the outside world
The family must also relate itself to the outside world through some, if not all, of its family members in order to satisfy its needs, including the generation of family capital. Since, as already suggested, the concept of the family concerns a unit that is by definition not

capable of being fully self-reliant, its needs, however defined and refined, cannot be fully met within the family's restricted domain. It is important to bear in mind that what we are concerned with here is the outside activity of family members qua members. This is to be distinguished from their possible activities in the outside world in their distinct capacities as atomic individuals.

In the former case, the same criterion that governs the question of family members' role differentiation within the family unit extends to their activities in the outside world. Accordingly, family members should also apply the criterion of care for the family as family members' common task to the questions of who should be active outside the family unit and what they are to undertake on behalf of their family. Similarly, the problem of interpreting the meaning and application of this criterion must be left up to the collective creative practices of family members in all the context specificity of their particular relationships.

This said, our analysis of the categorical syllogism in Chapter 7 suggests that there is one limit on family members' practices of interpreting their mode of ethical interaction with the outside world. We suggested that the persistent immediacy that characterises the categorical syllogism's form of unity, because it is only a particular unity, must also be exhibited by its external relationship to whatever falls beyond its unity. Correspondingly, family members' reflections on the relationship of their particular family to the outside world must give expression to this external relationship.

We want to suggest further that under the current condition of modernity the external relationship of the family to the outside world requires family members' reflections to take on a certain appearance. These reflections must appear as a response to the dichotomous differentiation of their family from the outside world. Due to the limits of modernity that we discussed in Part I of the book and, in particular, the dichotomisation of social spheres, the sphere of modern family life appears, not only as opposed to the outside world, but as hierarchically related to it. The family either takes on a valorised status or else it is subordinated to the wider spheres of civil and political life. We can find evidence for this contradictory state of affairs in the treatment of the family as at once offering a haven from the outside world and as constituting the domain of activities of lesser value. (Cf. Sennet, 1975; Waring, 1988.) In the current conditions of modernity, this constitutes the unavoidable framework within which the members of the modern family unit must reflect upon and determine their respective roles in the outside world.

It is also worth recalling here our suggestion in Part I of the book that the obstacles to social integration can be overcome with the transcendence of modernity's negative moment. Since the transition to a fully self-determining modernity would also impact upon the appropriate way to conceive the externality that defines the family's relationship to the outside world, it would also affect the way to address the question of the social roles of family members within an ethically integrated social system as elaborated by the Hegelian idea of the ethical state. Whilst we cannot go into this issue in any detail here, we note that on the interpretation of the idea of the ethical state that we proposed in Chapter 6 the logical structure of the family unit's mediating particularity must be governed by the integrated triad of syllogisms that logical objectivity makes possible.

Sexualities as multiple loving forms

Our analysis of the syllogism in Chapter 7 concluded, firstly, that the necessity of the contingency characterising the being of the categories in the position of extremes is constituted by a relation of difference to the unity of content exhibited by the middle term's objective universality. Secondly, we maintained that this relation must be exhibited by the availability of a multiplicity of forms in which the middle term's abstract essence might be expressed. Extending these ideas to our discussion of love, we can now say that the necessary contingency characterising the subjective aspect of familial love, as outlined in Chapter 8, must also be constituted by a relation of difference to the unity of content, the ethical substantiality expressed by loving feeling.

This relation gives rise to the idea of a multiplicity of loving forms. If love does indeed embody the common essence of persons that is abstract, the condition of abstractness is made explicit when love is expressed in different forms. When love is expressed in multiple forms the difference between them is shown to be other than that which determines that they are equally expressions of loving feeling in the sense elaborated in Chapter 7. In order for this difference to be exhibited the indifference of love towards the specifics of the form of its realisation must also be exhibited. In the next chapter we will argue that this indifference is manifested as the requirement that familial love be publicly recognised. For present purposes, however, the important implication that follows from our analysis is that familial love is exhaustively realised when it is expressed in a number of different yet symmetrically related forms in order that it not be exclusively and unjustifiably conceived as, or confined to, any one of these.

The possibility of a multiplicity of loving forms arises out of the role played by the necessity of contingency analysed in Chapter 7. A multiplicity of loving forms can be secured in a network of relations that recognises the value of differences in the constitution of sexualities. This means that, what matters from an ethical point of view is that there be differently constituted sexualities. It follows from this that gay male and lesbian sexualities are an indispensable part of the way in which the necessity of contingent being is constituted by a relation of difference to the unity of content embodied by love.

Homosexuality and the ontology of the contingent Our discussion of the subjective aspect and the objective significance of marriage in Chapter 8 showed how it is possible to allow for both the contingent and the necessary in this kind of spiritual union without valorising one of these at the expense of the other. On the basis of our analysis above, we can now say that the concept of homosexuality can be understood in terms of the dynamics of this interplay between the objective and the subjective. Homosexuality thus constitutes a spiritual self-affirmation of the contingent that familial love renders necessary.

The logical interdependence of multiple sexualities If the analysis above is correct, then not only is the ontology of homosexuality understood in terms of the notion of the necessity of contingency but, in addition, the relationship of homosexuality to heterosexuality is clarified in one key respect. Specifically, if multiple sexualities provide a multiplicity of loving forms, then these sexualities are logically interdependent to this extent. This interdependence shows that the content of a loving relationship cannot be justifiably reduced to its form and, as a result, any one form that love might take cannot justifiably be universalised.

The ethical significance of sexual difference

It follows from this analysis that sexual difference, that is, the difference constituted by differently sexed embodied beings, can be understood as one of a number of the contingent grounds for the existence of multiple loving forms. If, as it has been extensively argued in recent years, 'sex and sexuality are marked, lived, and function according to whether it is a male or female body that is being discussed' (Grosz, 1995, p. 213) then the morphology of sexed bodies plays a role in securing a multiplicity of loving forms. However, the attempt to give sexed bodies, like the attempt to give gender, any privileged role in an account of that which ensures multiple loving forms would be to deny a role to some 'transgressive' modes of desire, for example, those for which gender preference or the sex of a body do not define sexual object choice.[4]

A CRITICAL REVIEW OF RECENT SEXUALITIES DISCOURSES

The above account of the role that the idea of multiple sexualities plays in the Hegelian concept of familial love supplies a much needed framework for theorising sexualities. We will use it to assess a number of recent attempts to theorise the relationship of concepts like homosexuality and lesbianism to heterosexuality. In the rest of this chapter we will focus on three recent areas of discussion.

The valorisation of homosexuality over heterosexuality

In some recent philosophical investigations of the ontology of sexualities, in particular, of homosexuality and lesbianism, the logical interdependence of multiple sexualities has been overlooked with some unfortunate consequences. Consider the following as examples of this tendency. Elizabeth Grosz (1995, pp. 226-227) begins from the claim that due to its 'fundamental fluidity' human sexuality is potentially 'queer'. She then suggests that the existence of homosexuality poses a 'threat' to heterosexuality because the former has the power 'to infiltrate the very self-conceptions of what it is to be heterosexual' and to bring unstuck the 'apparently natural coupling of male and female lovers'.[5] Whilst we agree

---

4. Cf. Seidman, 1993, pp. 121-122. Sedgwick (1993, pp. 56-59) has emphasised the pervasive 'yoking of contradictions' that has presided over 'all the thought on the subject' of 'homosexuality in terms of overlapping sexuality and gender' even after having formalised (by abstracting from the asymmetries of gender and heterosexist oppression) what she calls 'the impasse of gender definition' as linked to homo/hetero sexual definition'. On her analysis this impasse is constituted by conflicting 'separatist' and 'inversion' models of gender definition that tend to be linked to respectively conflicting 'universalising' and 'minoritising' definitions of homosexuality. Our analysis would suggest that the conceptual incoherence that Sedgwick identifies results from the imposition of models aimed at ordering interrelationships between and within the categories of gender and sexuality onto that which is inherently open ended and not structured in any one way.

5. The same point is made by Calhoun (1994, p. 569) about the effects of transgressive sexual behaviour, though she relies on Judith Butler's notion of repetitive gender performances in order to distinguish lesbian from feminist sexual politics.

with her claims regarding the fundamental fluidity and openend-edness of sexuality, claims that the Hegelian conception of the necessity of contingency can well accommodate, we would make two critical observations.

Firstly, Grosz is right about the 'threat' of homosexuality to the extent that heterosexuality is conceived as the universal norm. Conversely, the threat of homosexuality does not merely arise in virtue of its very existence but has to do, importantly, with this being a denied or unrecognised existence. We will take up the question of the meaning and significance of recognition in the next chapter. The point here is that Grosz's target should be heteronormativity in its ontological distinctness from heterosexuality.

Secondly, we maintain that the power of homosexuality that Grosz invokes derives from the logic of the necessary interdependence of different forms of loving relations that we have analysed. If this is correct, then it would be a mistake to conceive the defining power of any one of these forms as uni-directional, as Grosz seems to here. Since the logical character of the contingency of sexually related beings suggests that there is a fundamental symmetry regarding the necessity of the contingency of different sexualities, this, in turn, would suggest that any 'power of infiltration' must be multi-directional.

The valorisation of 'woman-identified' lesbianism

From our analysis so far it follows that heteronormativity can be understood as the logical consequence of viewing the defining relationship of homosexuality to heterosexuality in a uni-directional way that privileges the latter. But the failure to recognise the ontological interdependence of different forms of loving relations also underpins the lesbian feminist demand that women reject heterosexuality as an institution of male domination. In other words, it is not just heteronormativity but 'woman-identified' lesbianism that can be understood as mistakenly denying the interdependence of multiple loving forms.[6]

---

6. Defenders of this view of lesbianism might see our argument as contributing to what Bat-Ami Bar On (1992) has recently identified as 'the containment' of lesbian feminism's radicalism and the consequent reprivatisation and depoliticisation of intimate relations. (Our position could be mistakenly seen as contributing to the tendency to view female erotic life in isolation from female friendship and solidarity, a tendency in response to which Adrienne Rich (1993, p. 240) proposed the notion of a 'lesbian continuum'. Bat-Ami Bar On argues that this containment began with the 'normalisation' of lesbian feminism as one amongst a variety of feminisms and has recently been reinforced by the focus on

The same problematic conceptual commitments continue to underlie more recent attempts to develop a notion of specifically lesbian love in contrast to the perceived earlier subsumption of lesbian love under a notion of 'woman-identified' love directed to the class of women. This brings us to a recent paper by Ruth Ginzberg (1992). Drawing on the work of Audre Lorde,[7] Ginzberg presents lesbian love as derived from specifically lesbian experience. However, she also wants to acknowledge the 'contributions' of non-lesbian women to the conception of what she sees as lesbian love. To this end she invokes Lugones' notion of world travelling and suggests that non-lesbian-identifying women are travellers in lesbian worlds who are not also 'at home ' in them as are women who identify as lesbian. In other words, Ginzberg suggests that the 'contributions' of non-lesbian-identifying women to the concept of love are made possible by such women's lesbian feelings, in spite of the way in which they, themselves, happen to experience loving feeling. The problem with this account is that it ultimately reverses a value hierarchy in favour of what is assumed to be the lesbian aspect of women's experiences.

In contrast, the account we have proposed on the basis of our analysis of Hegel's *Logic* need rely on no such hierarchical structuration. On the one hand, it makes room for the distinctness of lesbian eros as drawn from lesbian experience which it leaves to lesbian lovers to explore and elaborate. On the other hand, it proposes a sense in which lesbians must presuppose the (objective universal) framework of love within which any elaboration of the subjective and the specific takes place. If our analysis of the dynamic interplay between the subjective and the objective aspects of love is correct, what is presupposed, here, is drawn neither from distinctively lesbian experience nor from that which is not lesbian.

---

stigmatised sexualities resulting in the separation of lesbian politics from gender politics. (See, however, Calhoun (1994) who argues that without this separation a specifically lesbian theory focusing on lesbian desire cannot be fully developed.) The problem with Bat-Ami Bar On's argument about the containment of lesbian feminism's radicalism is that it takes for granted the vanguardism of this view of lesbianism. This, however, has been rightly called into question. See for example, Phelan, 1989, pp. 37-58.

7. As regards Lorde's conception of love we believe it possible to demonstrate that, in contrast to the emphasis of Ginzberg's reading (1992, pp. 73-75), its strength derives from its having eloquently captured the dynamic interrelationship of the objective universality and the subjective aspects of loving relationships that the Hegelian concept of love highlights.

The misconception of lesbian desire

As explained in Chapter 8, the Hegelian account of a loving union creates space for the participants themselves to explore and create the concrete meaning of the terms of their interaction as sexual beings. This entails that, whilst communal and cultural values and practices might be taken up by lovers, the latter have no special authority over them.[8] Our analysis of the ontology of homosexuality would suggest further that not only are the specificities of the practices of lovers a matter for the participants to explore for themselves, this is also the case for the very terms in which such processes of exploration take place. For this reason it is inappropriate for theories of erotic desire to pre-empt the ways in which the exploration of aspects of loving relations or desire might proceed. To illustrate this point consider Grosz's treatment of 'lesbian bodies and pleasures'. Noting the relative underrepresentation of lesbians in some key discourses, Grosz (1995, p. 219) describes 'lesbian desire and sexual relations between women' as 'the area which still remains the great domain of the untheorised and the inarticulate'.

> Is this [underrepresentation of lesbians as lesbians in key discourses] a lapse in the regime of sexuality, a sign of its imperfections and its capacity to create sites of resistance? Or is it a mode of further delegitimising lesbianism, a ruse of power itself? This is not an idle question, for whether one reads it as a shortfall of power, or as one of its strategies, will dictate whether one seeks to retain the inarticulateness, the indeterminacy of lesbian desire—my present inclination—or whether one seeks to articulate lesbianism as loudly and as thoroughly as possible (Grosz, 1995, p. 221).

Grosz (1995, p. 221) attributes the latter position to Marilyn Frye and comments:

> Frye seems to believe that the silence on the details of lesbian sexual relations is an effect of the obliteration or subsumption of women under heterosexist sexual norms.... Frye seems to yearn for a language and a mode of representation for lesbian sexual practices. She implies that without an adequate language, without appropriate terms, women's experiences themselves are less rich, less rewarding, less determinate than they could be.

---

8. Thus our conceptual framework lends support to the criticism by Martindale and Saunders (1992) of the style of lesbian ethics they call 'lesbian ethics in the upper case' even if they are mistaken about who in fact advocates such a position. On the latter see Shogan (1993).

Grosz basically argues that it might be a mistake to assume that female sexuality (in contrast to male sexuality) is knowable and capable of articulation. Instead, theorising female sexuality may not be a matter of

> simply *how* to know woman (what theories, concepts and language are necessary for illuminating this term); but rather, the *cost* and *effects* of such knowledge, what the various processes of knowing *do* to the objects they thereby produce (Grosz, 1995, p. 224).

So, she links her response to the position she attributes to Frye about lesbian sexuality to a more fundamental question of the theorisation of female sexuality. This enables her to imply that Frye is buying into a conception of language and knowledge that does not enable her to see that 'articulateness and representation' may not 'in themselves' be 'a virtue' as far as lesbian sexuality is concerned (Grosz, 1995, p. 222).

Our view is that, in this exchange with Frye, Grosz offers a misplaced choice over whether 'to retain the inarticulateness, the indeterminacy of lesbianism, and of female sexuality' or 'to articulate lesbianism as loudly and as thoroughly as possible'. On our analysis this is not the sort of question to which theorising can or need provide an (one?) adequate answer or, indeed, quasi-universalising pronouncements of the kind Grosz makes here. This is not to say that the question she addresses cannot be written and spoken about productively. Rather, our concern is that she conflates philosophical articulation, for which the fundamental question of the theorisation of female sexuality is a concern, with human and lesbian practices of meaning creation more generally. Adapting an expression of hers, we might say that such practices include the 'philosophically sayable' (Grosz, 1995, p. 189), but they are not limited to them.

Our account of the subjective aspect of the ontology of homosexuality and, in particular, our claim that its multiple shapes develop within specific relationships, suggests that Frye's position has more merit than Grosz is prepared to allow.[9] Rather than juxtaposing to Frye's concerns a philosophical framework in which lesbian sexuality is subordinated to the problem of theorising female sexuality,[10] we would stress the importance of Frye's concerns

---

9. Grosz (1995, p. 222) allows that lesbians may need 'modes of representation to affirm and render these [delegitimated social and sexual] practices viable and valuable'.

10. Indeed Grosz (1995, p. 222) treats them as identical. We do not want to

for the process of exploring the (subjective and intersubjective) meanings of lesbian sexual practices. From within our conceptual framework we need not judge Frye's claims as resulting from her failure to appreciate the negative effects of 'the subsumption of women under heterosexist norms'. Instead, there emerges a more subtle way of understanding (a) her observation that in her experience 'lesbian "sex" is ... *in*articulate'; and (b) her comment that this restricts the meaning generating potential of lesbian experience.[11] She can be understood as drawing attention to the lived, as distinct from theorised, effect of the inarticulateness in question. Inarticulateness understood as a lived constraint upon the meaning generating potential of lesbian experience is open to a variety of different reflective responses depending on the vast range of factors that have to do with the specifics of beings and interactions.[12] So, Grosz's 'present inclination' to seek 'to retain the inarticulateness, the indeterminacy of lesbian desire' turns out to be unnecessarily limiting.

In another, initially more restrained, attempt to theorise lesbian desire, Grosz (1995, pp. 173-174) sets out to investigate 'what kinds of terms may be appropriate for understanding [her] own' 'sexual practices, fantasies and desires' rather than to explain or judge lesbian sexual practices. Here, she opposes to the dominant

object to this position but to its effect as evidenced in Grosz's essay. It renders invisible the possibility of reflection on lesbian sexuality that is neither derived from nor identified with female sexuality as such.

11. Cited in Grosz, 1995, p. 221. In the passage Grosz cites, Frye notes that most of her 'experience in the realms commonly designated as "sexual" has been prelinguistic, non-cognitive' and that as regards these areas of experience she has 'no linguistic community, language and, therefore in one important sense, no knowledge'.

12. Grosz's desire to assess the political value (presumably for lesbians' struggles) of lesbians' attempts to articulate the structure of (their) lesbian desire(s) tends to underestimate the variable dynamics of the contingent, even as she warns against the 'taming and normalisation' effects of theoretical discourses on lesbian desire. This would explain why she concludes her review of de Lauretis' *The Practice of Love* by suggesting that the time has come (she does not say for whom) to rethink what discourses lesbians should be using to theorise lesbian desire, even though she makes a point of acknowledging that de Lauretis's reworking of a psychoanalytic conception of lesbian desire may be an attempt at self-understanding (Grosz, 1995, p. 171). In contrast to Grosz's approach, we believe that the strength of the practice of 'queer theorising' lies in its efforts to resist classification and categorial colonisation (Butler, 1990) and to transgress and transcend categorial 'ideological liabilities' (de Lauretis, 1994, p. v). Its weakness, on the other hand, lies in its inability to say precisely what, if anything, marks the limits of politically significant transgressive behaviour.

concept of desire as ontological lack that of 'the subordinated tradition within western thought' in which 'desire is primarily seen as production' (Grosz, 1995, pp. 179-180). Drawing on the work of Deleuze, Guattari and Lyotard, Grosz (1995, p. 180) advocates a reading of lesbian desire in terms of 'bodies, pleasures, surfaces and intensities'.

> To use the machinic connections a body-part forms with another, whether it be organic or inorganic, to form an intensity, an investment of libido, is to see desire, sexuality as productive. Productive, though in no way reproductive, for this purpose can serve no other purpose, have no other function, than its own augmentation and proliferation ...
>
> If we are looking at intensities and surfaces rather than latencies and depth.... Their effects rather than any intentions occupy our focus, for what they make and do rather than what they mean and represent (Grosz, 1995, p. 183).

Grosz draws two insights from her discussion of this 'positive' conception of desire. First, as regards lesbian desire, she notes that 'becoming-lesbian' is a question of 'what kinds of lesbian machine we invest our time, energy and bodies in' (Grosz, 1995, p. 184). Second, as regards theorising, her proposal is presented not as

> a vision of things to come, an ideal or goal, but a way of looking at, and doing things here and now, with concepts and ideas in the same ways we do with bodies and pleasures, a way of levelling, of flattening the hierarchical relations between ideas and things ... of making them level and interactive, rendering them productive and innovative, experimental and provocative. That is the most we can hope from knowledge or desire (Grosz, 1995, p. 185).

Whilst there is much to commend attempts to produce desire in its radical particularity, we think that here, too, Grosz's discussion shows signs of advocating an unnecessarily restrictive understanding of desire. For, part of the way in which she presents desire as productive is through its opposition to desire as lack, an opposition which, as she recognises, has the effect of denying the ontology of any desires with inner depth, like lovers' sharing of a rich inner life. Whilst we have no objections to the suggestion that for some of us nothing may be lost by abandoning such an ontology of desire in favour of an exclusive focus on 'machinic connections', it is worth noting that Grosz goes beyond offering an understanding of lesbian desire in the restricted terms she initially suggests.

This is most evident in her concluding comments on the production of concepts and ideas when Grosz assigns a restricted place to knowledge. In the second passage cited above she advocates that the production (in her sense) of concepts and ideas (of desire) proceed 'in the same ways' as do the productive activities of bodies and pleasures. Presumably, this is possible because, and in so far as, bodies and pleasures are productive. Yet rather than render this relationship between the ontology and the concept of desire visible, much of Grosz' text is devoted to clarifying her intentions through a series of disclaimers. If the very ontology of desire is purely productive and if it can be linked to the production of concepts in the way that Grosz claims, then Grosz should not be trying to convince others of the value of producing concepts. Rather she needs to show the productive activity in action. This is precisely what we take the categories of Hegel's logic to be doing. Their creative power is not, however, premised on the opposition and substitution of one concept of desire for another. As we hope our discussion makes clear, rather than offering an either-or choice between machinic and what we referred to as ethical connections, it is possible within the Hegelian conceptual framework to engage bodies and pleasures at the level Grosz advocates without having to deny another spiritual orientation of desire. This is due to the space created for the necessarily contingent by the interplay of the subjective and objective aspects of loving beings.

11. THE FAMILY AND THE LAW

Our aim in this final chapter is twofold. Firstly, we want to outline what we consider to be a central feature of the Hegelian understanding of the logical ground of family law. Secondly, we want to draw out some implications of this understanding for two issues of current concern. The first of these is the question of the legal recognition of same sex relationships and the second is the legal conceptualisation of the post divorce family.

Before turning to the first of our aims we note that a defence of Hegel's theory of law is beyond the scope of our present discussion. Instead, we hope merely to indicate why a suitably elaborated Hegelian approach to the concept of law has the potential to supply a much needed theoretical framework within which to resolve complex issues surrounding the role of law in its relationship to the family. Contemporary approaches to the theorisation of this relationship have recently been reviewed by Martha Minow and Mary Lyndon Shanley (1996). The authors find fundamental weaknesses in contractarian, communitarian and rights based thinking about family law.

> Contract-based theories promote individual freedoms but neglect social values and concerns about inequality and dignity; community-based theories articulate shared values but risk constraining individual freedoms and social pluralism while prompting greater social conflict. Rights-based theories invigorate as social values respect for certain individual freedoms, but they historically lack a rich understanding of relationships, including their preconditions, their responsibilities, and their consequences (Minow and Lyndon Shanley, 1996, p. 20).

In our view, the problems that Minow and Lyndon Shanley correctly identify are due to the tendency within each of the three approaches they discuss both to over emphasise and to under emphasise

what we described in Chapters 7 and 8 as the atomic and the necessarily intersubjective aspects of family members' identities.

We also believe that the interplay between these two aspects
of the loving identity has not just been overlooked by current contractarian, communitarian and rights based approaches. In contemporary legal discourse it has also been under theorised by
thinkers, like Minow and Lyndon Shanley (1996, p. 23), who advocate a focus on 'relational rights and responsibilities'. We will,
therefore, begin our discussion with an outline of the central
claims of these authors. We will try to show how our Hegelian approach, which has a similar focus on relational rights and responsibilities, supplies a more adequate theoretical grounding for such
rights and responsibilities.

THE LEGAL RECOGNITION OF RELATIONAL RIGHTS AND RESPONSIBILITIES

Minow and Lyndon Shanley (1996, p. 23) maintain that were it
to draw attention to 'the claims that arise out of relationships of
human interdependence' family law theory would be better positioned to accommodate 'two paradoxical characteristics of family life and the family's relationship to the state'. The first of these
paradoxes is that 'the individual must be seen simultaneously as a
distinct individual and as a person fundamentally involved in relationships of dependence, care and responsibility'. Here, Minow
and Lyndon Shanley implicitly point to the need for the public recognition of both the atomic and necessarily intersubjective aspects
of family members' identities.

They go on to suggest that attention to relational rights and
responsibilities would require courts that decide cases like child
custody disputes between parents 'to consider each party to such
actions both as separate adults and as individuals-in-relationship'
(Minow and Lyndon Shanley, 1996, p. 23). On this approach certain kinds of cases that are especially vulnerable to the distortion
of the relational aspects of parenting would be better handled by
the courts. For example, in cases involving pregnancy contracts
and disputes between same sex parents one of whom is biologically related to their child it would not be open to courts to make their
rulings by reducing these sorts of cases to the mere enforcement
of a contract or to the protection of the biological parent's interests
(Minow and Lyndon Shanley, 1996, p. 22).

Whilst we agree with these observations about the potential benefits of a relational approach to the legal conceptualisation of family

relationships, the authors' discussion starts from the assumption that the law ought to have a role in the recognition and regulation of intimate relationships. Their analysis does not address the concerns of critics of family law concepts, such as radical and lesbian feminists. They have argued, for example, in favour of the deregulation of marriage and for the resolution of property and child custody disputes outside the legal system.[1]

Indeed, the second paradox that Minow and Lyndon Shanley (1996, p. 22) identify is that 'family relationships are simultaneously outside of yet shaped by the political order'. They suggest that recognition of this fact would require legal institutions to have regard to the ways in which family life is framed and influenced by wider social practices. Illustrating the application of this claim, they maintain that the question of the legalisation of same sex marriages calls for a consideration of 'the place of such proposed relationships in the lives of those immediately involved and those in the surrounding community' (Minow and Lyndon Shanley 1996, p. 23). In attempting to recognise the undeniable influence of wider cultural practices on the internal life of families the authors attribute to 'the surrounding community' a significant role in the determination of the meaning of fundamental legal concepts like marriage. Yet, their suggestion leaves unexplained why an appreciation of the socialising effects of wider cultural practices should lead to a recognition of any role for particular communities in the determination of the meaning and application of such concepts. Their own proposal seems potentially to suffer from the problem that they attribute to a community based approach, namely that it risks constraining social pluralism.[2] We will come back to these concerns once we have outlined a view about the meaning and significance of the public recognition of family relationships based on the analysis we offered in the

1. Card, 1996; Robson, 1992a and 1992b. Calhoun (1997, pp. 132-135) offers an overview of radical and lesbian feminist arguments against marriage, motherhood and the family.

2. Midgley and Hughes (1997) conceive of the problem with the notion of the family in a slightly different but equally problematic way. They suggest that it is ambiguous because it is definable from two perspectives that represent conflicting interests. On the one hand, an administrative perspective that looks down on the family unit from the outside views it as a political and economic unit and, so, values its stability and potential for self-regulation and self-maintenance. On the other, individual family members view it as an emotional and supportive network and, so, they value its permanence to the extent that it has the potential to sustain loving supportive relationships (Midgley and Hughes, 1997, pp. 61-62). They conclude that 'what the family is and where family values lie can look quite different from these two perspectives' (Midgley and Hughes, 1997, p. 62).

preceding chapters. An outline of the role of such public recognition will enable us to explain the logical ground of the legal recognition and regulation of family relationships.

Law and the public recognition of family relationships

Why is the public recognition of family relationships necessary? Our discussion of mutual recognition in Chapters 7 and 8 suggests that in the present context recognition concerns the objective aspect of familial ties as this is expressed in marriage, family property and parenting. Developing this idea further we can say, firstly, that on the Hegelian approach the objective universality embodied in a loving couple's mutual recognition also calls for recognition of the loving union by non-members. The reason for this has to do with the objective universal essence that, as we argued, lovers presuppose as the framework within which to practice their love. The logical priority of this objective universal essence is concretely expressed in the public recognition of a loving union by non-members.

Secondly, this requisite public recognition must be institutionally embodied in law precisely because what is in need of this kind of recognition is the objective aspect of family relationships alone and not their subjective aspects. Recall that the objective aspect of marriage, the formal moment of family life, consists of the embodiment of the abstract common essence, as distinct from specific natures, of the participants of a loving relationship whereas family property and children constitute substantive embodiments of the objectivity of familial love. Significantly, for reasons that we need not go into here, in the Hegelian system the law is understood in terms of the institutional embodiment of persons' abstract essence, irrespective of whether this essence is intersubjectively or atomically constituted. The combination of these two elements is what makes the institution of law particularly suited to satisfying the requirement that family relationships be publicly recognised.

This is why we believe that Hegel is consistent with the demands of his system of logic when he refers to the family as a 'legal entity' (1981, §171) and insists on the legal recognition and regulation of marriage, divorce, family property and parenting (1981, §164, §176-§179). This part of his analysis can be severed from his assumption that the gender based administration of family property should similarly be legally recognised since this assumption follows from his distorted elaboration of gender roles that we examined in the previous chapters.

An internal objection to the family as a legal entity The above mentioned references to the family as a legal entity have led Theunissen (1991, p. 7) to complain that, although he presents the family as the first moment of 'Ethical Life,' Hegel assumes that 'the mates belong to civil society and live in a state'. Yet, according to Theunissen (1991, p. 18) consistency would require Hegel to view the family as becoming a legal entity only upon its dissolution into a plurality of families which gives rise to the concept of civil society as the second moment of 'Ethical Life'. Our discussion above points to the reason why this objection to Hegel is misplaced. We have seen that the rational principle underlying the law's role in intra familial relations is conceptualised through a consideration of the family against the background of the abstractly understood non-familial. Neither the second nor the third moments of ethical life, which respectively elaborate the internal workings of civil society (the systems of the economy, civil and criminal law, government and corporations) and the state (constitutional law, international relations and world history), need be assumed for the elaboration of the dimensions of the concept of the family which are public in nature when all that is at issue is the family's recognition by the instituted outside per se. The question of the extent of justifiable legal regulation of the internal affairs of family life is a further issue to which we will return shortly.

The ethical significance of commitment ceremonies A different kind of objection to our suggestion above about the role of family law could be put as follows. Whilst there is some basis for the public recognition of on going coupled relationships, given the constraints that are inevitably imposed on intimate relationships as a result of their legal regulation, the need for public recognition might better be satisfied through community practices like commitment ceremonies in the presence of friends. Hegel (1981, §164) acknowledges the role of kin and community in the recognition of a couple's bond and he realised that state sanctioned marriage makes divorce more difficult (Hegel, 1981, §176).

We do not wish to detract from the seriousness of the concern that people should be just as free to end their intimate relationships as they should be to enter them. Nor do we deny the cultural significance of the practice of commitment ceremonies in the presence of friends and family. Nevertheless, our response to this suggestion is to point out one unattractive consequence of adopting this approach. As communitarian theorists have shown, the strength of face to face community practices lies in the fact that they engage participants in their totality as fully concrete beings who view each other accordingly. We suggest that this is precisely the reason why such practices cannot play the role we attribute to family law. Since lovers are viewed as whole beings within their communities, were communities to be pressed in the service of the public recognition of love's objective universality the subjective aspects of familial love would be at risk of unwarranted interference.

From the point of view of the relevant logic what would be lacking were the public recognition of a marriage not provided by the institution of law is exclusive regard to lovers' objective universal essence on the part of those giving the recognition. If lovers' objective universal essence is not the exclusive focus of public recognition then it cannot be effectively distinguished from the irreducible differences that also define their identities as loving beings. The irreducible differences defining the identities of loving beings cannot, in turn, be safeguarded from the possibility of being exposed, as a result of meeting the demand for public recognition, to processes that undermine the freedom to address the subjective aspects of familial relationships.

The need for a clear difference in the treatment of the relationship of the law to the subjective and the objective aspects of family relationships is overlooked by Minow and Lyndon Shanley (1996) when they advance the idea of focusing on relational rights and responsibilities. As a result, their approach fails adequately to explain the basis of the legal recognition and regulation of family relationships and to set limits to the relevance of community concerns in the determination of such questions. Despite having aptly drawn attention to the undesirable tendency within communitarian thought to generate disputes about which family values society should endorse through its legal and other regulatory institutions (Minow and Lyndon Shanley, 1996, pp. 13-16), their own approach does not seem to have the conceptual resources to avoid this problem.

LEGAL RECOGNITION AND PLURAL SEXUALITIES

On the basis of our Hegelian understanding of the rational principle underlying the legal recognition of family relationships we can now account for the forms of sexual relationship that justifiably fall within the scope of legal recognition. Let us bring together the observation, made above, that legal recognition should extend only as far as the objective aspect of familial love and our conclusion, in the

previous chapter, that this objective aspect must remain indifferent
to specific loving forms.[3] We can now say that the law's exclusive
recognition of heterosexual love and, indeed, legal discrimination
on the basis of the specific form of a loving relationship, contradict
the logical ground of the need for suitably instituted public recognition of family relationships.

Same sex marriages

Three important points follow from the above analysis for the debate concerning the legal recognition of same sex relationships.
First, there is a logical basis for dislodging the legal concepts of
marriage, family property and parenting, from definitions derived from heterosexual experiences. This is because the legal
recognition of long term coupled relationships which involve the
potential to acquire family capital and to raise children cannot
be grounded on the fact that heterosexuals engage in this mode
of relationship. So, our position supports the view advanced by
Calhoun (1997, p. 135) that

> it does not follow from the fact that heterosexual marriage and
> family has been oppressive for heterosexual women and a pri-
> mary structure of patriarchy that any form of marriage or fam-
> ily, including lesbian ones, is oppressive for women and a pri-
> mary structure of patriarchy.

In addition, our analysis shows why the legal concept of the family need not remain linked to a heterosexual form, whether patriarchal or not.

Second, when grounded in an analysis of the objective universality of loving relationships, the demand for the legal recognition
of same sex marriages amounts to a demand to treat the forms
of love as irrelevant from the point of view of the law since such
forms come into play only from within familial love's subjective
domain. It follows from this that, whilst the demand in question
should not be conceived in terms of seeking the same treatment
as heterosexuals,[4] it also should not be conceived in terms of treatment that recognises same sex couples' differences from heterosexuals. Comparative assessments are altogether out of place here.[5]

---

3. This indifference need not be the homophobicly constituted space of 'un-
knowing' that Sedgwick (1993, pp. 51-52) discusses.

4. Cf. Weitzman, 1974; Mohr, 1994; Pierce, 1995.; Wolfson, 1996. Critics of
this position, such as Robson, 1992b, and Card, 1996, correctly maintain that it
amounts to complicity with the heteronormativity of legal discourses.

5. We do not believe that we are defending a view that naively assumes the

Finally, what of the question faced by lesbians and gay males about whether or not to support the legal recognition of same sex relationships given the cultural and historical links of the legal categories of marriage, parenting and family to heteronormativity? It is important to recognise that the issues at stake here can be confined to political strategic considerations as distinct from theoretical or conceptual ones.[6] That is, if our analysis is correct, then only considerations characteristic of any political struggle to do with effectiveness (priorities, timing and the like) remain open questions. These should not be confused with the conceptual issues that we have been discussing. So, for example, Ruthann Robson's (1992b) opposition to lesbian marriage on the strategic ground that it threatens 'lesbian solidarity' by creating divisions between 'good' and 'deviant' lesbians, (like her related claim that it exposes feminists to the law's gender bias), should be distinguished from a quite different, we would say conceptual, claim, that she conflates with this argument from solidarity. This is her suggestion that lesbian marriage threatens 'lesbian survival' because it 'domesticates' lesbians in the sense of oppressively over legalising their lives and eroding their power to define their lesbianism (Robson, 1992b, p. 18). Robson (1992b, p. 127) concludes that lesbian 'energy is better directed at abolishing marriage as a state institution'.

Our differentiation between strategic and conceptual arguments enables us appropriately to assess the merits of each kind of argument. The strategic argument from lesbian solidarity calls for assessment of contingent factors like the character and strength of lesbian solidarity at any given time and the specifics of legal doctrine. Such questions might, in turn, need to be considered in the light of the need to render visible the outlaw status of gay and lesbian families. With this political goal in mind, Calhoun (1997, p. 137) advances the strategic counter argument that by pressing for legal recognition of their families and child custody rights gays and lesbians oppose the enforced restriction of their families to 'queer non-marital and non-parenting relationships'.

neutrality of law. Rather we take the view that the proper target of sociologically oriented critiques of law, that draw attention to such matters as law's race, class, gender and sexuality biases, is law as it operates in liberal theoretical and institutional frameworks. Although we cannot argue the point here, we believe that Hegel's account of law in the ethical state does not suffer from the same limitations.

6. We believe that the current tendency to treat all theoretical questions as strategic ones arising out of various discursive power struggles is ultimately unhelpful.

Whatever one makes of the above sort of disagreement, Robson's domestication argument is flawed because it fails to appreciate the difference between the objective and subjective aspects of coupled loving relationships and the relevance of the law to the former. Consequently, it can see no positive and productive way of relating the categories of family and law. The limitations of Robson's position become clear when she discusses lesbians' child custody and access disputes and the possibility of extending the legal category of parent to include both lesbian parents. In line with her goal of 'centering' lesbians rather than the law (Robson, 1992b, pp. 20-21) Robson (1992a) insists on treating differently the intralesbian situation from that in which non-lesbians are also involved. In the latter type of case she advocates the privileging of lesbian choices over the interests of children or paternal rights.

In the former type of case in which it is not possible to resolve conflicts by centering lesbians' choices, Robson opposes the expansion of the legal category of parent which would give the non-biological mother of a disputing lesbian couple a basis for claiming child custody or access rights. She urges lesbians to resolve the disputes amongst themselves by another 'non-domesticating' process available to them. This process effectively amounts to invoking lesbian categories that Robson (1992a, p. 183) only explains in terms of their opposition to legal categories. Her view is that the law (a) is unnecessary in a world of lesbians and (b) should be opposed where relationships between lesbians and the dominant non-lesbian culture is concerned (1992b, pp. 23-25). Thus, her approach unrealistically refuses to countenance the possibility that lesbians amongst themselves are capable of reaching an impasse when their personal relationships end and they are still linked together through involvement with their children. In the final section we will turn to a brief consideration of the legal conceptualisation of the post divorce family.

THE POST DIVORCE FAMILY

Our examination of the relationship between the concepts of family and law has enabled us to attribute a certain role to family law which properly includes the regulation of divorce for the reason that marriage partners' decision to end their marriage, like their decision to enter into it, concerns their objective universality. Thus, the Hegelian approach inevitably gives rise to the question of how the law should deal with property and child custody disputes between divorcing parents. We think that the key to an

appreciation of the Hegelian position on this question is the differentiation between the ideas of the 'natural dissolution' of the
family and its 'ethical dissolution' that we outlined in Chapter 9.
Recall that whereas the latter necessarily comes about as a result of
the development of the children of a family into their atomic individuality, the former results from the death or divorce of parents.
Thus in the Hegelian approach it is conceivable that a family that
has come to its natural end has yet to reach its ethical end. This
observation has some interesting implications for the legal conceptualisation of post divorce relationships between parents and
between parents and children. We can best draw these out of a
comparison of the effects of a family's natural dissolution on family capital and children.

Significantly, the natural dissolution of the family results in
the dissolution of the family's necessarily intersubjective will. In
thus putting an end to their family's substantial personality, relative to each other divorcing parents revert back to their respective
atomic individualities. This change in the ethical and legal status
of family members, in turn, grounds, the respective claims by the
members of a post divorce family to have their family capital transformed into private shares. In this case, family capital, the collective property that signifies on going 'labour and care for a common possession' loses its spiritual source. Consequently, it must
revert back into private property items that can severally embody
the formal personalities of each one of the (potentially) atomic individuals who had formerly constituted the family's substantial
personality. Divorcing partners thus become entitled to a share
as do their children in their capacity as (potentially) formally free
persons. This said, the Hegelian approach does not provide any
objectively universal principle, such as a contribution principle,
on the basis of which to determine the amount of specific shares.
Instead, this question is left to the contingencies of time and place.
Principles of distribution may well focus on considerations that
are determined either communally (and codified in law) or by the
parties involved (when they make pre-nuptial agreements).

By contrast, the conceptualisation of the post divorce relationship of divorcing parents to their children relies on an entirely different feature of the Hegelian concept of the family. Children, as
we explained in Chapter 9, are taken to embody the family's substantial unity, namely parents' love for each other as distinct from
their love in the form of a substantial personality. We can, therefore, distinguish between (a) parental love as the objectification

of parents' love for each other and (b) parental love as the objectification of parents' love for each other that takes the form of a substantial personality. In the case of the natural dissolution of a family, because the divorcing parents no longer form a necessarily intersubjective identity their parental love in the first sense just described must simply take the new form of atomically interrelated individuals relating to their children.

Interestingly, the fact that divorcing parents no longer feel the love of each other except as love of their children brings the children of divorcing parents to the centre of their continuing familial ties. As long as divorcing parents' responsibilities for raising their children have not reached the ethical end of developing the children's atomic individuality, divorcing parents can be said to continue to belong to their children's family. The post divorce family can thus be conceptualised as the continuation of a substantial ethical unit that, nevertheless, takes on a new form as a result of the dissolution of its substantial personality.

We believe that were family law discourse to distinguish adequately between what the Hegelian approach refers to as the natural dissolution of the family and its ethical dissolution the difficult task of conceptualising the post divorce family would be significantly advanced. To illustrate this claim we would like to end our discussion by revealing the limitations of the position advanced in a recent otherwise insightful paper on this issue by Elise Robinson et. al. (1997).

According to Robinson et. al. (1997, pp. 93-94) empirical research into (legally enforced) child custody arrangements following the divorce of parents shows that such arrangements tend to favour giving custody to women and they reinforce values that underlie the model of the sentimental family. Significantly, this model invokes respect for the privacy of the family and of its gendered division of labour. Furthermore, the authors suggest that within the model of the sentimental family children are viewed as fragile objects in need of protection. Their own perspective on their new situation is not taken into account and the perspective of parents is privileged. Consistent with the assumptions underlying the model of the sentimental family, most accounts of a post divorce reality involving children

> suggest that either two new families are formed, with the children being part of one or both, or that one new single-parent family is formed, made up of the children, the residential parent, and (perhaps) any new partner the residential parent may come to have, but not including the outside parent (Robinson, 1997, p. 96).

Robinson et. al. challenge these beliefs about the impact of divorce on the families of divorcing parents by drawing on the experiences of children of divorcing parents. The authors offer a description of children's post divorce situation which for the most
part is consistent with the Hegelian approach we have proposed.
They argue, correctly in our view, that children benefit from family life through relationships with intimate others and not through
'residence in a sentimental household' (Robinson, 1997, pp. 95-
96). Relationships provide the conditions that contribute to their
identity and agency formation. It follows from this that when living arrangements change following parental divorce the household splits into two but the child's family, in the sense of his or
her relationships with his or her specific intimate others, endures
(Robinson, 1997, pp. 99-100).

Indeed, from the child's perspective, which (decisions about)
child custody arrangements typically overlook, the child's post
divorce family is still a single, even if larger, unit (Robinson,
1997, p. 96). It 'has now expanded to flow into two households
instead of one' (Robinson, 1997, p. 100). This more fluid model
of the post divorce family allows children of divorcing parents to
access the 'special moral context' that families supply. This is a
context in which familial ties play an important role in revealing who the child is as a moral agent at a time when his or her
actions do not as yet reveal his or her moral identity to outsiders
(Robinson, 1997, p. 98).

To be sure, the authors' attention to the experiences and perspectives of children of post divorce families enables them to
make some important observations about the nature of the post
divorce family. They identify the advantages of viewing it in terms
of the continuity of ethically enriching familial ties. Still, the development of their position relies upon the assumption that the
different perspective of children is somehow more credible than
that of parents. Thus, even though they locate the source of the
problem with alternative accounts of the post divorce reality in
the apparent failure of such accounts to incorporate the perspective of children, the authors do not explain why or when it is appropriate to draw upon children's perspective in preference to the
parental perspective.

This lack of a principled inclusion of the perspective of children
in the process of defining the post divorce reality leads Robinson
et. al. to conclude their discussion of their preferred model of the
fluid family with suggestions, drawn once again from the child's

perspective, about the special moral benefits of growing up in a post divorce family. Here is how they represent the advantages to a child of having access to two households:

> by giving the child two households to be connected to, the child gets the good of living in two different worlds. When one world becomes tiresome or stale, the other world holds out, perhaps, the freshness of a different style of personal interaction, a different ambience, an alternative world view, a change of scene. It can be comforting, when there is a quarrel or dispute in one of the child's worlds, to retreat at least mentally to the other world, where this particular altercation does not exist (Robinson, 1997, p. 100).

Notice, firstly, how the authors' appeal to 'the good of living in two different worlds' is explained in terms of being given two households. Their discussion started by invoking the distinction between the household and relationships with intimate others in order to point out, against the model of the sentimental family, that what matters morally is relationships and not households. Yet, the authors collapse the distinction in their own appeal to the child's access to different worlds. Nothing more is said about what makes these 'worlds' different in any morally significant sense.

Secondly, the authors' illustration of 'the good of living in two different worlds' presents relationships that supposedly define the child's moral identity as resources for the alleviation of boredom or means for avoiding the cultivation of a sense of shared responsibility for the resolution of family problems. The psychological benefits referred to in the above cited passage can no doubt be an important part of the experience of children who grow up in plural households. Nevertheless, the authors' attempt to attribute to this experience some special moral significance in the elaboration of their conception of the post divorce family confuses the issues. (Are they implying that good child rearing requires parents to 'give' their children more than one household?) Having implied that the perspective of children is authoritative, they do not have any way of limiting its supposed authority.

By contrast, the Hegelian approach we presented above suggests that it is not the child's perspective, but his or her position, that should be taken to be ethically significant. Children, we have suggested, move to the centre of an adequate conceptualisation of the post divorce family. From this position they mediate the now atomic interrelationship of their divorced parents and, where appropriate, they also mediate the interrelationship of their divorced parents and their parents' new partners. A recognition of the central position of children within the post divorce family supplies a principled way of determining child custody issues and disputes that end up coming before the courts.

BIBLIOGRAPHY

Abelove, H., Barale, M.A. and Halperin, D.M. eds. (1993) *The Lesbian And Gay Studies Reader,* Routledge, London.

Agamben, G. (1993) *The Coming Community,* M. Hardt, trans., University of Minnesota Press, Minneapolis and London.

Aristotle (1941)'Nichomachean Ethics', Book 18, in R. McKeon, ed., *The Basic Works of Aristotle,* Random House, New York.

Arthur, C. (1980) 'Personality And The Dialectic Of Labour And Property: Locke, Hegel, Marx', *Radical Philosophy,* Vol. 26, pp. 3-15.

Arthur, C.J. (1987) 'Hegel On Political Economy', in D. Lamb, ed., *Hegel And Modern Philosophy,* pp. 102-118.

Avineri, S. (1980) *Hegel's Theory Of The Modern State,* Cambridge University Press, Cambridge.

Bar-On, B. (1992) 'The Feminist Sexuality Debates And The Transformation Of The Political', *Hypatia,* Vol. 7, No. 4, pp. 45-58.

Baynes, K. et. al. eds. (1987) *After Philosophy: End or Transformation?,* The MIT Press, Cambridge, Massachusetts.

Beiser, F.C. ed. (1993) *The Cambridge Companion To Hegel,* Cambridge University Press, New York.

Benhabib, S. (1984) 'Obligation, Contract And Exchange: On The Significance Of Hegel's Abstract Right', in Z.A. Pelczynski, ed., *The State And Civil Society,* pp. 159-177.

Benhabib, S. (1992) *Situating The Self: Gender, Community And Postmodernism In Contemporary Ethics,* Polity Press, Oxford.

Berry, C.J. (1977) 'From Hume To Hegel: The Case Of The Social Contract', *Journal Of The History Of Ideas,* Vol. 38, No. 3, pp. 691-703.

Berthold-Bond, D. (1980) 'Hegel on Metaphilosophy and The Philosophical Spectator', *Idealistic Studies,* Vol. 16, No. 1, pp. 205-17.

Berthold-Bond, D. (1989) *Hegel's Grand Synthesis: A Study Of Being, Thought, And History*, State University of New York Press, Albany.

Bethke Elshtain, J. (1981) *Public Man, Private Woman*, Princeton University Press, Princeton, New Jersey.

Blum, L. A. (1980) *Friendship, Altruism and Morality*, Routledge and Kegan Paul, London.

Bradford, J. and Sartwell, C. (1997) 'Addiction And Knowledge: Epistemic Disease And The Hegemonic Family', in H. Lindemann Nelson, ed., *Feminism And Families*, pp. 116-130.

Brod, H. (1992) *Hegel's Philosophy Of Politics: Idealism, Identity And Modernity*, Westview Press, Boulder.

Burbridge, J.W. (1995) *On Hegel's Logic: Fragments Of A Commentary*, Humanities Press, New Jersey.

Butler, J. (1990) *Gender Trouble: Feminism And The Subversion Of Identity*, Routledge, New York.

Calhoun, C. (1994) 'Separating Lesbian Theory From Feminist Theory', *Ethics*, Vol. 104, pp. 558-581.

Calhoun, C. (1997) 'Family Outlaws: Rethinking The Connections Between Feminism, Lesbianism And The Family', in H. Lindemann Nelson, ed., *Feminism And Families*, pp. 131-150.

Callahan, S. (1997) 'Gays, Lesbians, And The Use Alternate Reproductive Technologies', in H. Lindemann Nelson, ed., *Feminism And Families*, pp. 188-202.

Card C. (1996) 'Against Marriage And Motherhood', Hypatia, Vol. 11, No. 3, pp. 1-23.

Castoriadis, C. (1997) *The Imaginary Institution Of Society*, Polity Press, Cambridge.

Cieskowski, A. (1979) *Selected Writings*. A. Liebich, ed. and trans., Cambridge University Press, London.

Cooper D.E. (1984) 'Hegel's Theory of Punishment', in Z.A. Pelczynski, ed., *Hegel's Political Philosophy*, pp. 151-157

Cornell, D. Rosenfeld, M. and Carlson, D.G. eds. (1991) *Hegel And Legal Theory*, Routledge, London.

Dallmyr, K-H. (1971) 'The Structure Of Hegel's 'Philosophy Of Right'', in Z.A. Pelczynski, ed., *Hegel's Political Philosophy*, pp. 90-110.

de Lauretis, T. (1991) 'Queer Theory: Lesbian And Gay Sexualities: An Introduction', *differences*, Vol. 3 No. 2, pp. iii-xvii.

de Lauretis, T. (1993) 'Sexual Indifference And Lesbian Representation' in H. Abelove et. al. eds., *The Lesbian And Gay Studies Reader*.

de Lauretis, T. (1994) *Lesbian Sexuality And Perverse Desire*, Indiana University Press, Indianapolis.

Dean, J. (1997) *Solidarity Of Strangers: Feminism After Identity Politics*, University of California Press, Berkeley.

Dove, K.R. (1970) 'Hegel's Phenomenological Method', *Review Of Metaphysics*, Vol. 23, No. 4, pp. 615-641.

Dunn, J. (1993) *Western Political Theory in the Face of the Future*, Cambridge University Press, Cambridge.

Easton, S. M. (1987) 'Hegel And Feminism', in D. Lamb, ed., *Hegel And Modern Philosophy*, pp. 30-35.

Findlay, J. N. (1972) 'The Contemporary Relevance Of Hegel', in A. MacIntyre, ed., *Hegel*, pp. 1-20.

Firestone, S. (1970) *The Dialectic of Sex: The Case For Feminist Revolution*, Bantam Books, New York.

Flay, J. (1980) 'Comment', in D.P. Verene, ed., *Hegel's Social and Political Thought*, pp. 167-175.

Fox Keller, E. (1985) *Reflections On Gender And Science*. Yale University Press, New Haven.

Fromm, E. (1984) *To Have Or To Be?*, Abacus, London.

Fromm, E. (1985) *The Art Of Loving*, Thorsons, London.

Fukuyama, F. (1992) *The End of History and the Last Man*, Penguin Books, New York.

Galston, W.A. (1993) 'Cosmopolitan Altruism' in E.F. Paul, F.D. Miller Jr. and J. Paul eds., *Altruism*, Cambridge University Press, Cambridge.

Gare, A. (1996) *Nihilism Inc.: Environmental Destruction And The Metaphysics Of Sustainability*, Eco-logical Press, Como, Australia.

Gare, A.E. (1995) *Postmodernism And The Environmental Crisis*, Routledge, London.

Gaskins, R.H. (1990) 'The Structure Of Self-Commentary In Hegel's Dialectical Logic', *International Philosophical Quarterly*, Vol. 30, No. 4, pp. 403-417.

Gaylin, W. (1987) *Rediscovering Love*, Penguin Books, New York.

Ginzberg, R. (1992) 'Audre Lorde's (Non-essentialist) Lesbian Eros' *Hypatia* Vol. 7 No. 4, pp. 73-90.

Gorz, A. (1988) *Critique Of Economic Reason*, Verso, London.

Gorz, A. (1994) *Capitalism, Socialism, Ecology*, Verso, London.

Grimshaw, J. (1986) 'The Critique Of Individualism' in *Feminist Philosophers: Women's Perspectives On Philosophical Traditions*, Wheatsheaf, Brighton, Sussex, pp. 162-186.

Grosz, E. (1992) 'A Note On Essentialism And Difference' in S.

Gunew, ed., *Feminist Knowledge: Critique And Construct,* Routledge, London, pp. 332-344.

Grosz, E. (1995) *Space Time And Perversion: The Politics Of Bodies,* Allen and Unwin, St. Leonards, Australia.

Habermas, J. (1987) *The Philosophical Discourse Of Modernity,* Polity Press, Cambridge.

Habermas, J. (1992) *Postmetaphysical Thinking: Philosophical Essays,* Polity Press, Cambridge.

Halley, J.E. (1993) 'The Construction Of Heterosexuality', in M. Warner, ed., *Fear Of A Queer Planet: Queer Politics And Social Theory,* pp. 82-102.

Hardimon, M. O. (1994) *Hegel's Social Philosophy,* Cambridge University Press, New York.

Hardwig, J. (1997) 'Privacy, Self-Knowledge And Pluralistic Communes: An Invitation To The Epistemology Of The Family', in H. Lindemann Nelson, ed., *Feminism and Families,* pp. 105-115.

Harris, E.E. (1983.) *An Interpretation of the Logic of Hegel,* University Press of America, Maryland.

Harris, E.E. (1987) Formal, Transcendental And Dialectical Thinking, State University of New York Press, Albany.

Harris, H.S. (1983) *Hegel's Development: Night Thoughts (Jena 1801-1806),* Clarendon Press, Oxford.

Harris, H.S. (1995) *Hegel: Phenomenology And System,* Hackett Publishing Company Inc., Indianapolis and Cambridge.

Hartmann, K. (1972) 'Hegel: A Non-Metaphysical View', in MacIntyre, A., ed., *Hegel,* pp. 101-124.

Hartmann, K. (1984) 'Towards A New Systematic Reading Of Hegel's Philosophy Of Right', in Z.A. Pelczynski, ed., *The State And Civil Society,* pp. 114-136.

Hayim, G.J. (1990) 'Hegel's Critical Theory And Feminist Concerns', *Philosophy And Social Criticism,* Vol. 16, No. 1, pp. 1-21.

Hegel, G.W.F. (1970) *Philosophy Of Nature: Part Two Of The Encyclopaedia Of The Philosophy Of Sciences.* M.J. Petry, trans., Allen and Unwin, London.

Hegel, G.W.F. (1975) *Logic: Part One Of The Encyclopaedia Of The Philosophical Sciences (1830),* W. Wallace, trans., Clarendon Press, Oxford. We indicate references to remarks and additions to Hegel's text respectively with the letters 'R' and 'A'.

Hegel, G.W.F. (1977) *Phenomenology Of Spirit,* A.V. Miller, trans., Oxford University Press, Oxford.

Hegel, G.W.F. (1981) *Philosophy Of Right*. T.M. Knox, trans., Oxford University Press, Oxford. We indicate references to remarks and additions to Hegel's text respectively with the letters 'R' and 'A'.

Hegel, G.W.F. (1985) *Philosophy Of Mind : Part Three Of The Encyclopaedia Of The Philosophical Sciences (1830)*, W. Wallace, trans., Clarendon Press, Oxford. We indicate references to remarks and additions to Hegel's text respectively with the letters 'R' and 'A'.

Hegel, G.W.F. (1986) *The Philosophical Propaedeutic*. A.V. Miller, trans., M. George, and A. Vincent, eds., Oxford University Press, Oxford.

Hegel, G.W.F. (1989) *Science Of Logic*, A. V. Miller, trans., Humanities Press, Atlantic Highlands.

Held, V. (1993) 'Non-Contractual Society: The Post-Patriarchal Family As Model' in *Feminist Morality*, University of Chicago Press, Chicago, pp. 192-214.

Heller, A. (1990) *Can Modernity Survive?*, Polity Press, Cambridge.

Hill Collins, P. (1991) *Black Feminist Thought*, Routledge, New York.

Hinchman, L.P. (1982) 'Hegel's Theory Of Crime And Punishment', *Review Of Politics*, 44, pp. 523-545.

Hinchman, L.P. (1984) *Hegel's Critique Of The Englightenment*, University Press of Florida, Florida.

Hobsbawm, E. (1995) *Age Of Extremes*, Abacus, London.

Honneth, A. (1991) *The Critique Of Power: Reflective Stages In A Critical Social Theory*, K. Baynes, trans., MIT Press, Cambridge.

Honneth, A. (1996) *The Struggle For Recognition: The Moral Grammar Of Social Conflicts*, Polity Press, Cambridge.

hooks, b. (1984) *Feminist Theory: From Margin To Center*, South End Press, Boston, Massachusetts.

Hyppolite, J. (1989) *Genesis And Structure Of Hegel's Phenomenology Of Spirit*, North Western University Press, Evanston.

Ilting, K-H. (1971) 'The Structure Of Hegel's *Philosophy Of Right*', in Z.A. Pelczynski, ed., *Hegel's Political Philosophy*, pp. 90-110.

Ilting, K-H. (1984) 'The Dialectic Of Civil Society', in Z.A. Pelczynski, ed., *The State And Civil Society*, pp. 211-226.

Jagentowicz Mills, P. (1979) 'Hegel And 'the Woman Question': Recognition And Intersubjectivity', in L.M.G. Clark, and L. Lange, eds., *The Sexism Of Social And Political Theory:*

Women And Reproduction Form Plato To Nietzsche. University of Toronto Press, Canada, pp. 74-98.

Johnson, P. O. (1988) *The Critique Of Thought: A Re-Examination Of Hegel's Science Of Logic*, Avebury, Gower Publishing Company, Aldershot.

Jordan, B. (1989) *The Common Good: Citizenship, Morality And Self-Interest*, Basil Blackwell, Oxford.

Kaplan, M.B. (1991) 'Autonomy, Equality, Community: The Question Of Lesbian And Gay Rights' *Praxis International*, Vol. 11, pp. 195-213.

Kaplan, M.B. (1994) 'Philosophy, Sexuality And Gender' *Metaphilosophy*, Vol. 25, No. 4, pp. 293-303.

Kean, J. (1988) *Democracy And Civil Society*, London, Verso.

Knowles, D. 'Hegel On Property And Personality', *The Philosophical Quarterly*, Vol. 33, No. 130, pp. 45-62.

Kojeve, A. (1991) *Introduction To The Reading Of Hegel: Lectures On The Phenomenology Of Spirit*, Cornell University Press, New York.

Kolakowski, L. (1983) 'The Death Of Utopia Reconsidered', in S. McMurrin, ed., *The Tanner Lectures on Human Values*, Vol. 4, University of Utah Press.

Kolb, D. (1988) *The Critique Of Pure Modernity: Hegel, Heidegger And After*, The University of Chicago Press, Chicago.

Kortian, G. (1984) 'Subjectivity And Civil Society', in Z. A. Pelczynski, ed., *The State And Civil Society*, pp. 197-210.

Kow, J.P. (1993) 'Hegel, Kolb And Flay: Foundationalism Or Anti-Foundationalism?', *International Philosophical Quarterly*, Vol. 33, No. 2, pp. 203-218.

Krell, D.F. 'Lucinde's Shame: Hegel, Sensuous Woman, And The Law', in D. Cornell, et. al. eds. *Hegel And Legal Theory*, pp. 287-300.

Kristeva, J. (1989) 'Stabat Mater', in T. Moi, ed., *The Kristeva Reader*, Basil Blackwell, Oxford.

Kyrkilis, J. (1991) *M. Bakunin On Liberty And Society*, MA Dissertation, School of Philosophy, Faculty of Humanities, La Trobe University, Australia.

Laclau, E. ed. (1994) *The Making of Political Identities*, Verso, London.

Laing, R.D. (1985) *The Politics of Experience and the Bird of Paradise*, *Penguin* Books, , New York.

Lamb, D. ed. (1987) *Hegel And Modern Philosophy*, Croom Helm, New York.

Lindemann Nelson, H. ed. (1997) *Feminism And Families*, Routledge, New York and London.

Lloyd, G. (1984) *The Man Of Reason: 'Male' And 'Female' In Western Philosophy*, Methuen, London.

Lorde, A. (1993) 'The Uses Of The Erotic: The Erotic As Power', in H. Abelove et. al. eds., *The Lesbian And Gay Studies Reader*, pp. 339-343.

Lucas, J.R. Jr., ed. (1986) *Hegel And Whitehead: Contemporary Perspectives On Systematic Philosophy*, State University of New York Press, Albany.

Luhmann, N. (1981) 'The Economy As A Social System', in S. Holmes and C. Larmore, trans., *The Differentiation Of Society*, Columbia University Press, New York, pp. 190-225.

Lukes, S. (1973) *Individualism*, Basil Blackwell, Oxford.

MacIntyre, A. (1988) *Whose Justice.? Which Rationality?*, University of Notre Dame Press, Indiana.

MacIntyre, A. ed. (1972) *Hegel: A Collection Of Critical Essays*, Anchor Books, New York.

MacIntyre, M. (1985) *After Virtue: A Study In Moral Theory*, Duckworth, London, 2nd edition.

Mae Brown, R. (1995) 'The Furies Collective', in P. A. Weiss, ed., *Feminism And Community*, Temple University Press, pp. 125-134, Philadelphia.

Marcuse, H. (1987) *Hegel's Ontology And The Theory Of Historicity*, MIT Press, Cambridge.

Martindale, K. and Saunders, M. (1992) 'Realising Love And Justice: Lesbian Ethics In The Upper And Lower Case' *Hypatia*, Vol. 7, No. 4, pp. 148-171.

Marx, K. (1978) *Economic And Philosophic Manuscripts Of 1844*, in R. C. Tucker, ed., *The Marx-Engels Reader*, W. W. Norton & Company, New York.

Mathews, F. (1991) *The Ecological Self*, Routledge, London.

McCumber, J. (1993) *The Company Of Words: Hegel, Language And Systematic Philosophy*, Northwestern University Press, Illinois.

Merchant, C. (1990) *The Death of Nature: Women, Ecology and the Scientific Revolution*, Harper and Row, New York.

Midgely, M. and Hughes, J. (1997) 'Are Families Out Of Date?', in H. Lindemann Nelson, ed., *Feminism and Families*, pp. 55-68.

Minow, M. and Lindon Shanley, M, (1996) 'Relational Rights And Responsibilities: Revisioning The Family In Liberal Political Theory And Law', *Hypatia*, Vol. 11, No. 1, pp. 4-29.

Mohr, R. D. (1994) *A More Perfect Union: Why Gay America Must Stand Up For Gay Rights*, Beacon, Boston.

Moller Okin, S. (1979) *Women In Western Political Thought*, Princeton University Press, New Jersey.

Moller Okin, S. (1989) *Justice, Gender And The Family*, Basic Books, New York.

Moller Okin, S. (1994) 'Gender Inequality And Cultural Differences', *Political Theory*, Vol. 22, No. 1, pp. 5-24.

Moller Okin, S. (1997) 'Families And Feminist Theory: Some Past And Present Issues' in H. Lindemann Nelson, ed., *Feminism And Families*, pp. 13-26.

Moody-Adams, M.M. (1997) 'Feminism By Any Other Name', in H. Lindemann Nelson, ed., *Feminism and Families*, pp. 76-89.

Nardi, P. (1992) 'That's What Friends Are For: Friends As Family In The Gay And Lesbian Community' in *Modern Homosexualities: Fragments Of Lesbian And Gay Experience*, K. Plummer, ed., Routledge, London and New York.

Narr, Wolff-Dieter (1985) 'Toward A Society Of Conditional Reflexes', in Habermas, J. ed., *Observations On 'The Spiritual Situation of The Age'*, MIT, Cambridge, Massachusetts.

Navickas, J.L. (1976) *Consciousness And Reality: Hegel's Philosophy Of Subjectivity*, Martinus Nijhoff, The Hague.

Nicholson, L. (1984) 'Feminist Theory: The Private And The Public' in C. Gould, ed., *Beyond Domination: New Perspectives On Women And Philosophy*, Rowman and Allenheld, New Jersey, pp. 221-232.

Nicholson, L. (1997) 'The Myth Of The Traditional Family', in H. Lindemann Nelson, ed., *Feminism And Families*, pp. 27-42.

Nicolacopoulos, T. (1997) *Is Resisting Liberalism Unreasonable?*, PhD Dissertation, School of Philosophy, Faculty of Humanities and Social Sciences, La Trobe University, Australia.

Noddings, N. (1984) *Caring: A Feminist Approach To Ethics And Moral Education*, University of California Press, Berkeley.

Norman, R. (1981) *Hegel's Phenomenology: A Philosophical Introduction*, Humanities Press, New Jersey.

Oldfield, A. (1990) *Citizenship And Community: Civic Republicanism And The Modern World*, Routledge, London.

Pelczynski, Z.A. (1971) 'The Hegelian Conception Of The State', in Z.A. Pelczynski, ed., *Hegel's Political Philosophy*, pp. 1-29.

Pelczynski, Z.A. (1984) 'Political Community And Individual Freedom In Hegel's Philosophy Of State', in Z.A. Pelczynski, ed., *The State And Civil Society*, pp. 55-76.

Pelczynski, Z.A. (1984) *Hegel's Political Writings,* Oxford University Press, Oxford.

Pelczynski, Z.A. ed. (1971) *Hegel's Political Philosophy Problems And Perspectives: A Collection Of New Essays*, Cambridge University Press, Cambridge.

Pelczynski, Z.A., ed. (1984) *The State And Civil Society: Studies In Hegel's Political Philosophy*, Cambridge University Press, Cambridge.

Perkins, R.L. ed. (1984) *History And System: Hegel's Philosophy Of History*, State University of New York Press, Albany.

Person, E. S. (1990) *Love And Fateful Encounters: The Power Of Romantic Passion*, Bloomsbury, London.

Phelan, S. (1989) *Identity Politics: Lesbian Feminism And The Limits Of Community*, Temple University Press, Philadelphia.

Pierce, C. (1995) 'Gay Marriage', *Journal Of Social Philosophy*, Vol. 28, No. 2, pp. 5-16.

Pinkard, T. (1985) 'The Logic Of Hegel's *Logic*', in M. Inwood, ed., *Hegel*, Oxford University Press, New York, pp. 85-109.

Pinkard, T. (1991) 'The Successor To Metaphysics: Absolute Idea And Absolute Spirit', *The Monist*, pp. 295-328.

Pippin, R.B. 'You Can't Get There From Here: Transition Problems In Hegel's Phenomenology Of Spirit', in F.C. Beiser, ed. *The Cambridge Companion to Hegel*, pp. 52-85.

Pippin, R.B. (1989) *Hegel's Idealism: The Satisfaction Of Self-Consciousness*, Cambridge University Press, Cambridge.

Plant, R. (1980) 'Economic And Social Integration In Hegel's Political Philosophy', in D.P. Verene, ed., *Hegel's Social And Political Thought*, pp. 59-90.

Plant, R. (1983) *Hegel: An Introduction,* Basil Blackwell, Oxford.

Plant, R. (1984) 'Hegel On Identity And Legitimation', in Z.A. Pelczynski, ed., *The State And Civil Society*, pp. 227-243.

Plant, R. (1991) *Modern Political Thought*, Basil Blackwell, Oxford and Cambridge, Massachusetts.

Plumwood, V. (1993) *Feminism And The Mastery Of Nature*, Routledge, London.

Polikoff, N. (1993) 'We Will Get What We Ask For—Why Legalising Gay And Lesbian Marriage Will Not Dismantle The Legal Structure Of Gender In Every Marriage', *Virginia Law Review*, Vol. 79, No. 7, pp. 1535-1550.

Poole, R. (1991) *Morality And Modernity*, Routledge, London.

Purdy, L.M. (1997) 'Babystrike!', in H. Lindemann Nelson, ed.,

Feminism And Families, pp. 69-75.

Rawls, J. (1993.) *Political Liberalism*, New York, Columbia University Press.

Redding, P. (1996) *Hegel's Hermeneutics*, Cornell University Press, Ithaca, New York.

Rich, A. (1993) 'Compulsory Heterosexuality And Lesbian Existence', in H. Abelove et. al. eds., *The Lesbian And Gay Studies Reader*, pp. 227-254.

Richardson, H.S. (1989) 'The Logical Structure In Sittlichkeit: A Reading Of Hegel's Philosophy Of Right', *Idealistic Studies*, Vol. 19, pp. 62-78.

Riedel, M. (1984) *Between Tradition And Revolution: The Hegelian Transformation Of Political Philosophy*, W. Wright, trans., Cambridge University Press, Cambridge.

Robinson, E.L.E., Lindemann Nelson, H. and Lindemann Nelson, J. (1997) 'Fluid Families: The Role Of Children In Custody Arrangements', in H. Lindemann Nelson, ed., *Feminism and Families*, pp. 90-101.

Robson, R. (1992a) 'Mother: The Legal Domestication Of Lesbian Experience', *Hypatia*, Vol. 7, No. 4, pp. 172-185.

Robson, R. (1992b) *Lesbian (Out) Law: Survival Under The Rule Of Law*, Firebrand Books, Ithaca, New York.

Rosen, M. (1982) *Hegel's Dialectic And Its Criticism*, Cambridge University Press, New York.

Rubin, G.S. (1993) 'Thinking Sex: Notes For A Radical Theory Of The Politics Of Sexuality', in H. Abelove et. al. eds., *The Lesbian And Gay Studies Reader*, pp. 3-44.

Rundell, J.F. (1987) *Origins Of Modernity: The Origins Of Modern Social Theory From Kant To Hegel To Marx*, Polity Press, Oxford.

Ryan, A. (1997) 'Liberalism', in R.E. Goodin and P. Pettit, eds., *A Companion to Contemporary Political Philosophy*, Blackwell, Cambridge, Massachusetts, pp. 291-311.

Schlink, B. 'The Inherent Rationality Of The State In Hegel's *Philosophy Of Right*', in D. Cornell, et. al. eds., *Hegel And Legal Theory*, pp. 347-354.

Schmidt, D.J. (1988) *The Ubiquity Of The Finite: Hegel, Heidegger And The Entitlements Of Philosophy*, The MIT Press, Cambridge, Massachusetts.

Sedgwick, E.K. (1993) 'Epistemology Of The Closet', in H. Abelove et. al. eds., *The Lesbian And Gay Studies Reader*, pp. 45-61.

Seidman, S. (1993) 'Identity And Politics In A 'Postmodern' Gay

Culture: Some Historical And Conceptual Notes', in M. Warner, ed., *Fear Of A Queer Planet*, pp. 103-142.

Sennet, R. (1975) *The Fall Of Public Man*, Vintage Books, New York.

Shklar, J. (1976) *Freedom And Independence: A Study Of The Political Ideas Of Hegel's Phenomenology Of Mind*, Cambridge University Press, Cambridge.

Shogan, D. (1993) 'In Defence Of A Wordly Separatism', *Hypatia*, Vol. 8 No. 4, pp. 129-133.

Siebert, R.J. (1980) 'Hegel's Concept Of Marriage And Family: The Origin Of Subjective Freedom', in D.P. Verene, ed., *Hegel's Social And Political Thought*, pp. 177-214.

Sinfield, A. (1994) 'Sexuality And Sub-Cultures In The Wake Of Welfare Capitalism', *Radical Philosophy*, 66, pp. 40-43.

Singer, B.J. (1991) 'Intersubjectivity Without Subjectivism', *Man and World*, 24, pp. 321-338.

Skolimowski, H. (1992) *Living Philosophy: Eco-Philosophy as a Tree of Life*, Arkana, London.

Smith, S.B. (1989) *Hegel's Critique Of Liberalism: Rights In Context*, The University of Chicago Press, Chicago and London.

Smith, T. (1993) *Dialectical Social Theory And Its Critics: From Hegel To Analytical Marxism And Postmodernism*, State University of New York Press, Albany.

Stace, W.T. (1955) *The Philosophy Of Hegel: A Systematic Exposition*, Dover, New York.

Stack, C. (1974) *All Our Kin: Strategies For Survival In A Black Community*, Harper and Row, New York.

Stein, E. (1994) 'Why Sexuality Matters To Philosophy: An Introduction', *Metaphilosophy*, Vol. 25, No. 4, pp. 233-237.

Steinberger, P. J. (1988) *Logic And Politics: Hegel's Philosophy Of Right*, Yale University Press, Newhaven and London.

Stillman, P. G. (1980a) 'Person, Property, And Civil Society In The Philosophy Of Right', in D.P. Verene, ed., *Hegel's Social And Political Thought*, pp. 103-115.

Stillman, P. G. (1980b) 'Property, Freedom And Individuality In Political Thought', in J.R. Pennock and J.W. Chapman, eds., *Property*, New York University Press, New York, pp. 130-167.

Sunstein, C.R. (1994) 'Same-Sex Relations And The Law', *Metaphilosophy*, Vol. 25, No. 4, pp. 262-284.

Taylor, C. 'Hegel's Ambiguous Legacy For Modern Liberalism', in D. Cornell et. al. eds., *Hegel And Legal Theory*, pp. 64-77.

Taylor, C. (1980) *Hegel And Modern Society*, Cambridge University Press, Cambridge.

Taylor, C. (1983) *Hegel*, Cambridge University Press, Cambridge.

Taylor, C. (1987) 'Overcoming Epistemology', in K. Baynes et. al. eds., *After Philosophy: End or Transformation?*, pp. 464-488.

Taylor, C. (1989) *Sources Of The Self: The Making Of The Modern Identity*, Cambridge University Press, Cambridge.

Taylor, C. (1992) 'Inwardness and the Culture of Modernity' in A. Honneth et. al. eds., *Philosophical Interventions In The Unfinished Project Of Enlightenment*, The MIT Press, Cambridge, Massachusetts, pp. 88-110.

Teichgraeber, R. (1977) 'Hegel On Property And Poverty', *Journal Of The History Of Ideas*, 38, pp. 47-64.

Theunissen, M. (1991) 'Being, Person Community', in D. Cornell et. al. eds., *Hegel And Legal Theory*, pp. 3-63.

Tugendhat, E. (1986) *Self-Consciousness And Self-Determination*. P. Stern, trans., The MIT Press, Cambridge, Massachusetts.

Vannoy, R. (1990) *Sex Without Love: A Philosophical Exploration*, Promitheus Books, Buffalo, New York.

Vassilacopoulos, G. (1994) *A Reading Of Hegel's Philosophy*, PhD Dissertation, School of Philosophy, Faculty of Humanities, La Trobe University, Australia.

Ver Eecke, W. (1980) 'Relation Between Economics And Politics In Hegel', in Verene, D.P. ed., *Hegel's Social And Political Thought*, pp. 91-101.

Verene, D.P. , ed. (1980) *Hegel's Social And Political Thought: The Philosophy Of Objective Spirit*, Humanities Press, New Jersey.

Walzer, M. (1987) *Interpretation and Social Criticism*, Harvard University Press, Cambridge, Massachusetts.

Waring, M. (1988) *Counting For Nothing: What Men Value And What Women Are Worth*, Allen and Unwin, Wellington.

Warner, M. (1993) 'Introduction' in M. Warner, *Fear Of A Queer Planet: Queer Politics And Social Theory*, pp. vii-xxxi.

Warner, M. ed. (1993) *Fear Of A Queer Planet: Queer Politics And Social Theory*, University of Minnesota Press, Minneapolis and London.

Weitzman, L. (1974) 'Marriage Contracts', *California Law Review*, Vol. 62, No. 4, pp. 1169-1258.

Westphal, K. (1993) 'The Basic Context And Structure Of Hegel's *Philosophy Of Right*, in F.C. Beiser, ed., *The Cambridge Companion To Hegel*, pp. 234-269.

Westphal, M. (1984) 'Hegel's Radical Idealism: Family And State As Ethical Communities', in Z.A. Pelczynski, ed., *The State And Civil Society*, pp. 77-92.

Wolfson, (1996) 'Why We Should Fight For The Freedom To Marry', *Journal OF Lesbian, Gay And Bisexual Identity*, Vol. 1, No. 1, pp. 79-89.

Wood, A.W. (1990) *Hegel's Ethical Thought*, Cambridge University Press, Cambridge.

Zack, N. (1997) '"The Family" And Radical Family Theory', in H. Lindemann Nelson, ed., *Feminism And Families*, pp. 43-51.

Zimmerli, W. (1989) 'Is Hegel's *Logic* A Logic? Analytic Criticism Of Hegel's *Logic* In Recent German Philosophy', in W. Desmond, ed., *Hegel And His Critics: Philosophy In The Aftermath Of Hegel*, State University of New York Press, Albany, pp. 191-202.

Žižek, S. (1991) *For They Know Not What They Do: Enjoyment As A Political Factor*, Verso, London.

Lightning Source UK Ltd.
Milton Keynes UK
UKHW040800060323
418105UK00001B/277